Crime and Punishment in the England
of Shakespeare and Milton, 1570–1640

THE WITCHES OF NORTHAMPTON-SHIRE.

Agnes Browne. ⎫ Arthur Bill.
Ioane Vaughan. ⎬ Hellen Ienkenson ⎬ Witches.
Mary Barber. ⎭

Who were all executed at *Northampton* the 22. of *Iuly laſt*. 1612. James 1st

LONDON,
Printed by *Tho: Purfoot*, for *Arthur Iohnſon*. 1612. James 1

Crime and Punishment in the England of Shakespeare and Milton, 1570–1640

John W. Weatherford

McFarland & Company, Inc., Publishers
Jefferson, North Carolina, and London

Frontispiece: On their way to visit a colleague, three witches travel by sow, demurely riding sidesaddle. Bodleian Library, University of Oxford, Ma1709 (1).

Library of Congress Cataloguing-in-Publication Data

Weatherford, John W., 1924–
    Crime and punishment in the England of Shakespeare and Milton, 1570–1640 / by John W. Weatherford.
        p.   cm.
    Includes bibliographical references and index.

    ISBN-13: 978-0-7864-0963-1
    ISBN-10: 0-7864-0963-0
    (softcover : 50# alkaline paper) ∞

    1. Punishment—England—History. 2. Trials—England.
3. England—Social conditions. I. Title.
KD7882.W43 2001
345.42'077'09—dc21   2001023079

British Library cataloguing data are available

©2001 John W. Weatherford. All rights reserved

No part of this book may be reproduced or transmitted in any form or by any means, electronic or mechanical, including photocopying or recording, or by any information storage and retrieval system, without permission in writing from the publisher.

Cover images ©2000 Art Today

Manufactured in the United States of America

McFarland & Company, Inc., Publishers
  Box 611, Jefferson, North Carolina 28640
    www.mcfarlandpub.com

For Gretchen

Contents

Introduction   1

I. Issues of Crime and the Time   9

II. Removing Obstacles to Wealth   16
Deadline (1595) 17; *A Fresh Start* (1591) 17; *One Way Out* (1598) 19; *Jeopardies* (1603–1621) 21; *The Mediator* (1605) 26; *"Oblivion Was Their Motto"* (1620) 29; *Dangerous Real Estate* (1624) 32

III. Murdering Children for Their Own Good   39
Born Free (1605) 39; *Save the Children* (1616) 46; *The Rescuing Spring* (1621) 47; *The Last Picnic* (1637) 51

IV. Murdering to Resolve Triangles   54
Parental Muddle (1591) 55; *The Magnetism of a City Wife* (1573) 57; *The Endgame* (1582–1604) 61; *Horning the Parson* (1609) 62; *The Collector from Hell* (1641) 67; *A Note on Ratsbane* 68; *The Chattel Fights Back* (1635) 70; *Oatcakes for All* (1604) 71

V. Robbery on Land   74
Home Fires Burning (1608) 74; *The Maid in the Garden* (1612) 78; *The King's Chapel* (1612) 79; *Tom and Bess* (1635) 79; *Picaresque Characters* 82; *Picaresques: You Know the Way* (1609) 82; *Picaresques: Ratsey* (1605) 84; *Picaresques: Courtney* (1612) 88

VI. Robbery at Sea   91
Pirates at Work (1608) 91; *Captain Harris* 91; *Captain Jennings* 94; *Captain Longcastle* 100; *Captain Downes* 101; *Down to Wapping* (1609) 103

Contents

VII. Fraud and Blackmail ... 106
Chancery (1616) 106; *Worldly Possessions* (1599) 107; *Freed from the Iron Gate* (1608) 109; *Proud Rascal* (1623) 112

VIII. From Sex to Disaster ... 115
The Wish List of Youth (1643) 115; *The Mad Squire* (1605) 116; *Instead of Abortion* (1614) 119; *In the Warmth of the Kilns* (1614) 121; *"The Seed of a Varlet"* (1631) 122; *Downfall in Dublin* (1640) 132; *Vicar Is Showing Off Again* (1641) 133

IX. Corruption ... 135
The Handsome Duke (1592–1628) 135; *Spirits of the August* (1626) 136; *Allegations of a Scot* (1628) 139; *Curing Doctor Lambe* (1607–1628) 144

X. Shades and Witches ... 152
The Witches of Northamptonshire (1612) 154; *Whisked Out of Pinner* (1592) 155; *Mother Sutton's Dip* (1613) 156; *The Devil Wags His Tail* (1621) 160; *Lads Will Be Lads* (1643) 163

XI. From Religion to Disaster ... 165
Catholics versus Protestants 165; *Doctrine at the Half Moon* (1607) 165; *A Happy Conversion* (1618) 166; *Newgate Protestants on Strike* (1642) 167; Protestants versus Protestants 168; *How Windows Lie* (1631) 168; *Not Conforming* (1634) 169; *Schism on the Ladder* (1609) 176; *An Anabaptist Drunk* (1643) 177

XII. Conclusion ... 178
Threads 178; Justice 183; Coarsening 186; Evidence 187

Appendix A: Shakespeare's Purse ... 191
Appendix B: "Appeal" by Next of Kin ... 193
Notes ... 195
Works Cited ... 203
Index ... 213

Introduction

This book is a study of crimes and their punishments in the England of Shakespeare and Milton. Its author has written accounts of criminal cases based on various sources, but especially on narratives printed for popular consumption at the time of the event. These narratives illuminate the nature and causes of crime and the workings of law enforcement; they also reveal their authors' attitudes toward the criminals they encountered. In the process of relating these themes, writers less consciously reveal notions about women, households, and the supernatural.

The book examines certain Elizabethan attitudes and preoccupations in these matters, and compares them with our own. The purpose of making comparisons of this sort is to lead readers to reexamine two contradictory assumptions that we sometimes hold of the past and present:

1. Newer is better. The practices of four centuries ago lack rational explanation, and their absurdity is the result of people not knowing what we know.

2. Older is better. Our beliefs are right because they have "always" been held.

Formal indictments often declared that the accused was instigated by the Devil, and any exploration of the causes of crime was truncated by the convenient conclusion of clerics, criminals, and victims alike that crime was the Devil's work. Though we can, if we wish, still plausibly trace most of these cases to the seven deadly sins, today we generally do not regard criminals as the pawns of Satan.

Instead we are prone to look to environment for the causes of the crimes described in these old narratives. We find them in certain rigidities of society, such as an insoluble poverty resulting from demographic pressures; economically motivated arranged marriages unrelieved by the availability of divorce; and the participation of the nation-state in the doctrinal conflicts of stubborn Catholics, Anglicans, and nonconformists. Offenders were then confronted with the further rigidity of reified law, relieved only fitfully by mercy or corruption.

Sources

Elizabethans who did not care to watch public executions could sometimes get their crime news by buying a pamphlet. This was an ancestor of newspapers. Those attending an execution could buy a pamphlet on the spot, so it was also an ancestor of play and game programs. Some accounts, on a single large sheet or broadside, were ballads to be sung to some well-known tune; most, however, were in prose.

The need for timeliness put pressure on their producers, who had to work with printers setting every letter of type by hand. Occasionally this pressure produced a generic or recycled account, in which whole passages would be inserted from an earlier pamphlet. In any case, production was quick and dirty. Even so, most narrators took the time to set a didactic tone, ranging from how counterproductive it is to murder somebody, to the wondrous machinations of God the Detective.

Nearly all were printed in London. The publishing industry hummed by day in neighborhoods that were dangerous by night: Smithfield and the Barbican (where the first collected works of Shakespeare were printed). Much of the book trade clustered about St. Paul's Cathedral, which was larger then. All day, business and social contacts went on in the cathedral. It was so long from east to west that north-south traffic cut through it: pedestrians, porters, peddlers with baskets. Shabby genteel types and others down on their luck took shelter in it. Men who fancied themselves dashing blades made rendezvous. Gamblers and other cheats picked up their victims, or "conies." Against the vast bulk of St. Paul's leaned St. Gregory's Church, and completely inside the crypt of the cathedral, like a stony pregnancy, snuggled still another church, little St. Faith's. One of the cathedral towers held the Bishop of London's jail cells.

No wonder, then, to find printers' shops clustering all around the building. Several printers gave their addresses as St. Paul's churchyard, a couple as the great north door, at least one as Paul's Cross, an elaborate freestanding pulpit. Others operated nearby in Paternoster Row, which remained a publishing center until it was bombed out in 1940. The printers, like other businesses, hung out signs: the Fleur de Lys and Crown, the Green Dragon, the Mermaid, the Spread Eagle, the Bishop's Head, the Bible, the Lamb, the Sun, the Talbot.

The accounts in the pamphlets are too informative to ignore, and too inhibited by authority to be swallowed whole. Many were written by clergymen ministering to condemned persons. These men did not wish to offend the authorities on whom their privileges depended, and they treated not only the judge but the prosecutor as infallible. In any case, all printing during this period was subject to censorship. Tightening earlier regulations, the court of star chamber in 1585 decreed that presses could operate only in London or its suburbs, except for one press each at Cambridge and Oxford universities. All presses had to be registered with the Stationers, the printers' own guild. All new publications had to be first perused by either the Archbishop of Canterbury or the Bishop of London. The wardens of the guild could inspect any printer's shop at any time, and had to destroy any unregistered presses or unlicensed printed matter they found. Besides these costly forfeitures, the offender could suffer 12 months' imprisonment. This was not the only danger printers or authors faced. They were occasionally prosecuted for seditious libel or treason, depending on the subject matter, and suffered various punishments, ranging from the pillory, through cropping of the ears, to a traitor's death.

As political and religious tensions grew, the government in 1637 further tightened control. Only 20 printers were allowed to operate. Even bookbinders, type founders, and the makers of presses were regulated, on pain of whipping, the pillory, and prison. Censorship was extended even to the reprinting of books that had passed the censor before. Bookshops were subject to periodic searches. No books could be imported without license. Law books were censored by the three chief justices, books on history and politics by one of the secretaries of state; books on heraldry by the earl marshall; divinity, philosophy, poetry, and every other kind of book, by the Archbishop of Canterbury, the Bishop of London, or the chancellors of Oxford or Cambridge. This last miscellaneous category included not only medicine but plays. These rules applied only to printing; permission to *perform* a play still rested with the lord chamberlain.[1]

Most of our cases come from these pamphlets, some from published trial records. Nearly all are rare, and some are the last copy known to survive to our time. (Their provenance is given in the endnotes.) Lack of polish makes them all the more revealing, as they let slip attitudes and random details, and freeze unposed subjects like a camera. Their readers would have felt a familiarity with the scene that we could not recover even if we wished. The grisly ends of feckless, wicked, or unlucky wretches were part of everyday life. Over hotheads like Marlowe and Jonson, the gallows always cast a threatening shadow, but it was also part of the landscape of those who did not brawl. Shakespeare and Milton for a time lived near Cripplegate and its adornment of traitors' quarters, and whenever the Bard chose not to commute by water to his work at the Globe Theatre, he had to walk under the heads stuck up on London bridge.

The Framework

Our first question about law and order must be, How could there be any? Elizabeth and James had no standing army. We would not recognize any policemen. Obviously law enforcement existed, or there would be no cases, but the few police were night watchmen or constables. Constables were ordinary, untrained subjects selected periodically by the village or city to enforce the law. This service was not coveted, as it might require one to apprehend a friend or neighbor. Worse, it could be dangerous. Both the constable and his neighbors had a general duty to prevent crime and seize suspects. The neighbor, as a mere subject, was normally liable for damages if he injured a suspect (unless the "hue and cry" had been raised, when he was free to kill him if he resisted arrest). A constable, on the other hand, was not liable as long as he was working within the law. This umbrella of sovereign immunity left much to be desired. If a suspect injured a constable, the constable's remedy was no better than any other man's: He could only sue the suspect for damages. A woman could be made a constable, on the grounds that she could hire a male substitute.[2]

Public order becomes less mysterious if we remember that, for every few hundred persons, there was one man who knew the families in his neighborhood well, and who was usually held in respect or even awe. This was the parson. The parish was his ancient beat, divine wrath his truncheon.

The foundation of the judicial system was the local justice of the peace (or magistrates, in boroughs). In each shire there would be men of substantial family, reputation, and assured loyalty, from whom the crown would name a few to be justices of the peace. They may have spent a year in an inn of court like many of the young gentry, but they were not lawyers. Each had summary judicial powers; two together had more power than one; and each quarter the JPs of the shire met with lawyers to deal with the knottier problems. Even in serious cases, justices of the peace conducted the preliminary examination of suspects, and performed much of the detective work, though it seems from our cases that anybody could and did dabble in detection. Inquests upon doubtful deaths were conducted, with the aid of a jury, by the coroner of the shire.

The main officer above the justices of the peace was the sheriff, who, in addition to important fiscal and administrative functions, was responsible for law and order in the whole shire. He too was appointed, or rather "pricked," by the sovereign, who signified the royal pleasure (and still does) by sticking a pin through the list of candidates next to the chosen name. The custom is quaint now but would originally have been a protection against forgery or alteration. The sheriff had assistants, but no regular police. He could summon subjects to his aid as a *posse comitatus*, an institution that survived in the Wild West after it had died out elsewhere. Usually there was one sheriff per shire. London had two, and one of the city's privileges was to elect them.

It is tricky to envision the old law courts. Wigs would be an anachronism, but not red robes. The civil cases would be especially puzzling to us. The lawyers would be pleading in a strange language:

"*Issint que act de parliament ou act del ley poet faire ceo en divers cases a severall respects, mes home per ses parols ne poit faire ceo, & nosment un estate a cesser quant al un, & a continuer quant al auter, a faire un mesme home halfe alive, & halfe dead ... donques touts Wardshippes poient estre defeate....*"[3]

It looks like some kind of French, but it would have been mysterious to the ear of a Frenchman, because the lawyers would be pronouncing much of it as if it were English. It had once been Norman French, so corrupted and specialized over centuries that it came to be called Law French. If we looked over the lawyer's shoulder, we might see some of his papers also in English, and some in Latin.

The criminal courts would be more recognizable, with a row of shackled prisoners standing and waiting their turn for trial. When one's turn comes, the shackles are removed and matters proceed with dispatch. The defendant has no lawyer. If he (or she) has already been convicted or acquitted of this same charge, he can have the trial stopped. If he pleads not guilty, a jury is brought in, and he can challenge its membership. He cannot testify or call witnesses of his own, but he can confront and question prosecution witnesses. If he pleads guilty, or the jurors find him guilty, he can state any technical factors affecting sentencing, such as qualifying for benefit of clergy. It is at this stage that a convicted female would plead pregnancy to postpone execution. If the jurors find the prisoner not guilty, that is the end of the case as far as the king is concerned, and all his horses cannot put it together again. As we shall see, acquittal did not necessarily end the recourse of the victim's family.

A defendant had to plead to be tried. If he refused to plead, he met a death more unpleasant than hanging. He was stretched flat on the ground while attendants piled weights on him until at last he either chose to plead or died of suffocation. After a certain number of weights, of course, he no longer had enough breath to tell anybody if he had changed his mind. This practice, the *peine forte et dure*, was common enough for one of the courtyards behind Newgate to be known as the pressing yard. A man might choose this painful alternative if he had property, because if he were tried and found guilty his property could be confiscated and his family impoverished. If he refused to plead, his property descended intact to his heir after his last labored breath.

Capital cases were high treason, petty treason, murder, grand larceny, robbery, rape, sodomy, witchcraft, coining, forgery, burglary, arson, and others in growing numbers. Most had been committed in the past few weeks; most found guilty were sentenced to death; and most of those sentences would be carried out within the week. In the margin of his notebook the judge jotted by the convict's name, "*sus. per col.*," the only written authorization to hang him, and went to the next case.

Outside London and Westminster, important cases generally had to await a travelling court. All over the realm, this was the assizes, visitations by royal justices to certain privileged towns, located so that court would be no more than a day's ride away for subjects. The justices of assize made their tours every other quarter, the Easter, Trinity, Michaelmas, and Hilary terms, arriving in town with a herald, and such pomp and trumpets as befitted the representatives of a just and dread sovereign. Contested capital cases were tried before a jury. The jurors sometimes mitigated a penalty by returning a verdict for a lesser offense, for example by undervaluing stolen goods so as to reduce a grand larceny to a petty larceny. A judge could exercise mercy in sentencing, but from his sentence there was virtually no legal appeal. We shall see however that a condemned person might receive a royal reprieve or pardon.[4]

Technical Notes

The calendar employed in England at this time was Julian, already lagging ten days behind the Gregorian calendar of Western Europe. The old-style new year began on the first day of spring, even though the first day of January was perversely called and celebrated as New Year's Day. A writer referring to February 1610 meant the year that we would call 1611; but his December 1610 is also our 1610. By the 1640s this practice was in flux, with some people writing both years.

Money often figures in these cases. Comments on its value, arithmetic, and coinage appear in Appendix A, "Shakespeare's Purse."

I have used the term "Elizabethan" loosely, to include the subsequent two reigns, feeling that it is on balance more convenient than misleading. I have the precedent of scholars such as E.M.W. Tillyard.

A few editorial conventions have been adopted. In direct quotes, the original inconsistent spellings have been retained, though the letters U and V, which were then interchangeable, have been distinguished as they are today. The same is done for the letters I and J. In citing titles, capitals follow modern convention; in all other quotations, the printer's blithely erratic decisions rule. Punctuation in all quotations follows the original. Colloquial exchanges not in quotation marks are abridgements or extrapolations of statements in the original.

I

Issues of Crime and the Time

Elizabeth, James, Charles, and their subjects have not been summoned back to support any psychological or social hypothesis. By observing them, we see ourselves better. We recognize enduring questions about crime, punishment, poverty, the status of women, family continuity and cohesion, abortion, homosexuality, bigotry, and superstition. Our interest is attested to by thousands of modern books and articles, and hundreds of web sites that are being trampled by paper-writing students in their hundred thousands. In these it often appears that liberals and conservatives find the answers to these questions easy. It is broadening to encounter different answers that other people once found just as easy.

Capital punishment is an example. Today it enters election contests and fills letter columns. Opponents call it barbarous; the European Union will not accept countries that keep it; and several nations cannot extradite a criminal to face it. Opponents point out that those American states most reliant on executions were among those most reliant on slavery. They consider it an instrument for controlling the lower orders, or catering to the unhealthy vengefulness of victims' families. They argue that it does not deter crime.

Advocates argue that it does, especially among the executed, and welcome it as an instrument for encouraging testimony against accomplices, and as a psychological balm for the agony of surviving victims. Some may also feel that, as long as there are lower orders, they had better be controlled. Both opponents and advocates cite, in their own support, the sacredness of life.

Elizabethans too held life sacred, but capital punishment was an institution that they felt no urge to examine. It had existed at all times and in all lands. Viewing the state as analogous to the human body,[1] they found it as natural as a bodily function for the commonwealth to "spew forth" its malefactors, as one of those malefactors put it on the gallows. They were content to administer plain punishment, severed from any further purpose, though obviously they also put great faith in the deterrent power of public punishment. The powerful modern argument that execution makes judicial mistakes irreversible had no place in a literature that could not entertain the possibility of a judicial mistake. Nor was rehabilitation an alternative to execution. When we speak today of rehabilitating criminals, we mean rehabilitation for this world. Elizabethans meant rehabilitation for the next world, and it must have seemed only charitable to send penitent culprits there before they could botch their salvation again.

Punishment, by definition, has to be worse than normal life. Innocent folk were already prisoners of pain or the dread of it, knowing no anesthesia stronger than alcohol,[2] and barred from the other escape by their knowledge that the Almighty had "fixed his canon 'gainst self-slaughter." So much of Elizabethan life was painful, that to make punishment sufficiently distinguishable from the norm required more brutality than we happy moderns can stomach. There was of course a practical side to punishment. People had pigs to raise, shops to run, children to accumulate in the race against child mortality, and a try to make, against the odds, at a quick taste of the sweets of life. The severity with which they treated interferences such as theft and witchcraft is understandable, and especially when we realize that there was no such thing as insurance.

The heat of the capital punishment debate today stirs popular emotions so disproportionate to its actual frequency (100 executions in the United States in 1999) that it plainly must possess some intrinsic emotional power. It thus seems now more a proxy than a free-standing issue, joining such other transformations of symbol into substance as flag-burning, and that compulsive pursuit of euphemisms which Molière called precious and we call politically correct. But the intrinsic emotional power existed then too, and was used by society to drive home its messages.

We have also made homosexuality a popular issue. The Elizabethans used "deviant" to describe bad arrows, not bad humans, and managed somehow to live without the word "deviance." True, they plainly found some kinds of behavior intolerable. Odd religious sects, centering on trances or free love, were beyond acceptable norms; but then to Protestants so were Catholics, and *vice versa*. Yet heresies and witchcraft overshadowed homosexuality, about which they showed not so much tolerance as a pragmatic ambiguity, as if they were saying, "Don't ask, don't tell."

Male homosexuality, as a branch of sodomy, had been an ecclesiastical offense long before the dissolution of monasteries, both in the sense that it was an occupational hazard among cloistered monks, and in the sense that everybody committing it fell under the jurisdiction of the ecclesiastical courts. When Henry VIII expelled the courts of Rome, sodomy briefly ceased by default to be an offense at all, until his parliament made it a felony for the first time. This statute alone might explain why Elizabethan men, effusive in declaring their love for each other, did not say whether Agape or Eros governed it. Yet some tacit, blinking toleration must have existed. A modern man as overt in his attentions to handsome youths (and his own codpiece) as King James, we might expect, would now be ejected from any straight bar and probably some gay bars. The great lawyer and philosopher Sir Francis Bacon was said to be a pederast, yet those who sought his fall were content to achieve it by charging bribery alone.[3] Such sodomy prosecutions as we possess presented aggravating circumstances. The punishment could be drastic, but as we shall see in one case, some details had to be settled among the judges, suggesting a scarcity of precedent. In the ordinary world, 1,631 crimes reported in Sussex between 1592 and 1640 included only two buggery cases,[4] and 5,980 indictments in three counties between 1559 and 1603 included only 17.[5]

Female homosexuality had not even a name in law, and did not loom on the horizons of either statesmen or churchmen. Was this male ignorance or indifference? Did a man feel that a lesbian was not stealing his property when she had to do with his wife? Unawareness and indifference would be consistent with the general subservience of women. They had limited identity in business and at law, and their permissible literary publications were overwhelmingly works of religious devotion. Prosperous widows probably enjoyed the greatest freedom and power, though we shall see that they too might be ruthlessly exploited. Women probably benefited from traditional courtesies, and the fact that the favorite monarch of the period was Elizabeth. Some members of the clergy, males still smarting from Eve's initiative, presented women as foolish and inconstant, though Portia, Rosalind, Beatrice, Mrs. Page, Mrs. Ford, and others testify that Shakespeare's audiences must have thought better.

It might seem from the literature that women committed more murders than now, but probably their crimes (witchcraft aside) were simply more newsworthy for being less expected. Now and again, our authors allowed a murderess a glimmer, not of justification, but of recognition. One had had an unwanted marriage forced on her by her parents after they had led her to believe her lover would be welcome as her husband. The manipulation of another by her lover and his pander made her the least blameworthy of those three conspirators. One who poisoned her husband had been battered routinely. Yet each had a crime to repent, and to atone with death.

As victims, women usually earned sympathy from the authors. When one husband lodged his paramour on two successive wives, neither of them showed any meekness, and the author stayed on their side, though usually authors expected endless patience from wives, and applauded them (posthumously) when they found it. A servant who bashed his master was the sort nobody expected to come to any good, because he had rejected and bullied his pregnant wench. An odd exception is the nameless woman used as a target by Puritan soldiers; the author quite accepted their tale that she was a witch, making her the culprit and the soldiers her potential victims, saved only by their heavenly cobelligerent. A philandering bishop's wife received little attention from an author preoccupied with protecting the public image of the church.

Men's fear of women, and women's frustrations with that, probably encouraged the interest of both sexes in witchcraft. Ministers had no sympathy for witches, who after all had to befriend the Devil to qualify. The politic chaplain-in-ordinary at Newgate prison professed to distance himself from the question of witches, in the very pamphlet that he wrote about one of them. The playwright Dekker's *Witch of Edmonton* was something of a victim who became a witch because her neighbors were already treating her like one. The real witch of Edmonton's lay jury of Londoners at the Old Bailey showed some hesitancy about the evidence of witchcraft, though in the end they let themselves be overborne by a rural justice of the peace who affected expertise in such things. Witches could be of either sex, but among our cases only one was male. Each of the women seems to have thought herself a witch, at least part of the time; the male probably never.

Besides witchcraft, women might assert themselves in other ways, for example adultery, infanticide, and abortion. Adultery produced several fatal triangles. Infanticide warranted few pamphlets. It was the killing of an infant born alive, commonly determined by examining its lungs, which would be pink if it had taken a breath.

When life begins has become a passionate debate. When did it begin for Elizabethans? Their answers may not satisfy modern partisans on either side. Abortion had immemorially been a sin in the Church. It became an offense in Anglican canon law only in 1588. In 1591 the rule was relaxed to allow bishops discretion in dealing with persons committing or contemplating it in the first 40 days of gestation. In English common law, abortion had not been prohibited by statute when Henry VIII replaced the pope. "An intentionally induced abortion was at common law a misdemeanor," according to a modern law dictionary. Sir Matthew Hale, lord chief justice in the 1670s, wrote that inducing an abortion was neither murder nor manslaughter under the common law, because even after the fetus shows signs of life, it is not yet "*in rerum natura*." In the next century, Justice Blackstone explained that for there to be a murder, the victim had to be "a reasonable creature in being.... To kill a child in its mother's womb is not now murder, but a great misprision...."[6]

Blackstone's contemporaries elaborate:

> As soon as an infant is able to stir in its mother's womb, it becomes an object of protection in the eye of the law; therefore if a woman is quick with child, and by a potion or otherwise she killeth it in her womb; or if anyone beat her, whereby the child dieth in her body, and she is delivered of a dead child; this, though not murder, was by the ancient law accounted homicide or manslaughter; but latter authorities have thought it to be a great mispris[i]on only. But if the child be[ing] born alive, afterwards die of the potion or bruises it received in the womb, it is murder in such as administered or gave them.[7]

Thus only one born alive could be murdered. To destroy a fetus once it "stirred" or seemed "quick" was a misdemeanor, and possibly not even that in an earlier stage of its development. Inducing and attempting abortion, "quick" or not, were made illegal by statute in 1803. For our period, Sir Matthew Hale's opinion more likely represents the common law.

Pregnant women were routinely respited from execution until they could give birth. On its face, this practice appears to recognize that the unborn had a right to life. It might however have been a right of the child's family, as against the crown, to keep the child. In either case, the unborn child had to be "quick" to win this respite. Yet a woman under sentence could not prolong her life by getting pregnant again and pleading her belly a second time. Blackstone explains, not quite to the point, that "she may now be executed before the child is quick in the womb, and shall not, by her own incontinence, evade the sentence of justice."[8] Although opportunities to plead one's belly twice must have been rare, this rule raises the theoretical question, What has happened to any right of the second fetus to life, or of its family to the child?

The rights of an unborn child were contingent on its achieving live birth in other respects as well. For example, it might inherit and sometimes even be given property despite its obvious inability to take possession, but only if it were later born alive.[9] Among all these vague frontiers, the only clear boundary was live birth.

Our authors did not argue that poverty pushed people into crime. They preferred to recite the crimes of persons who had plunged into poverty from a happier condition. Doubtless, poor people died for acts that were desperate enough, but too drab to merit a pamphlet. There was more drama in a downfall, and a higher probability that those able to buy pamphlets would identify with the protagonist, and feel a twinge of the pity and terror essential to tragedy.

Prosperity and poverty coexisted then as now, but more intimately then, before there was any zoning, and when some servants regularly shared their betters' bedrooms. Although parishes still cared for their poor, only grandparents could recall the time when there were rich priories and monasteries to share the burdens of charity. As population grew, the City of London endured a stream of migrants arriving in the metropolis from a countryside that had no more room or hope for them, forcing the merchant oligarchy to regulate the London poor in more detail than the rest of the nation. The city fathers would deny that they were making poverty a crime, but to subsidize idle strangers offended them spiritually and materially. They cut off able-bodied persons from city pensions. They licensed begging, restricting permits to imprisoned debtors and the disabled. Citizens were required to report any sturdy beggars they saw, or be fined three shillings four pence. A constable who looked the other way was fined twice as much.

Indigents also tried to make ends meet as thieves or prostitutes. The city fathers carried out raids on their roosts, especially bowling alleys, alehouses, and the few theatres that had not moved beyond their jurisdiction. Vagrants were arrested in the streets during church services. Country vagrants were sent back to the parish from whence they came. The carter who had brought them to London was compelled to cart them back home— if he could be found. Innkeepers who took them in were ordered either to support them or send them back. Vagrants with diseases were taken to St. Thomas's or St. Bartholomew's Hospital. Orphans were sent to Christ's Hospital unless it was full, and then they would be sent to one of the parishes for care. Ministers were asked to persuade their parishioners to take these orphans into their homes, and see that they were educated. The city fathers revealed their own laudable priorities when they specified the subjects they considered essential: reading, writing, grammar, and music. Each parish had some money for the poor, from its property taxes. If this ran out, the City helped from a central fund, as long as that lasted. After that, nothing.

Sturdy urban vagrants were put in Bridewell, a former palace of Henry VIII sited where the Fleet River flows into the Thames. As the overloaded Fleet evolved into an open sewer, Henry's son Edward VI gave his smelly palace to the City of London, and soon it became the first workhouse. The governors of Bridewell estimated that, to care for 200 inmates, they needed about £2,000 a year. Foreigners, often blamed for unemployment in London, were not supposed to work, and their foreign goods could be confiscated. Foreigners were not only Dutch and so forth, but English who were not Londoners. The net proceeds from these confiscations went into the City fund for the poor, and supported Bridewell.

Bridewell inmates were fed a "thin diet, onely sufficing to sustaine them in health," so they could work to repay their food and shelter. They made shoes for the poor from rejected leather, and also nails, pins, combs, yarn, candlewick, wire, knives, and tennis balls. The strongest hauled sand. If their work would compete unfairly with a trade guild, they were given to guild members as apprentices. If they proved lazy or defiant apprentices, they were whipped. Inmates were let out if their work required it, but if they were caught begging, they too were whipped. A Bridewell apprentice caught deserting his master was treated like an escaping inmate. That meant having a hole bored through one ear, a primitive kind of recordkeeping, to ensure that if he escaped again his captors would know it was a second offense. Since the second offense was a felony, there might be no opportunity for a third. The way out of Bridewell was to get work, by way of apprenticeship or employment as a servant. Free-lance prostitutes were put in the women's wing of Bridewell, which a discreet bawd could probably visit, working the system to get the pick of promising girls.[10]

II

Removing Obstacles to Wealth

Families of four centuries ago ran broad and deep. Their property, even if modest, descended, in most shires, by a rule known as male primogeniture with postponement of females. The eldest son inherited the estate to the exclusion of all his brothers and sisters. Only if a family had no son would daughters inherit, and then they would all share the estate equally. The purpose of male primogeniture was to preserve estates intact and build up the wealth, status, and power of a family. That was certainly its effect. A corollary of this system was that the head of the family more or less looked after younger brothers, unmarried sisters, and other family dependents. In this way the family extended further in breadth than now.

Families with property also knew their ancestors and connections, and there were those whose land holdings, great or small, went back at least four centuries, or to that dim legal time whereof the memory of man runneth not to the contrary. Their past line of descent made them what they were; their future line of descent formed the beacon of their earthly purpose. Descent and alliance had a language of their own in heraldry. Today we visit a parish church and muse over the escutcheons and lozenges, knowing they are in a language of some kind now legible only to antiquaries and heralds. Those whom they commemorate were able to read them, and tell what family had provided a grandmother, or whom a woman had married and whether she had died a widow or before her husband. Upward mobility may not have been rapid, but it was achievable through the patient building of the estate for children and grandchildren. One who did not have a coat of arms might some day apply successfully for one to the heralds, as Shakespeare did. They granted him, in their language, this coat of arms:

"Or, on a bend sable, a tiltingspear of the field." During long sermons, armigerous fathers and mothers must have browsed among the hatchments, quarterings, and charges on the walls and floor of the church, mentally trying out matches that would some day bring a neighbor's manor under their family name. The tough thread woven of family, continuity, and property, enduring quietly through times of strife and distress, could be snapped by private disasters like those that follow. Ambition, and impatience with so slow a process as alliance and descent, led to ruinous homicide.[1]

Deadline (1595)

On Christmas Thomas Chambers would come of age, and under his late father's will inherit £200 in cash as well as real estate worth £30 a year. If for any reason the youth did not live till then, his sister, Mrs. Graygoose, and mother, Mrs. Wright, would inherit the estate. At Candlemas Mrs. Graygoose's husband John reckoned that with less than 11 months until Christmas his young brother-in-law showed every sign of good health. Graygoose rode over from his home in Epping to Corbett's Tie, where Thomas and his mother lived with her second husband, John Wright. Graygoose had a private chat with the stepfather on how their wives would inherit, and enrich each of them, if Thomas did not make it to Christmas. John Graygoose and John Wright agreed that whoever saw Thomas first during Whitsun holidays would kill him.

Thomas's friends began to miss him even as the holidays began, but did not find him until Monday, 19 June, when the persistent baying of a greyhound in the forest led them to Thomas. His brains had been dashed out by a single blow from a post ripped off a nearby stile. People remembered that Wright had been absent from his usual haunts a few evenings before, and had said something or other that now seemed suspicious. He broke down before the magistrate, implicating Graygoose. They were hanged at Rumford on 14 July, 1595, before they could share in their widows' Christmas inheritance.[2]

A Fresh Start (1591)

To a Kentish farmer named Lincoln, becoming a widower at 50 represented an economic opportunity. In this fertile countryside, it did not take him long to call on a widow of "reasonable wealth," but she briskly told him that his four children made him an ineligible suitor. They were a "great charge." She had not achieved her reasonable wealth by assuming great charges. Lincoln went home and "sate downe in great heavinesse by the fireside." A married laborer who worked for Lincoln found him moping by the fire.

Why so pensive?

Sit down. I can't be merry.

Why don't you find a good wife? You have wherewithal to keep one.

Oh, said Lincoln ("fetching a great sigh"), there is none will have me, because of my great charge of children. As the evening wore on, Lincoln offered his man a deal: 40 shillings and a cow to do away with the four children. All this scared the laborer badly. Lincoln added a promise, never to swear he was the murderer. For some reason this promise reassured the laborer. Besides, 40 shillings! And a cow! They agreed.

A Saturday morning in November started as usual with breakfast at home: the father, the laborer, and the four children. Then Lincoln set out to market in Ashford, taking with him his eldest son of about 15. The laborer went part way with them and then returned to the house, where he knocked the two boys and the girl on the head with a hatchet, and slit their throats. Meanwhile at the market, their father bought them three pairs of little shoes. At the end of the day, Lincoln sent his son on ahead. The youth arrived after dark. He and the neighbors were finding the bodies just as the father arrived.

The neighbors blamed the laborer. They had seen him about the place earlier, and now he had disappeared. This opinion did not suit Lincoln, who had spared his eldest son only to cast him as the murderer. Managing his grief, he argued that the laborer was "a verie honest fellow." The culprit could not be the servant, he said, and so it must be his son. Whatever the neighbors made of this, they were offended to find that Lincoln just left the bodies where they were for three days, until a gentlewoman named West came around to lecture him. Lincoln's miserly concession was to dig a hole about two feet deep in the cellar and put the bodies in it. In another five days a leisurely coroner arrived, and found that springs in Lincoln's cellar had washed the bodies so they were now quite clear and white. By then the laborer had been arrested, denying any knowledge.

Everybody knew that murdered corpses would bleed or blush in the presence of their attackers. Sometimes they would even open one eye and fix the culprit with a baleful stare. So convenient a forensic tool was not to be ignored:

But [the laborer] beeing brought before the dead bodies of the children, the Father being there also, the woundes began to bleede afresh, which when the Crowner sawe, he commanded the partie apprehended to looke upon the children, which hee did, and called them by their names, whereuppon, behold the wonderfull workes of God, for the fact beeing still denied, the bodies of the children, which seemed white like unto soaked flesh laid in water, sodainly received their former colour of bloude, and had such a lively countenance flushing in theyr faces, as if they had beene living creatures lying asleepe, which indeed blushed on the murtherers when they wanted grace to blush and been ashamed of theyr owne wickednesse. Which wonderfull miracle caused the murtherer there present not onely to confesse and acknowledge himself guiltie of the damnable deede, but also to accuse the Father of the children as principal procurer of their untimely deaths.

Both were tried in Canterbury and hanged near Ashford. At the last minute the father confessed, explaining that he needed a fresh start.[3]

One Way Out (1598)

Henry Robson had never given debt much thought until he fell into a financial black hole all too familiar to his fellow subjects. He was put into Rye Jail by his creditors. Henry could make money only by fishing, which is notoriously bad in jails, and so he faced possible life imprisonment. His wife visited him loyally, and by working hard she helped him with his everyday costs, but she had nowhere near the ready cash to buy his freedom. Could she have raised enough by selling everything she owned? If she could, she did not, perhaps foreseeing that after taking that irrevocable plunge into utter destitution she would still have the same feckless mate on her hands. She thought she knew her Henry. Henry believed firmly that her property was sufficient to pay his debts, but then if he had been good at arithmetic he would not have gone to jail. Doubtless the couple debated this issue during visits.

For company, Henry had a cellmate named Glasier, and the two men whiled the dragging hours discussing the problem. Glasier was sympathetic.

"Faith Harry I am sorie to see thee live thus in prison, and hast been so well beloved in this towne."

"Tush Glasier tis too late now to be sorie, when there is no remedie, for so long as my wife liveth, it is unpossible thatever I should come out."

"Faith then sure," reflected Glasier, "if my wifes death could procure my libertie, I would never be in bondage, or imprisoned."

"No why my wishes can never the sooner procure her death."

"I but your indevour may, without being once suspected: and if you will take my counsell and be secret, I will warrant you she shall not long live."

Henry's spirits lifted, and he promised to be Glasier's friend for life. They worked out a plan, which was to kill Mrs. Robson, sell her property, leave prison and England, and start afresh in the low countries. Soon after, Glasier was freed from jail. He went to a mercer in Rye named Fisher, invested one penny in ratsbane, and brought it back to Henry's cell. Friend Glasier's instructions were: Mix the ratsbane with some ground glass, and wrap a bit no bigger than a hazelnut in some shoulder of mutton skin, and on the night when next his wife should come to lie with him, convey it into what he called her privie parts. Then visitor Glasier departed.

A week later, Mrs. Robson found Henry more than usually affectionate. Although she had planned to go back home that night, he persuaded her to spend it in the cell with him "the dearest night's pleasure that ever woman had," observes the author. In the morning she returned home to resume the drudgery awaiting her. Soon she began to feel discomfort, then swelling, and then extreme pain as the ratsbane took command. So she lay for five days, visited by neighbors and several physicians. Some tried purges on her, but nothing helped. All suspected that she had been poisoned, and as soon as she was dead the physicians held up her burial and conducted an autopsy. Throughout her veins, they are said to have reported, they found ground glass and ratsbane.

They doubted that she could have ingested it through food or drink, but they could not imagine how else she might have done. The authorities combed Rye for recent purchases of ratsbane, and at Fisher's shop learned about Glasier. He had vanished, but the recorder, Master Boulton, examined his cellmate Henry.

"Neighbour Robson, we understand by one Glasier, that you had certain poyson of him which you caused him to buy; now wee have sent for you to know to what intent you bought it; for that you are suspected of the death of your wife, and by some manifestly accused." This was bluff. Henry did not know they had failed to find Glasier, but he said he was as ignorant as a newborn child of any poison.

"Nay, if you be so obstinate, we will bring Glasier forth, who to your shame shall testifie it, and then you are not only guiltie of the poyson, but also of the act doing: and therefor confesse the truth and shame the devill."

"Well, I had indeede Ratsbane; but what of that?"

"Why didst thou deny it then it shewes a guiltie conscience. But what didst thou with it, and to what intent didst thou buy it?"

"Why, the Courthouse is full of rats and I bought it to kill them."

"That is not so but the devill is the father of lyers, and I feare thou art his sonne: confesse the truth what thou didst with it."

"Well, if you will needes know, I will trulie resolve you. I have long been in prison and I have often heard that poyson will breake open any iron lock, and therefore I bought it thinking thereby to get my libertie. Now I have told the truth I hope you will pardon me."

"No thou hast not told the truth; for with it and glasse mingled together thou didst poyson thy wife; and therefore as thou lookest for any favour at our hands, confesse how and in what manner thou didst it, and who was the counseller in it."

"Well, then I perceive you glut after my blood, and if it will pleasure you you shall have it." Henry finally confessed and was hanged. Of eternal friend Glasier we hear no more. That is a pity, because he must have known of at least one previous use of this method of murder—cases very likely never solved.[4]

Jeopardies (1603-1621)

To small yeomen and the poor, common lands were an ancient right. To large landlords they were an antiquated inconvenience, like a sharp bend in a modern highway. The commons were an area open to all, where villagers could graze their animals. It was also land that, in the large owner's view, might as well be turned over to the growing herd of sheep that had been enriching him and the past few generations of his family. It was the wave of the future. In village after village, through the process known as enclosure, local commons were being turned over to the richer gentry by act of parliament, and the lesser countrymen were being fenced out of what had been their pasturage. There was not much anybody could do about an act of parliament. If a statute made a common part of some lord's estate, that was the law of the realm. Not every landlord bothered to go through this laborious and expensive process. Some of them simply seized the common, and relied on bullying and force to hold it. This practice naturally led to much friction.

In Market Rasen, Lincolnshire, just such a dispute had been gaining heat one Sunday in 1603, when, after evening prayer, the issue of enclosing the town fields was brought up in the church. Passions ran high. When the discussion took on a less and less Christian tone, pastor William Storre (M.A. Oxon.) intervened to suggest letting a few sober men argue the two sides. Nearly everybody agreed, and even asked him to arbitrate the dispute. Mr. Storre was uneasy. He had already had some friction with Francis Cartwright, the only son of one of the local landlords, and known for his "hotte stomacke."

After two or three refusals, Storre gave in, fearing to leave a vacuum for violence to enter. In the end, his arbitration went against the enclosing squire. The first person in the assembly to respond was Francis of the hot stomach, who shouted,

"The Priest deserveth a good Fee, he speaketh so like a Lawyer," and words our narrator refused to repeat. Francis's father kept him from stabbing the minister, but he stamped out into the market place and made a sort of proclamation: Storre was a scurvy, lousy, paltry priest. Whoever called Storre a friend or spoke in his cause was a rogue and a rascal. If it were not for the law he would cut the priest's throat, tear out his heart, and hang his quarters on the maypole.

Storre went to the justice of the peace for protection. The justice would normally have made Francis post a bond to guarantee his future good behavior, but this local dignitary was overawed by the Cartwrights, and pretended to doubt that he had sufficient grounds. He said he would bring it up to the next quarter sessions, when more justices of the peace would be sharing in the decision. Storre prepared to take his problem to the court of high commission in Westminster. Another Sabbath came around, and Storre preached a sermon on the text, "Except the Lord of Hostes had reserved unto us, even a small remnant, we had been as Sodome, and like unto Gomorrah," plainly referring to common lands. The preacher inserted "some sharpe and nipping reprehensions." Young Cartwright was furiously taking notes with his pen and inkwell in the family pew. Francis's "stomacke filled with raw humors." At a cutler's shop he bought a short, specially sharpened sword.

A day or so later, at about eight in the morning, on a road south of Market Rasen, a maid came upon Francis hacking away at Storre. When Francis fled, the maid tried to help the victim, who was lying in a red puddle, alive but with a great gash in his brain. He had many defensive wounds, as police would say now, including three severed fingers and cuts on both arms. His thighs and knees had been deeply slashed, a thighbone and pelvis broken in several pieces. A heel was doubled back to his calf. The maid's

The murder of William Storre by Francis Cartwright, 1603. Cartwright hacks away at his minister, ignoring the illegible biblical text indicated by the victim. The woman might be Mrs. Storre calling for justice, and perhaps showing the penury to which the murder has brought her. Bodleian Library, University of Oxford 4oE.17 Art (3).

alarm put Market Rasen in an uproar. Some ran about crying Murder, but others thought there must be a fire somewhere and rang the church bell. A few carried Storre into the constable's house and set about binding his many wounds. The next day a bonesetter and four surgeons arrived. Storre died six days later (at the change of the moon, notes the author).

Francis had run home to the protection of his father, where he was besieged by a great angry crowd. The father, fearing a lynching, was able to hold them off and persuade them to wait for constables. These took Francis to the justice of the peace, whose cowardice came into play again. He released Francis on slight bail, and Francis disappeared. Word of the murder and the fiasco soon reached the Archbishop of Canterbury, and the privy council summoned the justice of the peace to appear and explain himself. He managed to get out of this trip by pleading age and ill health, but he was relieved of his position pending review by the next assizes. The constable was bound over for contempt for letting Francis skip bail.

Francis became a fugitive, working his way to Berwick, hoping to escape into Scotland. He was caught by the Berwick garrison, but escaped. After much dodging he reached the safety of Rouen and later Delft. He was dependent on such money as his father was able to send him. A Mr. Trigg, another Lincolnshire parson, labored by letters to lead him to repentance. The Cartwrights finally gained Francis a conditional royal pardon, and he returned home.

"Scarce was I entertayned at home," complained Francis with obvious self-pity, "but least still I should nestle myself in secure slumber, another affliction arose to endanger mee. The wife of the slaine sueth an Appeale against me, notwithstanding my Pardon."

This astonishing old process is described in Appendix B.

In the end, Francis was saved by a technicality from the widow's appeal. Certain prominent persons, probably the archbishops, had been busy about King James, however. His majesty let it be known that, if any flaw could be found in his pardon of Cartwright, sentence of death should proceed. Francis was in a perilous position. Not surprisingly, he had enemies who realized that his fate was conditional on his good behavior, and they could now pick on the hot-stomached Francis with impunity. In this humiliating position, he was planning to go back into exile when his father died. He decided to remain in the country, and proposed marriage to a lady, a little unrealistically perhaps for one excommunicated. Nor had he made his peace with the hostile part of the county gentry. Four men attacked him and wounded him with halberds. When he recovered, he declared his contrition before the archbishop, bishops, and clergy in convocation. Having thus overcome his spiritual disability, he married. In recognition of his new state of grace, the Archbishop of York entertained Francis with his family and bride.

In time, he became a father. Francis said now he might hope he had paid his price, though surely the widow Storre would not have thought so. Now a new turbulence invaded his life. At Grantham one day a Mr. Rigge (a rash man, said the rash Francis) made it his business to pile insults on him, and when Francis refused to fight, Rigge wounded him with his sword. Responding at last, Francis killed Rigge. Francis was not as free to fly as he had been. He had to consider his wife and son. If he fled he would leave his family penniless. There followed a time he called "Imprisonment and Irons," in which he might have killed himself but for the visits of two ministers. Just at this point, Cartwright's only son fell so ill that his burial was being arranged.

Cartwright was led in chains "like a condemned Gally Slave" to see his son one last time. Do not punish him for my sins, he prayed. The little boy recovered after all, a sort of turning point even though Cartwright now faced trial for killing Rigge. He was given only one year in prison, because of the strong possibility that he had acted in self-defense.

When he stepped out of prison, he had spent much of his estate in payments to courts and lawyers, and possibly in a financial settlement with the widow Storre. Freedom felt so good that he started spending more on pleasures—nothing illegal, he tells us, but not prudent either. Soon he found himself hanging about at Westminster waiting for a kinsman of his wife's to find him employment. Waiting at court was expensive in itself. Down to the last of his money, Francis placed himself under vice-admiral Sir Richard Hawkins on board the *Vauntgard*, setting out on a diplomatic mission to the Dey of Algiers. His reputation travelled with him. The other gentlemen on board knew about his case, and played the jolly game of trying to goad him into some act that would be his ruin.

In the Mediterranean, the captain decided he had had enough of this and put him on another ship, the *Marigold*, returning to England. Off Malaga, the *Marigold* ran afoul of two other English ships and nearly wrecked. The sailors knew their bad luck came from having the unredeemed murderer Cartwright aboard. As if to prove their point, the ship was captured near Gibraltar by Algerian warships. The sailors' fate would normally have been a life of slavery, but for two lions that the *Marigold* carried in its cargo, presents from the Dey of Algiers to the King of England. The Algerians had to let the *Marigold* go. Cartwright landed at Deal and hired a coach, a crude, rocking wagon in which he managed to wound himself with his own sword.

As he recovered he asked: After my many wounds, my exile and other restless travels, the hostility of the Atlantic and Mediterranean, the hatred of gentlemen and mariners, the stalking of the Algerian, and this last accident, have I paid my dues, 18 years after hacking my pastor to death? To some, all his troubles were not as appropriate as hanging would have been, but at least he was not swaggering and bullying about Market Rasen. Perhaps age and his experiences were mellowing him, as he implied. When we last hear of him, poverty had forced him to serve in the European wars, and he was seeing little of his wife and growing son. His hardships, in the unlikely case that he was not grossly exaggerating them, cannot obscure the fact that even double jeopardy had not achieved justice.[5]

The Mediator (1605)

Old Mr. Browne, timorous owner of lands around Eastbridge, Suffolk, worth £600 a year, made all his plans by talking aloud to himself. To keep these from his loathed wife, he took long walks. He and Mrs. Browne had separate households within their house, separate servants, and separate meals. In the same house lived a memento of Browne's younger days, an illegitimate daughter of marriageable age whom he was bringing up to be a lady.

In the privacy of his woods, Browne recited his chief worries: First of all, somebody might kill you; but if that does not happen and you just go on like this, that too is a worry. If your wife dies first, you might be old and helpless without her. But if she does not die first, you will be old and helpless and at her mercy. That is more terrible yet. You need a plan.

Luckily, Browne had a gem of a servant named Peter Golding, able, devoted, and penniless. His loyalty was famous in Eastbridge. Peter had fallen in love with the daughter, a love sustained and deepened by his daily reflection on the difference between his servant's wages and £600 a year. Peter's own plans and his master's converged when Browne made his proposal: Care for me, and you can marry my daughter, and I will adopt you as my son. Peter had only to continue being loyal and valuable to become wealthy and independent. He was no ordinary servant, and handled much of Browne's business. Browne showed new heights of trust by sending him on a long visit to London to look after some litigation there.

The arrangement with Peter depended on a certain conventional passivity on the part of the daughter, and a steadfast mind on the part of her father. The daughter, however, loved not Peter the servant but Mr. Wentworth, the wealthy gentleman next door. While Peter was away, she married Wentworth. Was she an undutiful daughter? No. Dotty old men sometimes enjoy giving away the same asset twice. Browne, not at all steadfast, gave his consent. For all we know, he had sent his servant away so Browne and his daughter could accomplish the match with Wentworth. He told himself on his walks: You don't pass up a good catch like Wentworth. As for being looked after in your old age, your daughter and son-in-law will be just next door. After all, with money you can always find a good servant. Maybe you can make some new deal with Peter when he gets back from London. Oh, Peter's going to be furious, though. Maybe he'll kill you.

Yes, Peter was furious when he returned, and loud in his disappointment. There, there, Peter, his master urged, just be patient and I'll be a good master to you yet. To start with, Browne gave him outright a farm at Dunnage, worth £30 a year. The politic Peter quickly recovered, and continued to be the ideal servant.

Within the divided house there was ample opportunity for diplomacy. As might be expected, Mr. Browne's servants often had friction with Mrs. Browne's servants. Peter was able to reduce this diplomatically, and to ingratiate himself with old Mrs. Browne without offending her husband. The whole neighborhood of course knew about the quarrels of the two sets of servants, and Peter's new triumphs as peacemaker. Certainly Mrs. Browne liked him.

One day a nephew of hers, Brian Smith, came to visit. She and Brian and Peter sat in the parlor together, cosily chatting on various subjects, such as Life. Life was strange and uncertain: Some old men go on and on, some young ones die early. Wealth was strange too: Some start with nothing and die rich, and then somebody born wealthy dies a beggar. Smith said he envied Peter, who now had £30 a year certain. Peter deferentially said he owed it all to his master, but wished his estate were as good as Smith's. Alas, Smith said, there is nothing certain about my estate. If my aunt here dies before Mr. Browne, I shall get nothing. As all creatures are in God's hands, pursued Peter piously, what if my master should die before your aunt? Brian of course did not wish anyone to die, but in that case he would be happy if, of course, there is any bliss in earthly possessions. Peter made a sporting proposition. He would bet ten pounds against Smith's ten shillings that Mr. Browne would not live through the next 12 months. Brian felt there was something indecent about such a bet, but his aunt said there is nothing wrong with winning money, and if you don't take the bet I will. The deal was put in writing, witnessed by Aunt Browne.

Two days short of a year later, Mrs. Browne pointedly reminded Peter that he looked like losing his money. Death can act in a minute as well as a month, he said. In fact, he had tried several times, undetected, to help death act on old Browne. Now, with only a day or two before his self-imposed deadline, Peter prepared three ashwood clubs and distributed them in the coppice along the path Browne always took. The next day he went to town to collect some money for his master, and Browne began his walk. It took only minutes for Peter to stop on his way, bash Browne in the back of the head with the nearest of the waiting clubs, and go about his usual business with no noticeable gap in his alibi. Not that he needed an alibi. When two laborers found the body that afternoon, several names were whispered, but not Peter Golding's.

Mr. Morgan, the parson, and likely the best educated person in the area, puzzled over this event, a murder strangely lacking a suspect. Although everybody knew that the victim and Mrs. Browne had always fought, she was physically incapable of bashing Browne's skull. Mr. Morgan visited Peter. I know how much you loved your master, said Mr. Morgan, and he has told me of his love for you. I shall pray heaven, and do whatever is needed on earth, to discover this dark deed. And you should search "above the height of imagination" to ensure that the murder of so good an old man should not go unavenged.

Through his flowing tears, Peter was finally able to say, "O Maister Morgan, my Maister was to me as the Sunne to man, or raine to a parched sommer, the life of what I am, and the giver of what I have."

> We two together by the helpe of God, and God will help us to find out murtherers, wil know who killed him. Then tell me Peter, thou knowest who of his tenants were at oddes with him. I am to preach at his funeral. Invite them al thither, at which sermon if the Caine be there, I hope to utter such heavenly sentences, shall make his eyes stare, and his heart steale his blood out of his treacherous face.

At the funeral the heavenly sermon laid out with graphic clarity the terrifying future the murderer had to expect. The parishoners wept, all but Peter, who, dumb with terror, "sate like one had laine six daies in a grave." After the sermon, the observant Mr. Morgan suggested he spend the night with Peter. Long before dawn, Peter had confessed to him. The next day, when the magistrates quizzed him further, he implicated Mrs. Browne. She was burnt at the stake, and Peter was hanged with his ashwood club at his back.[6]

"Oblivion Was Their Motto" (1620)

Norton, gazing beyond the fine Suffolk estate that was his to the neighboring estate that was not his, came to covet it as he realized that even the income he already enjoyed might not indefinitely support the costly and riotous life he had adopted. It only inflamed his hankering to know that its owner was the widow Leeson, and that her three sons and daughter were all minors.

He developed an ambiguous sort of relationship with the widow and her family. First came generosity: a little money here and there to help her out, a little money to the children. Then the transactions grew more complicated. His benefactions continued, but flowed in more businesslike channels. When the widow needed really serious money she found she could get it from Norton by mortgaging some of her land. At the same time, he played a rather perverse mentor to the children, teaching the sons the joys of heavy drinking, a subject in which experience had made him expert. Drunk or sober, behind Norton the friend always stood Norton the predator.

The eldest of the Leeson sons reached his majority, and as was customary he claimed the lands as his paternal inheritance. Norton engaged him in some trumped up lawsuit, and as his influence in the area was considerable, he was able to have the youth imprisoned, corrupting the jailer so that Leeson was held incommunicado. Somehow Leeson died in prison.

The second son, John, was not frightened enough to give up his claim when he in turn came of age. For a time, Norton bought his silence with money, but John soon saw that it was not the allowance but the estate that was the main show. When Norton found that the son would no longer be bribed, he called on his henchmen, one Worlish and a weaver named Land. They invited John one afternoon to another of those drinking bouts, this time at a more distant tavern on Mill Hill. The drinks flowed freely and the youth was entertained with dice and other games until darkness fell. Then Land and Worlish took him out, crushed his head, carried him to a nearby pond, and sank him, tied to a block and stake. John's disappearance

The murder of the Leeson sons, 1620. Years are compressed in this print to show the murder of the fourth Leeson youth in the presence of the Devil, the cleaning of the pond, and the examination of the remains of the three older Leesons. Reproduced by permission of the Huntington Library, San Marino, California.

was ostensibly a mystery in the intimidated community. At some time, Worlish told the widow that he had seen John in the Netherlands and was the last person to be with him when he died.

The third son was indeed frightened of Norton and his brutal followers, but in about two years he too came of age. He went to court to clear his estate, and got a subpoena out of chancery summoning Norton to appear in the suit. The son was afraid to serve the subpoena on Norton face to face, so, bringing his sister as witness, he tried to hang the document on Norton's door. There Land and Worlish seized them both, murdered them, and staked them down in the pool next to their brother. When friends missed them, Land said he had heard the pair were off to Ireland. Whatever the credibility of such a statement from such a source, the inhabitants of Halsworth, including the widow Leeson, knew better than to question it.

After six years, the farmer who owned the pond felt an odd urge to have it cleaned. His wife rightly complained of the expense, but the farmer's urge grew until he had laborers dragging the pool bottom. Their horses displayed a will of their own, refusing to work where the men wanted to start, ambling stubbornly over to another part of the pool, and causing the discovery of the three bodies. The author saw in the inexplicable behavior of both farmer and horses nothing less than *digitus dei*, the finger of a God who had decided the time had come for justice. Of the victims, the usually prosaic author wrote, "The bottom of the pond was their grave, and oblivion was their Motto."

The bones were raked up and assembled with some care. After six years it was too late, as the author explains, for the corpses to accuse the culprit by bleeding afresh. Nobody was sure whose bones they were, so the neighbors were asked to view the skeletons. They were measured and searched for identifying marks. The second son, John Leeson had been an unusual six feet tall, and so was one of the skeletons. Netherlands indeed! The third son had been missing two teeth on one side, and by this his mother and friends were able to identify him. Ireland indeed!

After this forensic triumph, it is sad to report that the authorities lost the skull. That is because Land took it to a local barber (barbers were the dentists and surgeons of the day) and asked him to remove more teeth from it. The barber was unable (he said) to do so. The author saw this as a miraculous refusal on the part of his dental instruments; we might think it was a dentist keeping out of trouble. Land then took the skull to a smith. We are not told what opinion the smith's tools held, but he also put Land off, and turned witness against him. By now of course Land's actions were the talk of the town and he was in much worse condition than before.

Worlish fled to Yarmouth, where he fell ill (*digitus dei* again) and was easily retrieved. Worlish's problem was that he had never been to the lowlands where he had claimed to see the second son die. Worlish was tried at Bury assizes before Lord Chief Justice Montague. His lordship solemnly speculated that by "lowlands" the defendant may have meant the bottom of the pond—an early example of that judicial wit that has long haunted English courts.

At the trial, dozens of witnesses appeared for the prosecution. The silent community had lost its terror. They had seen Land and Worlish and John Leeson go to the tavern on Mill Hill. They had heard Land and Worlish in their cups making dark jokes about what would happen if anybody poked about in a certain pond. Land and Worlish were taken to the gallows together. Land was hanged but Worlish was taken off the ladder and given a few more days to make a better confession—one that would seal Norton's fate. Norton, the force behind this whole story, had not been tried yet when the author went to press, but there seemed little doubt of his fate, for the lord chief justice had already told him that he was the main culprit. The author is less enlightening about Norton than he might have been, because he is more interested in Norton's being a Catholic, and in all the criminological conclusions to be drawn from that fact. The minister, however, recognized that Protestants too could be sinners, and puritanically suggested that the victims' fate was punishment for their own heavy drinking. The widow Leeson remains either a total mystery or an extreme example of female subservience.[7]

Dangerous Real Estate (1624)

There were other kinds of property that did not descend by blood, but could be acquired by eliminating its possessor. Certain governmental offices, for example, might be property whether they were sinecures or not, and ingenious incumbents found ways to turn them into cash by selling remainders, or the right to the office after the incumbent's death. Even the probability that a position would go to a certain person might tempt him to eliminate the incumbent. A sophistication of this kind upset the simple life of a village, during one of its immemorially ancient solar festivals.

As the shortest night of the year descended, if Old Cleeve was like other Somerset villages, a few shadowy figures would wait in the church porch, to learn who was going to die in the coming year. (They did this by watching to see who seems to walk into the church on midsummer's night, but does not come out again.) Most of the parishoners, however, would have been gathering in the churchyard, preparing for the more congenial ceremony, of "clipping," or hugging the church. They would turn their backs to the church and hold hands until they had encircled it. They were not sure why they did this every midsummer. Some thought it was to keep out the devil for another year. They probably did not know it was a fossil pagan rite. Better to do it, because the grandparents had done it, and because it just might keep the devil out, and anyway it was social.

The parson took no part in the clipping; parsons discouraged or gingerly tolerated such folk rites. In some parishes, midsummer in the churchyard got rowdy as its ancient erotic elements reemerged. Then a parson would forbid what he called the desecration of the graves. But those who lay in the graves were the celebrants' forebears, not the parson's, and some clippers probably owed their March births to the youthful midsummer romps of those whose rest was now alleged to be disturbed. In the parish of Old Cleeve, the Reverend Mr. Trat (M.A. Oxon.) took the opportunity today to ride off on his horse with some groceries for his mother.

Trat was not seen again. One Sunday came and went without him, and then another. After 15 days those passing his house were assaulted by a smell that insistently transcended the usual blend of community manures. However it stank, Trat's house was still his castle, and it was only after getting a warrant from justices of the peace in Saint Decuman and Creech that villagers broke down his door.

In the nauseating manse, they found two large earthenware pots on the ground floor next to one of the walls. One pot held somebody's arms and legs, neatly severed and packed parallel. They had been parboiled and salted, the method by which the country folk regularly prepared what they called "powdered beef" for preservation. One wonders how these searchers faced this dietary staple the rest of their lives. The salting had been botched, though the butchering was neat and competent. The other large pot held internal organs. Upstairs, the searchers found a cloth-covered tub containing the trunk, quartered like a beef. They found no head.

Masters Windham and Cuffe, the justices of the peace, knew something of investigating murders, from the recent cases of a man at Saint Audrey's murdered by his wife and her lover, and of a man at Otterhampton murdered by his brother in law. They took notes and directed the gathering of evidence. An especially promising clue turned up in the house, an old green suit that nobody had seen in the village before. In case it had been left by the murderer, Windham and Cuffe had it "cried" or displayed over the next few days at several nearby markets, the best way to reach persons from isolated dwellings. Behind a pile of rue and other pungent herbs stood a pot of blood, which a local named Andrew Baker took up. A justice told him to carry it out carefully and not spill any evidence. Andrew's response was to dump it on the floor, so the justices arrested him. They also arrested Alice Walker, whose oracular mutterings suggested guilty knowledge. Alice had been saying that if the minister "did not come home the sooner, his powdred Beefe would stinke before his comming."

Both Andrew and Alice were servants of the Smithwickes, a local family with more influence than money. The head of the family came to the aid of justice at this point. He bailed Alice out of jail, mounted his horse, and announced that he was setting out in search of the fugitive parson Trat. On some hunch that nobody understood, he chose to ride south to Taunton rather than west to Devon or east to Bridgewater. In Taunton he found a bowmaker named Ford who told him Trat had passed by headed for Ilminster just after midsummer's day. Smithwicke explained the situation to Ford and got him to report his story to a local justice. Smithwicke then rode on a dozen miles to Ilminster, where he found someone who remembered Trat asking the way to Blandford, Dorset. This was a good 35 miles farther, but Smithwicke rode on and was rewarded by finding a minister named Sacheverell.

Yes, he said, Trat had come by. He and Sacheverell had been students at Magdalen together long ago. They had not seen each other again until a few days ago, when Trat had ridden up to his door in the dusk. He had invited Trat in, but Trat said he did not have time to dismount. He was in some trouble back home. It seems that coming back from Dunster market he met some beggar just over from Ireland. He gave the Irishman two pence and took him home for supper and a bed. In the morning he caught the Irishman crossing himself at the breakfast table and scolded him for his papistical and superstitious practices. The two men fought, and he stabbed the beggar. He was not sure whether he had killed him. Sacheverell urged him to go back because a surgeon might yet be able to save the man, but he turned and rode off into the night. Smithwicke told Sacheverell the man had indeed died, and easily persuaded him to come forward and testify so the wrong parties might not be blamed.

Windham and Cuffe examined Ford and Sacheverell closely. They found that Ford did not really know Trat: How did you know the rider was Trat? He said so. As for Sacheverell, he had not seen his old college mate for many years, and the rider who called himself Trat had remained mounted in the dusk. In the end, neither would swear that the person they had met was Trat. In the meantime, Windham and Cuffe had learned more. One of the quarters showed stab wounds. A finger bore a small mark that one man remembered seeing on one of Trat's fingers.

Then too, the Smithwicke servants were behaving strangely. Alice Walker, unable either to tell the truth or to suppress it effectively, had accused a neighbor woman of spreading tales about Alice's involvement in the murder but this was before either the neighbor or the public knew there had been a murder. Just after the discovery, Cirill Austin, a day laborer for the Smithwickes, went off to work in a field 12 miles away. Somebody rode up to his group full of the exciting news of the murder, though he said there was still a lot he did not know yet. Cirill, bursting with importance, happily filled in some details. Sweating in the summer sun as he carried on, he wiped his face with a cloth. A girl in the crew thought it had bloodstains, and asked him about it. Cirill clammed up as his situation seemed to dawn on him. He tore the cloth in two, threw it down, and kicked dust over it. To his surprise, this did not allay their suspicions, so he fled.

Cuffe had him sought by hue and cry, but Cirill had a head start and fled Somerset. Across the border in Wiltshire, he knocked at a substantial house to beg a bit of hospitality. As Cirill's kind of luck would have it, the lady at the door already knew he was wanted (the country grapevine at work). Worse yet, this was the home of Mr. Long, justice of the peace. Long put him in jail. Cirill remained reasonably comfortable in jail, where prisoners ate according to what they could pay. He explained to visitors that he did not have to worry about money because somebody would pay for it. (His phrase was "smoak for it"). This was taken to refer to Peter Smithwicke.

Andrew Baker, who had called attention to himself by dumping the blood, attracted further suspicion by calling out in his sleep, "Let us flye Mr. Peter, let us away or else wee shall bee all vndone and hanged." So at any rate swore those who said they had overheard him.

It was plainly time for a search of the Smithwicke farm. This turned up the bloody reins of Trat's bridle hanging in the stable, though the parson's horse was never found. In a fireplace some human teeth and pieces of skull and neckbone were found among the ashes. With this discovery, the searchers had accounted for every part of the body except the genitalia, which they speculated were burnt. Somebody had taken a shine to his work.

Young Smithwicke had been variously heard to threaten to cut Trat into pieces, and "to shew him such a tricke as was never heard off in Summersetshire." He had also damaged his alibi by overinsistence, telling a friend he met on his ride to London to make sure he remembered seeing him on that particular day, which turned out to be the day of Trat's disappearance. No evidence pointed directly to Smithwicke senior, beyond his false pursuit of Trat after the murder, but he was kept in prison in Ilchester pending further study. In July, before the investigation was quite finished, and even before Peter had returned from London, the summer assizes arrived. The visiting justice, Sir Lawrence Tanfield, postponed the case to the next summer, and dismissed the existing grand jurors. These included friends and relatives of Smithwicke senior, who at one time had been a grand juror himself. The new grand jury indicted Peter Smithwicke, Andrew Baker, Cirill Austin, and Alice Walker. At their trial all were sentenced to death.

The four prisoners kept silent. They were descended on by at least five clergymen urging them to confess and repent. Often such visits brought results, but none of these four would respond. They probably hoped that, given the circumstantial nature of the evidence, they might be reprieved. In any case, it should have occurred to all that if these prisoners were the sort who could be moved by ministers of the gospel, they would not have quartered and salted one. Alice shed the only chink of light when a minister asked her if the four had taken an oath of silence. Something of that, she said. Only good oaths are binding, he argued. Come back tomorrow, she said. By then she had changed her mind, returning, as one exasperated minister said, "like a dogge unto the auntient vomit of her stubbornnesse and deniall."

The story ended on Friday, 25 July, 1625, when the four were taken from Taunton out to waiting spectators at a place called Stone Gallows and hanged, still silent. What had been their motive? It was no mystery to the villagers. They knew the background.

A frugal parson in a rustic parish, Trat had survived a couple of scandalous tales. Old Cleeve is on a steep hill atop a cliff (or "cleeve") washed by the Bristol channel. Incoming tides brought limpets that clung to the cliffside. For thrifty people, limpets and fish made a welcome dietary supplement. Trat would go fishing near the beach while his wife scrambled over the high crannies to reach the isolated places where the other limpet hunters had not gone, and pry the stubborn little molluscs loose for supper. There is always a limpet just beyond safe reach, and Mrs. Trat, ailing and never very strong (to say nothing of being hampered by her ankle-length dress), fell to her death. Immediately, the word spread that he had thrown her onto the rocks. The justices of the peace looked into the rumor, but they found no basis, and scolded the Smithwickes for spreading it.

The next tale was not a rumor. An indignant country wife complained that Trat had accosted her in the dark, and offered her "some violence and uncivill behaviour." The justices learned that on the night in question Trat had been invited out to supper. His enemy had secretly put on his familiar cloak and distinctive clerical hat and sneaked out into the night to waylay the woman. Again the justices vindicated Trat, and this time they fined the plotters, another public humiliation for them.

Trat too struck at his enemies, using the considerable advantages enjoyed by parsons of his day. He had a captive audience of parishioners, who could be fined for not attending services. As he mounted the pulpit and stood above his flock, perpendicular gothic arches amplified his voice as he "did thunder and crye out against the vices of his Parish." This thunder spoke the name of Peter Smithwicke, a proud and unruly youth seething in his family's pew, shamed before the whole community.

Their quarrel was over a kind of property already familiar for a thousand years, which did not completely disappear from England until the 1960s. This was advowson, the ownership of the right to name a clergyman to a benefice or living in a particular church. This right was a material property, treated by the law as real estate ever since 1164. The owner of an advowson could sell his vacant benefice to a qualified clergyman, or he could sell the advowson itself. The benefice carried with it, besides ministerial duties, a home, glebe lands, and the tithes that parishioners had to pay the parson in money or commodities. The parson might hold more than one benefice, and farm out the duties to a low-paid curate, pocketing the difference. At first Trat was just such a curate, under the elderly Mr. Brigandine, parson of the adjoining parish of Quantoxhead.[8]

Two developments brought on the quarrel. Mr. Brigandine married Peter Smithwicke's widowed grandmother, making the income he received from Old Cleeve parish a part of the Smithwicke family fortunes—gossip said a very important part. But then Trat, who had saved up money by keeping no servant (and supping on limpets), bought Brigandine's Old Cleeve advowson from him. Shortly after, Brigandine also resigned his incumbency to Trat. Now Trat would get all the parish income instead of Brigandine and instead of the Smithwickes. Peter and his father "were much distasted." They protested that Brigandine had promised to leave them the advowson at his death—and who knows what old Brigandine might have told them? Then followed the slander about Trat's murdering his spouse, and the attempt to get him into trouble over a country wife, and the various humiliations of the Smithwickes. Young Peter said that he would cut

Trat into small pieces. These were not small enough for Alice, who let it be known that if Trat had gone to the latest Dunster fair, some of her Welsh compatriots there would have chopped Trat "as fine as herbs to the pot." The rest we have seen.[9]

The case has fewer loose ends than most. The identity of the masquerader is no great puzzle. His tour took place at the same time as Peter's journey to London, and the Taunton-Ilminster-Blandford route is not much out of the way for Peter's trip to London. That promising clue, the green suit, proved to be a red herring. Nobody ever identified it. It had been a plant to support the deception that fizzled before it could be effective. Smithwicke made the victim an Irishman. Did he choose a green suit with some Irish stereotype in mind, or make the victim Irish because the suit was green? Alas, there is no evidence that the Irish were green much before the 1790s.[10]

III

Murdering Children for Their Own Good

Inevitably this chapter heading will sound ironic, if not sarcastic. Yet these murdered children were all the victims of a parent. In all but the first case, the parent sincerely believed he or she was choosing the lesser of two evils by infanticide, and felt moved by a seemingly ineluctable logic. The first case is more complex. A father murdered two of his three children apparently to get his brother out of debtor's prison; but in the end he deliberately chose to end miserably by pressing, for the sake of the accidental survivor and heir of an ancient lineage.

Born Free (1605)

Caverley house stood in the West Riding, having sheltered at least five centuries of Caverleys as lords of several manors worth seven or eight hundred a year. The house, with the parish church, was the stage for all their major passages in life. The place of such gentry in the universe was beyond doubt. The occasional interruptions of life's natural flow were the familiar ones, for which provisions were well established. So when the head of the family died in about 1600 before his eldest son Walter was of age, Walter became the ward of a neighboring nobleman, a kinsman of that Lord Cobham, who, to prevent an aspersion on one of his ancestors, had had Shakespeare change Oldcastle's name to Falstaff. In that age of tireless negotiation for alliances and estates, the eligible young Caverley was visited by neighboring gentry with daughters. Caverley and one of these daughters fell in love. His guardian would not let him marry the girl during his minority, but Caverly made a contract for them to marry when he came of age. When Caverley was called by his guardian to London on business, the young couple parted with tears and vows.

London had a faster pace than Yorkshire. Within days Caverley was introduced to Phillippa Brooke, niece of his guardian and Lord Cobham's granddaughter. With the minimum wait possible the couple were wed in London. Caverley's minority had suddenly ceased to be a problem. This match had obviously been his lordship's game all along. A letter announcing the marriage reached the betrothed girl waiting in Yorkshire. She tore it in pieces. She lost weight, and pallor replaced her cheery country ruddiness; but she brought herself to say properly, "I intreate of God to grant both prosperous health and fruitfull wealth to him and his, though I am sicke for his sake."

In a few months bride Phillippa was also sick for his sake. A startling change had come over him. Outwardly it was all too simple: Caverley was spending more money than his estate brought in. This would not have been easy. Mere heavy drinking at a penny a quart could never dent his income, and many a sober horse protected its drunken rider from mishap. Trollops could be more costly, but to full financial ruin, dicing offered the fastest road. Having a financial, as opposed to an agricultural, problem was utterly alien to the young Yorkshire squire. Bewildered, he would sit long spells in sullen silence, or "walke melancholy, bethinking continually, and with steddy lookes naild to the ground, seeme astonisht." Phillippa, whether she guessed the problem or not, kept begging to share his worries. Either he would sit without any response, or stride away shouting, "A plague on thee, thou art the cause of my madnesse."

A few years passed, in coldness and despair, and even so they had three sons. She kept begging him to say what she was doing wrong, how she could help. One day she got her answer: "I now want money, and thou must help me." She offered all her jewellery. At least now she could be some part of events. Even if you do not care for me, remember the children and try to restrain your expenditures, she told him. Your land is mortgaged, you are in debt, and friends who have signed your bonds are in danger of being undone by you. Caverley stopped her.

"Base strumpet (whom thogh I maried I never loved) shall my pleasure be confined by your wil? If you and your bastards be in want, either beg, or retire to your friends, my humour shall have the ancient scope. Thy rings and jewels I wil sel, and as voluntarie spend them, as when I was in the best of my estate."

"Sir, your will be done," she said, but he went on.

"I protest by heaven I will ever hereafter lothe thee, and never lie with thee, til thou give consent thy dowre shall be solde, to maintain my pleasure and leave thy selfe and children destitute of maintenance."

"Sir, in al this I will be a wife. What in all this the law will allow me to doe, you shall commaund."

"See thou doest it, for no longer than I am full of money shalt thou pertake from me a taste of kindnesse."

To sell her dowry she had to consult with her uncle. He had a fair idea of the financial destruction that was going on, and from his recent guardianship he was familiar with Caverley's estate. He would have noticed that she was no longer wearing her jewels. Questioned, Phillippa answered like a dutiful little automaton, "I am assured, and I prayse God for it, wee live like Abraham and Sarah, he loving to me, I obedient to him." Admirably spoken, commented the uncle, but I know about his debts. These "proceede of no other cause, but from the rash heate of youth, which will in time, no doubt be suppress by experience: and for that I believe your words be true, and ... to heare of his kindnes toward you, I will make such order for him, as he will continue still master of Caverley, in the same degree, or better than his ancestors here in Yorkeshire."

Caverley should go straight to the king's court, where a position awaits him. He must not let fear of his creditors keep him away, for I shall protect him. And so there is no need to sell the dowry lands now, is there? Phillippa was overjoyed. They were rescued. She could hardly wait to return to Yorkshire from London.

While she was absent, Caverley had gone on an especially intense binge of drinking and losing at dice. Being out of cash was an intolerable pressure. He hated his costly children. In public he said they were bastards, and his wife was a strumpet. The gentry in that part of Yorkshire knew both families, and some had attended the wedding. Caverley's fulmination did not sit well: "It was not fitte." Overcoming a strong feeling that no one should meddle between man and wife, some tried to quiet him. A childhood friend of Phillippa argued with him. Caverley shouted that the man was interested in his wife because he was something more than just a childhood friend. This insult led to a quarrel and they agreed to a duel. They met on the field, and after some swordplay, Caverley was wounded. Caverley in his rage would not give up.

Caverley's opponent could easily have killed him then and there, but lectured him instead: "Maister Caverley, you are a Gentleman of an antient house, there hath been much good expected from you, deceyve not mens hopes, you have a vertuous wife, bee kinde unto her, I forget my wrong, and continue your friend."

The wounded Caverley did not share these sentiments at all, but there was nothing he could do but blame his absent wife: "Strumpet, thou art the cause that I bleede now." His horse took him home, where his wounds were dressed. Phillippa arrived back from London, eager to share the good news from her uncle; but Caverley too had been looking forward to this moment.

His first greeting was, "What? Hast thou brought the money? Is the land sold?" Better than that, she told him. Uncle has promised you preferment at court.

"Have you been at London to make your complaint of me? You damnable strumpet, that the greatnesse of your friends might oversway the weakenesse of my estate? And I that have lived in that rank of will which I have doone, that freedom of pleasure should forsake it now, that I being a Caverley of Caverley stoope my thoughts so low to attend on the countenance of your alliance, to order my life by their direction, and neither doe nor undoe anything but what they list, which I refuse to doe, your complaints have so wrought with them, and you have so possessed them of my estate, they will inforce mee forsoothe for your good, and the good of my children. Was this your tricke to save your dowrie which I sware you should sell? Was this your going to London?"

She reminded him that the court preferment was something that most men would pay a lot to attain. She repeated her willingness to sell the dowry lands despite her fear of impoverishing the children. Caverley was about to hit her when he had an unexpected interruption. It was one of his servants, announcing a gentleman downstairs to see him, from Cambridge University. Caverley left, and his wife fell on the bed exhausted.

The visitor was no less than the master of Clare Hall, Cambridge, where Walter's younger brother was about to graduate. Like several friends, the younger brother had signed a bond for a thousand pounds for Walter, whose credit was so bad that he could no longer borrow on his own. Because Caverley had failed to repay the bond, his brother at the university had just been imprisoned for debt. The young man showed promise, said the master. Now was the very time when he should be seeking church preferment, but he could hardly look for it in prison. The master had put himself out to make this trip in order to stir Caverley's conscience, and to tell him that he would be a scandal before the world, and risk God's judgment, if he did not do something to free his brother.

"In that minute," writes the author, "he made him looke backe into the error of his life, which scarce ever in his life had done before this instant."

I shall wait for your answer, said the master, to know what to do with your brother.

Quietly Caverley thanked the master, ordered some beer for them, and had a servant take him on a tour of the grounds. When you come back, said Caverley, I will give you an answer and my brother will be a prisoner only a few hours after your return.

Left alone, Caverley stood for some time in the room. It is said he was drunk. Then a child's top whirled through a door, followed by William, his son of four, who looked up at him and said, "How doe you father?" Caverley lifted his son by the neck, drew his dagger, stabbed him, and bashed his head. Holding the son at arm's length as if to keep blood off his clothing, Caverley went back up to the room where his wife lay asleep. A maid was dressing Walter, aged 18 months, by the fire. Seeing Caverley with the bloody child and dagger, the maid caught up the baby and tried to escape the room. Caverley dropped William, picked up the maid, and threw her down the stairs. Back in the bedroom, he found his wife clutching his little namesake. He tried several times to stab him, but Phillippa kept interposing herself to protect her son. For a while the whalebones in her corset acted as a kind of armor, but at last he disabled her and finished off little Walter. In the meantime, the Cambridge master and the servant had returned from their tour to find the maid unconscious on the floor. They were uncertain whether to help the maid or investigate the horrid sounds coming from upstairs, when little William, barely alive, staggered to the head of the stair and tumbled down dying. The servant ran upstairs.

"Oh, sir, what have you done?"

"That which I repent not, knave," answered Caverley. A struggle followed and despite Caverley's wound and rundown condition he overcame the servant and ran out of the house. On the way he met the university master, who asked what was wrong. Nothing much, Caverley told him, I am going to look after my brother's problem as I promised. He ran to the stable, found a gelding saddled, and raced off, pursued by the visiting academic. Unable to overtake Caverley, he stopped to alarm the village. Caverley was not trying to escape, but to finish off his third son in the house where he had been placed to nurse. At the edge of the town Caverley's horse fell and ran off without its rider. He was hauled before Sir John Savill, justice of the peace, who knew

him, of course, and asked him what had made him such a monster.

"I have done that Sir I rejoyce at, and repent this, that I had not killed the other. I had brought them to beggary, and am resolved I could not please God better, than by freeing them from it." Caverley would normally have been taken to York, but in 1605 plague was raging there. It was decided to keep him in a Mr. Key's house in Wakefield, which also served as its new jail. Passing on the way by Caverley Hall, where his wife lay slowly dying, he asked to see her once more. This time they met in reconciliation. He was overcome with remorse, and she forgave him for all he had done to her and their sons. They spent a while holding each other and lamenting, but justice had a strict divorce to carry out. Caverley left his ancestors' home for the last time, just as his sons' bodies were being laid out on the front steps.

In Key's new jail he had changed his mind: "I would I had those beggars, either I to begge with them, or they to aske heavens almes for me."

Walter Caverly refused to plead and was pressed to death on 5 August, 1605, insuring the succession of Henry, the nursing infant whom he had not been able to kill. If he had killed him, his poor brother would have succeeded to the estate. Now the infant would succeed—under a guardian, of course, but perhaps not the one that Caverley had so resented. The Brooke family had fallen from political power a little over a year before Caverley's death. Lord Cobham and his brother Lord Brooke fell under suspicion of plotting with Spain to kill King James and to put his Catholic cousin Arabella Stuart on the throne. Lord Brooke was beheaded. Lord Cobham's experience was more bizarre. He had knelt for the axe to fall when a royal messenger rode up through the crowd with his reprieve. King James had staged this trick to see if Cobham would confess at the end. He did not, but he spent his remaining 18 years in the Tower.[1]

Facing Page, top: Squire Caverley murders his sons, 1605. (Bodleian Library, University of Oxford. 4oC16 Art.Bs [27].) He appears to be clubbing his victims, though the text of the pamphlet says he stabbed them. This discrepancy, and the presence of an unexplained dog, suggests that the illustration was taken from another case—possibly the woodcut at bottom (copyright Lambeth Palace), which was used for the Ashford, Kent, case of 1591. The two cuts are closely related, Devil and all, except that the background and a fourth corpse have been chiselled off the woodcut at top, and an axe has been converted to a club. The Ashford murderer did not use an axe, however, nor does the number of corpses match the text. The dog was unexplained in 1591 and it remained in 1605. From all this we conclude that there was a yet earlier account for which the woodcut was originally made, and that the Caverley print was altered from either the Ashford print or from a common ancestor.

Save the Children (1616)

In the spring of 1616, something made the people of Willesden think they owned the common lying in the three miles between them and Acton, so that they started turning their cattle onto the common where the Acton folk grazed theirs. This effrontery was not to be brooked. As soon as church services were over on Ascension Thursday, the men of Acton started digging earthworks to keep out the Willesden cattle. In a cause as urgent as this, the Acton women turned out to help, calling out the rest. Some of them went by the house of Jarvis Vincent, a gentleman, to pick up his wife Margaret. She had promised to help, but now she told them she was not feeling well, and the women marched on.

Jarvis and Margaret had been married at least a dozen years. With their three little children, they led a quiet life in the town. Margaret had an enquiring mind that was not satisfied with the gossip into which society usually channeled female curiosity. Instead she sought to learn as much as possible about theology. Her quest took her to divines beyond her parish—beyond her upbringing, in fact, for somewhere, at some time, either she found a lurking Catholic priest or he found her. To Protestants, these priests came as traitors, to introduce the oppression of European despots, the terrors of the Inquisition, and the horrors of civil war. Imagine Acton and Willesden, only with swords instead of shovels, and no justice of the peace to settle things in the end! Catholic priests were illegal in England. It was mortally perilous for them to visit, and Catholics looked on them as selfless and courageous men prepared for martyrdom. Religion aside, it is not hard to imagine Margaret being dealt with by the Anglican minister perhaps a bit routinely as part of the parish, and a female part at that, while the missionary priest listened to her and responded to her as an individual. Margaret converted. She tried to persuade her husband of the truths she had discovered, but the stodgy spouse would not budge from his Protestant roots. Not wanting any trouble, he said nothing about his wife's conversion.

Margaret's isolation was exacerbated by the impossibility of seeing her furtive Catholic priest as often as she wished. Spiritually alone, her seeming logic led her on to a fatal conclusion: Her beautiful little children, still protected by their innocence, stood in great peril of growing up Protestant, *ergo* damned.

What was a loving mother to do? While the men and women were mustering to save the common from the cattle of Willesden, Margaret saved two of her children by strangling them with a garter, while they were still safe in their cocoons of innocence. Affectionately she laid their bodies together on a bed.

After this supreme effort, she ravelled out. She could not think how to rescue her third child, who was put out to nurse in another house. She tried to strangle herself with the same garter, and when that failed she ran out the back door to drown herself in a pond, just as Margaret's maid Nan came through the back gate. One look told Nan something was badly wrong and she asked where the children were.

"Oh Nan, never oh never shalt thou see thy Tom more," cried Margaret, and gave the maid a great box on the ear. The maid held her and called for help, and soon the whole town knew what had happened. The people were at a loss what to do, and they stood crying in the Vincents' garden.

Jarvis finally burst out, "Oh Margret, Margret, how often have I perswaded thee from this damned Opinion, this damned Opinion, that hath undone us all."

"Oh Jarvis, this had never beene done, if thou hadst become ruld, and by mee converted, but what is done, is past, for they are Saints in heaven, and I nothing at all repent it."

Then constable Dighton arrived. Mr. Roberts, the justice of the peace (a Willesden man), signed the papers to commit her to Newgate prison. Evening had fallen on Ascension day, a long one for those who recalled how it had begun. Mr. Roberts lodged Margaret for the night with constable Dighton, who doubled conveniently as the landlord of the Bell Inn. The justice had her crucifix taken away, and gave her a Protestant bible, which she threw away. The constable and some neighbors spent the night trying to convert Margaret and to get her to repent. The next morning Margaret was carted the ten miles to Newgate, where numerous ministers came to her. It was no use, she said, she had done a deed of charity, making her children saints when they would otherwise have ended in hell. The ministers continued their arguments through Saturday and Sunday, until at last she said she wished she had her children back, and that she deserved hell for murdering them. Margaret's guilty plea before the court on Monday was an anticlimax. "Her offense was begot by a strange occasion," concluded the author, "but buried I hope with true repentance."[2]

The Rescuing Spring (1621)

The pleasant town of Ewell was unusual in two ways. Its people were spiritually underprivileged, because the stingy owner of the church living

III. Murdering Children for Their Own Good

Margaret Vincent murders her children, 1616. Here the Devil hands Margaret the cords to strangle the children. Bodleian Library, University of Oxford 4oG29 Art (4).

would not pay for a parson, but only a reader, and he was a nearly blind dotard. Ewell's other distinction was some fine drinking water that welled up from a spring in the cellar of John Rowse. Queen Elizabeth, Gloriana herself, that other moon, had this water delivered to her daily whenever she resided at nearby Nonesuch Palace.

Rowse had done well enough as a fishmonger in London to retire in his 40s and buy some land and a home in Ewell. Within six months, he had married a respectable local woman. He was on familiar terms with a gentleman or two. Because the couple needed a maidservant, and because the parish lay spiritually unguarded, the Devil sent John Rowse a wench named Jane Blundell, "who in short time was better acquainted with her masters bed then honesty required." When Mrs. Rowse found them out, peace left the household forever. John would not give up Jane, and the discordant trio bickered and recriminated in the house for two years, until Mrs. Rowse died—of a broken heart, said the villagers. John and Jane now had the house to themselves, and "he and his Whore were the more free to use their cursed contentments, and ungodly embracements."

Rowse remarried, choosing not Jane but another respectable local woman, to shore up his eroding status. Domestic warfare resumed immediately, because Rowse still kept his "lewd Trull" in the house. He began drinking and spending recklessly, and before long he was ruining the estate he had carefully built up. Mortgages were made and foreclosed, and still he owed over £200. The neighbors cut him.

He left his wife and two little children, returning with Jane to London, where an old friend from fishmonger days put them up for several weeks and advised Rowse to change his name and hide from his creditors, who seemed about to put him in debtors' prison. Since he had no prospects, he would die in prison and his children would go begging in the world, bearing his name.

At the friend's suggestion he fled to Ireland, but before he sailed, the friend drew up a trust in which Rowse handed over his remaining land to the friend in exchange for an undertaking to pay Rowse £260. Some thought Rowse was being cheated, but Rowse confirmed the deal in court.

Rowse did not thrive or stay long in Ireland. When he returned, the friend sent him off to the low countries, where he failed again. He began to suspect his friend, and regretted leaving his wife and children in Ewell, though by now he had children by Jane as well. He returned to London and demanded his property back, complaining that he had never received more than £20 of the promised £260. A deal is a deal, said the friend, and kept the money.

Rowse, to the end, felt sure he had been cheated, yet he asked the author not to mention the man's name (which may have been Carter, because the author coyly tells us you can find it on dice between sink and trey: cater). To be fair to "Carter": A true friend might well have concluded that Rowse was no longer competent in money matters and had to be rationed, as many trustees have rationed their wastrels. Rowse's notion that he had received only £20 may have been far from reality, but £20 would have been more than generous (7.7 percent) if the trustee's purpose had been to ration him and preserve capital. Alternatively, the friend could originally have decided that he might as well absorb the assets if Rowse were just going to throw them away.

Rowse now possessed nothing, and had just turned 50. Not London nor Ireland nor Holland had any room for him, and he returned to Ewell. His family, we are told, welcomed him as the prodigal father, but for him it must have been a miserable homecoming, every sight reminding him of better days and regrettable decisions, of friends now strangers, former lands, former money, former reputation, and a future that seemed to hold for him and his daughters of six and four only beggary from door to door. Early one morning he sent his wife on an errand to London. She was so troubled by his mood and her own overpowering premonitions that she rushed back early from London.

Where are the children? was her first question.

They are visiting a neighbor in town.

Then I'll fetch them.

No need, I'll bring them soon.

No, I'll fetch them now.

They are really four miles off in Sutton, and very well.

No, tell me the truth.

If you must know, they are upstairs. You will find them there.

Rowse had laid them on a bed, after carrying them into the cellar and holding their heads in Gloriana's crystalline spring. He drew his sword, but not knowing what to do next he laid it on the table and sat quietly until his wife rushed in.

I was loth, he told the constable, they should go about the town begging and bearing my name. They were mine, and I might do what I would with them. I gave them their lives and took their lives, and I am content to lose my life for them. Now their miseries are past. They cannot come to me but I hope I can go to them. John Rowse was hanged on 2 June, 1621, at Croydon.[3]

The Last Picnic (1637)

Bastardy was a liability in all classes, blocking inheritance and creating social inferiority. At upper levels, it could be somewhat overcome if the father used his wealth and influence to place his bastard well. At lower levels, it could be overcome if the father married the mother. Elizabeth Barnes knew that sometimes the father does not marry the mother.

She also knew what her eight-year-old daughter enjoyed. She liked to walk with her mother from their home in Battersea to a cousin in Fulham. She also liked apple pie, and raisins, and herring pie. Early in the morning of 14 March, 1637, they set out with a bundle of these favorites. By about 11 they were deep in Wormewall Wood, by Fulham. Elizabeth sat down to rest in the shade, and her daughter lunched on the pies and raisins. After this feast, the little girl dozed off in the quiet sylvan scene. Elizabeth drew a knife from the picnic bundle and slit her sleeping daughter's throat.

From the same bundle she drew a length of rope that she had also thought to pack, and looked for a place to hang herself. Amid hundreds of trees, she simply did not have the strength or experience to climb any of them or tie the necessary knots. An attempt to drown herself in a small stream also failed. Elizabeth walked to Kensington, found a barn, and hid in the straw. Soon the daughter's body was discovered, and Elizabeth was found and carted the three or four miles to Newgate prison.

As soon as Henry Goodcole heard this news he visited Elizabeth in his capacity as spiritual adviser to the condemned at Newgate. What made you do it? he asked her.

"None but the Devill alone." She asked Goodcole and others present to pray for her.

This was not good enough. He tried again later. Elizabeth told him that she had fallen into poverty and debt and did not know what to do. One thought lodged in her mind. Death will get you and your daughter out of this situation. Having nobody to talk to, she let the thought swell to an irresistible temptation.

How did you become poor?

I spent all I had on some man who pretended to love me. Goodcole could get her to say no more at the time, but by the day of her execution, 26 April, she had told the rest of her sad litle story. A Battersea tailor named Richard Evans had seduced her, and kept deluding her with hopes of marriage. When at last she had given him her last penny and found he had no further need of her, she murdered their little girl. Goodcole told

Elizabeth Barnes cuts her sleeping daughter's throat (1637). The fiendish expression does not match the mother's sad story. By permission of the Folger Shakespeare Library.

all his readers that the tailor's false dealing with Elizabeth should weigh heavily on his conscience. As for Elizabeth, he warned, it would have been much better if she had kept in touch with a minister, for a silent sinner is the Devil's secretary.[4]

IV

Murdering to Resolve Triangles

One might truly cherish a daughter or female ward and still labor to convert her from an economic liability to an asset by arranging her marriage. Even an artisan might match his best apprentice with one of his daughters. Heads of landed families contracted marriages as alliances to enhance the status of descendants yet unborn. The practice sometimes made intolerable mismatches. The surplus young daughter could be tied to a drunkard, or a lecher with the great pox. It was just as bad if the groom was a comely youth if he too was a victim of the alliance. He would be just as resentful as his bride of the calamitous sentence imposed on them. These mismatches endured until the death of a spouse, for among all but the mightiest subjects of the realm, there was no divorce. Occasionally a separation *a mensa et thoro* freed an incompatible couple from having to live together, but neither party could remarry while the other lived.

The lower orders retained a kind of folk divorce, in which the husband would bring his wife to market with a rope about her neck and auction her off. When he handed his end of the rope to the winning bidder, they went off confident, in spite of everything the church kept saying, that they had undone one marriage and made another. The ceremony could have been a collusive fiction in which the "bidder" was already identified. Some auctioned women must rightly have considered this degrading transaction good riddance of a bad husband. Neither the church nor the common law recognized divorce by sale. As a local custom, the neighbors would have recognized it, and if the participants were poor and unimportant, the temporal authorities might not waste much time on them.

With these exceptions, death alone brought freedom from a hated spouse. To a woman, widowhood also brought greater freedom in remarrying than she had enjoyed the first time around. No wonder then that freedom was sometimes won by hastening uncaring Nature with murder. The discontented spouses were not pursuing some abstract liberation. Each had a specific substitute already in mind, and already in bed. Murder to resolve triangles could occur whether marriage had been arranged or not, but a Devonshire case shows the havoc that foolish parents could wreak.

Parental Muddle (1591)

Everything was falling in place for George Strangwich when he finished his apprenticeship in London and came to Tavistock to work for a merchant named Glanfield. The Glanfields trusted him with the shop and were ready to trust him with the hand of his daughter. Better yet, Miss Glanfield had fallen in love with George. Everything ought to have gone so smoothly that there would now be no record of any of them but quiet little parish entries: marriage, baptisms, burial. Then mother and father Glanfield spoiled everything. They decided to move to Plymouth, and negotiated with a widower named Page to marry their daughter. This was a step up socially for the Glanfields, since Page was one of the chief citizens of Plymouth. But when the mother and father revealed their decision to their daughter, it was "sore against her will," for by now she felt betrothed to George, and on that assumption had been intimate with him. The girl's friends eventually persuaded her to obey her parents, but she made three fatal vows: never to love Page, never to stop loving George, and never to have children by Page.

In the first year of this marriage, she had two miscarriages. There is no way of knowing whether these were deliberate abortions, the result of stress, or some organic problem. Strangwich visited Plymouth whenever he could, and they made love whenever he did. From the beginning, the bride made several attempts to poison Page. Her recipe was inadequate, and though she made him very ill he was still alive after nearly a year. Page was vomiting blood, and might eventually have died of these administrations, but she and George were impatient. She bribed one of Page's servants, Robert Priddis, to kill his master for £40. Strangwich on his part found a Tom Stone, whom he paid to help Priddis. On Wednesday night, 11 February, 1591, Page was in his bed, just dozing off, his man Priddis still with him. Mrs. Page was spending the night in another room, recuperating from her second miscarriage. Stone knocked softly and Priddis let him in. Page jumped up and struggled with them, but they strangled him with his own kerchief while he tried to claw it away from his throat. To be thorough, they broke his neck on the edge of the bed. Then they tucked him back in, and smoothed his covers. Priddis stole to Mrs. Page's chamber to report success, and in about an hour the conspirators staged an amateur theatrical.

Priddis called, "Mistresse, let somebody looke into my Maisters chamber, methinkes I hear him grone." Mrs. Page and her maid, who was not in on the plot, went with a candle to investigate. Mrs. Page stopped at the chamber door while her maid went in and reported that Page's face was cold. Warm a cloth at the fire then and wrap it around his feet. Finally the maid caught on and cried out that he was dead. The new widow immediately took to her bed, and sent Priddis to notify her father and also one of Page's sisters, a Mrs. Harris. For the sister, the new widow added the silly lie that she should hurry if she wanted to see her brother alive, because he had fallen victim to some disease known locally as the "pull."

The sister arrived to find a convincing widow prostrate in her bed. All seemed as it was meant to seem, until Mrs. Harris, ministering to her brother's body, noticed a little blood on Page's chest. She removed his kerchief and found the scratch marks he had made on himself trying to claw it off. When she also found that he had a broken neck and abrasions on his knees, she went to the mayor, who with other worthies straightway inspected the corpse and arrested Priddis. Priddis immediately implicated Tom Stone. The next day was Stone's wedding day. He had just had time to get married, and was beginning the customary jollities, when the mayor's men came for him. Mrs. Page's arrest followed. The three were examined before the mayor and other city fathers, including none other than Sir Francis Drake, who less than three years before had fought the Spanish Armada. Mrs. Page simply told the truth: she "had rather dye with Strangwidge, then to live with Page."

Unaware of these developments, Strangwich came to Plymouth. He had changed his mind about murdering Page and was anxiously trying to find out whether the plot had truly been carried out. He learned soon enough when he was arrested. His defense was that he had written to Mrs. Page urging her not to go through with the murder. The letter, if he had really written one, had not arrived in time to alter Page's fate, or Strangwich's. Strangwich, Mrs. Page, Priddis, and Stone were all found guilty at the Exeter assizes and died on Saturday, 20 February, nine days after the crime.

This case has as little of the supernatural about it as can be, but some folk in Plymouth thought otherwise. Three days after the execution, somebody saw a fiery-eyed bearish creature wearing a linen cloth similar to the fatal kerchief. In the same week, too, a raven perched atop a ship's mast, wove a cord out of rope strands, and hanged itself by jumping off the mast with its wings closed in a most nonavian manner.

The author made one concession to the homicidal lovers. Although they had been tempted to their crime by the devil, the parents had also been led by the devil to the folly of marrying their daughter to Page instead of Strangwich.[1]

The Magnetism of a City Wife (1573)

George Saunders was run through with a sword on Shooter's Hill between seven and eight on Wednesday morning, 25 March, 1573. He just had time, kneeling in the road, to pray for his own soul and that of the stranger with the bloody sword. He did not know his killer, George Browne, but Browne knew him. While the dying Saunders prayed, Browne was busy eliminating a witness, a boy he had not planned to kill, but who was with Saunders by mere bad luck. After this reality overdose of stabbing a boy 10 or 11 times while being prayed for by his first victim, Browne paled and grew faint. He was unable to eat or drink for the rest of the day. He would have swooned indeed to learn that the boy he had left for dead was creeping painfully homeward.

For now, Browne proceeded according to plan, sending word of his deed to the widow Elizabeth Drewrie in London via his lookout and accomplice, "Trusty Roger" Clement, who was Mrs. Drewrie's servant. Then Browne melted into the throng at Greenwich Palace, only a mile away, where Queen Elizabeth and her entourage were residing. In the evening he rode to Mrs. Drewrie's house and picked up £20 from Trusty Roger. Though Wednesday had been a busy day, there was to be no rest for him. Thursday, Trusty Roger brought him another £6 and the message that he was being looked for and had better get out of England fast. Browne fled to Rochester to book a ship for Holland.

Because of the proximity of the murder to the queen's court, her privy council immediately took a hand in the case. The dying boy had managed to describe Browne to them. On Saturday, Browne was seized by the mayor of Rochester. The wounded boy lived to identify him to his face, dying the next Monday. Browne readily broke down and confessed to the councillors, implicating Mrs. Drewrie, who had planned and guided him in all this, and had promised to make a marriage between him and George Saunders's wife, Anne, "whom he seemed to love excessively."

Excessively and impulsively: At loose ends after coming over from Dublin, Browne had needed only one glimpse of Anne Saunders at Mrs. Drewrie's house to know he must marry her whatever the cost. Mrs. Drewrie told him that Anne lived next to St. Dunstan's in the East, across from Billingsgate. He called on her in the afternoon, while her husband was away. George Saunders was a solid citizen of London, a member of the merchant tailors' gild. He and his wife had very different notions about money. Recently, she had waylaid his messenger boy and taken the money intended for the payment of a debt due at the Exchange that day. Anne bought clothing with it. George lost face and credit on the Exchange. They had a row and she pouted.

Browne found Anne sitting just within her open door, watching the street traffic. He spoke some civil banality, and she responded with demure reserve; then in his impulsive way he declared his love. How matters went next we do not know, but she did not slam her door. Was it usual for middle class housewives to sit in their doors? Surely she was expecting Browne? Is this something Mrs. Drewrie did regularly for would-be lovers?

Soon after, the versatile widow Drewrie read Anne's palm. From the palm the two learned that her husband would die soon. The palm-reader's prescience was aided by her knowledge that already Browne and Trusty Roger were out stalking Saunders. His business took him about London in unpredictable ways, their first attempt at murder being aborted in Lombard Street when an acquaintance joined Saunders for a chat. In the second stalking, Saunders led Browne and Trusty Roger from his house to Cornhill, then after an hour to the Exchange, then home at midday, then to Lion Key to take a boat down to Greenwich, from which Saunders meant to return at six. Trusty Roger followed him to Greenwich, while Browne returned to the quay at six, planning to stab Saunders then and there. After all that, Saunders was saved inadvertently by none other than Anne, who unexpectedly showed up at the quay to meet her husband.

Plainly better coordination was needed, so Anne sent Browne a letter via Mrs. Drewrie, describing her husband's next moves. With this intelligence, Browne could ambush him. Saunders went to Woolwich, where he spent the night with an elderly couple of rustics named Barnes. In the morning he left for St. Mary Cray with John Beane, a boy who worked for

Barnes. Trusty Roger was hiding at a hedge corner at the foot of Shooter's Hill to make sure that the area was clear of witnesses. As Saunders and Beane neared this spot, the boy glimpsed Browne in the road ahead. When Browne disappeared into the bushes, the boy suggested they go back, knowing this spot was notorious for robbers. Saunders refused, and the two continued down the hill another minute or so to their deaths.

Browne was tried and condemned on Friday, 17 April, and was hanged at Smithfield the next Monday, 25 days after the murder, chivalrously maintaining to the last that Mrs. Saunders knew nothing of the matter and had never had sex with him. Browne's corpse was carted from Smithfield and hung up in chains near the site of his crime.

Mrs. Drewry and Trusty Roger, jailed, did not hesitate to implicate Anne, but she was not immediately picked up. Mother of several children, she was advanced in pregnancy: "at the tyme of hir husbandes death she looked presently to lie downe," and was soon delivered of a daughter. Next she must be "churched," an ancient religious cleansing ritual for mothers newly delivered. Once purified, she was arrested.

Mrs. Drewrie was accessory before the fact for planning the murder, and accessory after the fact for helping Browne flee. Mrs. Saunders's involvement before the fact had consisted of her furnishing Browne with her husband's itinerary, and after the fact providing money for Browne's escape, which she raised by pawning some of her and Mrs. Drewrie's silver. The two women were tried at the Guildhall on Wednesday, 6 May, and condemned to hang that Saturday. The case attracted much attention, and more than the usual number of clergymen sought to rescue the neglected souls of the two women. One of these, named Mell, accompanied Anne Saunders back to Newgate prison from her trial.

With less than three days in which to maneuver before her scheduled execution, Anne showed a sample of the manipulative power that had sent both her husband and her lover to undiscovered country. Mell was for some reason a suspended minister, and Anne quickly assessed her man. In the hectic Thursday and Friday between the trial and the scheduled execution, he fell in love with Anne and resolved to marry her, and on her instructions went to Mrs. Drewrie to give her advice. His counsel, not quite spiritual, was that Mrs. Drewrie should revise her confession so as to take all the blame and clear Mrs. Saunders. Her punishment, argued Mell, would after all be no worse if she did this kindly turn. Mrs. Drewrie balked. Mr. Mell pressed her, somewhat illogically threatening her soul with danger if she were to send an innocent woman like Mrs. Saunders to the gallows.

Mrs. Drewrie of course knew better, and must have told herself that a man who would believe this would believe anything. Yet, after all, Mell negotiated a deal with her. If she cleared Mrs. Saunders, Mrs. Drewrie's daughter would be given money for a dowry so she could make a good marriage. The money, like the idea, came from Mrs. Saunders. Armed with Mrs. Drewrie's revised confession, Mell prepared to go before the council and get a pardon for his beloved.

It is not surprising to learn that, before going to the council, this addled busybody fully explained the plot to a gentleman he thought would be sympathetic, but who was nothing of the sort. By the time Mell appeared before the council, their lordships knew what was afoot. They not only denied the pardon, but condemned Mell to stand in the pillory at the site and time of Anne's execution, wearing a sign that said, "For practising to colour the detestable factes of George Saunders wife."

For reasons of their own, however, their lordships chose to postpone the execution. They were trying to find a missing account book that would help the guardians of Saunders's children with his estate. They also felt that, having received Mell's spiritual guidance, Mrs. Saunders was probably in worse shape than most to meet her maker. Finally, she had not confessed to anything, and the council never liked the public to have lingering doubts. They resolved to reprieve her for a few days, but without telling her. Consequently on Saturday morning Anne thought that Mrs. Drewrie was to die that day, but was in the dark about her own fate. In this vulnerable and receptive state, she overheard two men (surely no accident!) commenting to each other that the scaffold was built strong enough for both women. She ran to Mrs. Drewrie and begged her to repeat her story despite Mell's bungling, but Mrs. Drewrie had had enough. She was going to tell the truth and so should Anne. At this, Anne broke down and at last confessed. The two were in fact not executed until Wednesday, 13 May. Mrs. Saunders spent her remaining time in repentance and asking forgiveness of her in-laws and her own family. Their lordships had achieved their purpose.

On the Wednesday, Anne, Elizabeth, and trusty Roger stood on a single cart beneath the Smithfield gallows. They had drawn a record audience. There were "personages of Honor and Worship," including the Earls of Derby and Bedford, representing the privy council. Smithfield was crammed. People sat in the windows and atop brick walls, stone battlements, and roof tiles. They had beaten down fences to improve the view, and some clung precariously from the steeple of St. Bartholomew the Less.

From the cart, Anne again confessed to instigating the murder out of lust for Browne. Elizabeth made the curious announcement that, contrary to rumors, she had not poisoned her own husband. Then turning to the Earl of Derby she told him that while she was his servant she had had nothing to do with the separation of the earl and his countess. The earl forgave her, all prayed, and the cart moved out from under them. We do not know Mell's thoughts as he witnessed all this from his vantage point in the stocks, the best view of all.[2]

The Endgame (1582-1604)

"Disquietly" is how Thomas Cash lived with his wife Ellen at Holton, Lincolnshire. Cash had a neighbor named Newton, and consoled himself for this disquiet with "the use of Newton's wife ... daily." Ellen became an invalid. No wonder, said the neighbors, considering Cash's "disloyalty and unkindenesse." Ellen was looked after by a servant, Anne Potter, who further complicated the geometry of this menage by planning to wed Thomas and become mistress of the house. After all, indissoluble marriage kept Newton's wife out of the competition. Thomas had the daily use of Anne as well as of Mrs. Newton. Thomas would now and then apologize to Anne for Ellen's stubborn perseverance on earth, and Anne would observe that it would be better for both Thomas and Anne if Ellen were put down. Better for poor Ellen too, she added. Good for Thomas, good for Anne, good for Ellen, and requiring only a whiff of euthanasia.

One morning, when Ellen tottered to the fire as usual, and asked her husband to fetch her something as usual, he strangled her. No struggle, no sound, no sign hinted that Ellen's short passage from frailty to death had been hurried by anyone. The neighbors who knew about the adulteries knew also about Ellen's health, and so they took her death to be natural. Cosy in their house, Thomas and Anne rejoiced: "Though long, yet now behold the end of our long continued trouble." Sunlit vistas opened before Anne.

How was she to know that Newton, in one act as inconsiderate as all of Ellen's impositions together, would suddenly die? In less than six months, Thomas and Newton's widow married. Anne, as an accomplice to murder, had to bottle all grief and fury in her churning spleen. She left Lincolnshire forever.

Thomas and his new wife stayed a while at Holton, but associations (or Ellen's ghost) haunted him and they moved a few miles to Long Oarsbie. After 14 years there, his second wife died. A year and a half later, Thomas married one Jennet Mowse and moved with her another few miles to Middle Rasen. The years drifted by. Jennet bore two children; Hamlet made his debut; the old queen died.

Then, in the ninth year of his third marriage, November, 1604, the sheriff's men appeared at Thomas's door and arrested him for murder. That time bomb, Anne Potter, had detonated. In 1604 she was living in St. Leonard's, Houndsditch, London. Feeling herself to be "sick unto death," she sent for the parson and uncorked her vintage story. The parson shared it with Sir Richard Hamcotes, sheriff of Lincolnshire. Thomas Cash, at about 50, would have been elderly by the standards of the time. He readily confessed to the justices of the peace, telling them he had been tormented by his conscience for a quarter century.

The story leaves a few mysteries. The convenience and timing of neighbor Newton's demise naturally raises the question, whether Mrs. Newton and Cash might have discussed what would really be best for Mr. Newton, just as Anne and Cash had discussed what would really be best for Ellen. Yet it would have been spiritually futile for Cash to confess one mortal sin and not another, and it seems more likely that he committed only Ellen's murder. Nor is there any evidence that Mrs. Newton murdered her first husband, with or without telling Cash.

Supposing Mrs. Newton innocent of Ellen's death, she may well not have known that Cash was guilty. Cash probably intended to marry Anne Potter, changing his plans only when fate offered him the wealthier of the two women. How had he broken this change to Anne? Get out, wench, you're sacked? Or things don't have to be any different between us just because I'm getting married? Or all things change, but I'll always miss you?

Anne and Thomas had played a slow game of musical chairs. Had she lived long enough, he might, when there was nothing left of this world for him to lose, have confessed first, and sent her to the gallows, for the good of his soul. In the event, it was she who won.

Horning the Parson (1609)

After the reverend Mr. Lowe got his pupil pregnant, her father, the squire, sacked him. The girl's family sent her on a visit somewhere and succeeded in keeping the birth secret. Lowe had wanted to marry the girl, but her father would not hear of it, having planned a much better match for her. The infant daughter, an unalloyed liability, was turned over to Lowe. In due course his ex-pupil came home a plausible *virgo intacta*.

Humiliated by the rejection or disappointed at not gaining the financial and social advantages that membership in the family would have brought, Lowe ineffectually sought revenge. One night he took some burning wood from his fireplace and threw it at the family's house, but he missed and his vengeance descended only on a grain crib. Suspicion fell on Lowe but he was not charged, for the squire wanted no publicity. Still, he had had enough of Lowe, and so had the village, where people spoke of other misbehavior that has not come down to us. Lowe was sent away with his little bastard.

Having put her out to nurse, he traveled from this nameless place to the village of Rockland, in Norfolk, and called on its parson, Mr. James. The parson held two churches, and took Lowe in as his curate for one of them, giving him room, board, and a small stipend. Lowe had a job, but he still had a baby. Even though it was at nurse elsewhere and nobody in Rockland knew it existed, he worried. The baby was a potential embarrassment, and the wetnurse was expensive. He sent a message to her, saying that he had heard the baby was not being treated well, and ordering her to send a man to meet him with the infant on a lonely heath outside Rockland. On the heath the infant was handed over, from horseback to horseback. As soon as the messenger rode out of sight, Lowe smothered it in his cloak. Having forgotten he would need a spade, he left the small body on the heath, fetched a spade from the parson's, and returned to bury it. Now at last his life was growing simpler.

Simplicity was not a state he knew how to maintain. He "next attempted, & obtained the love of Mistress James," the parson's wife, "a woman of good Parentage, vertuous education, and (to the outward eye) of civill and unblemisht reputation. This woman's chastity notwithstanding, he speedely attempts and effectually ... obtaines." They seem to have conducted their affair rather transparently, so it took the attentive villagers of Rockland little time to guess what was going on. Rockland's rustic wits, scandalized and delighted, were saying that, "Master Lowe dieted at Master James his board, and lodgde in his wives bed." When the trusting parson got wind of these rumors, it was not their truth that he investigated, but their origin. He traced them back to a few "first Authors" and threatened to take them to court if any more gossip reached him—in itself another delicious news item on the alehouse agenda.

For all his venereal triumphs, Lowe could see that he was once again in an inferior position. It galled him "that howsoever hee may seeme to embrace the shaddow of his content, the substance is still injoyed, and rests at the command of Master James his Master, and that hee but like a slave by stealth, and by Times allowance, sparingly and fearefully injoyes it." Just as his reflection on the problem of his infant had revealed no solution but to kill it, so his reflection on the problem of his cuckold parson left no choice but to kill him. Lowe accordingly made various attempts at murder. Whatever these were, he was no more effective than he had been when attempting arson. His efforts went unnoticed by the victim or anyone else.

So the 12 days of Christmas arrived at Rockland with nothing to mar the festive mood. As was the custom, the young men and women visited a different house each evening, enjoying traditional pastimes. For the last evening, the young people were invited to the parson's: Twelfth Night, 1609, eight years to the day after Mr. Shakespeare had first staged his *Twelfth Night*. The hosts seemed to enjoy watching them at their games, "especially Maister Lowe." When the party ended and the youths stepped out into the unseasonal thunder, lightning, wind, and rain, Mrs. James did not follow her husband to bed but retired to a room downstairs and at the other end of the house—perhaps by arrangement with Lowe, perhaps to nurse her baby (whose, by the way?). The parson went upstairs to his bed, bringing his eight-year-old daughter Moll for warmth. Lowe went to his room, just above the room where Mrs. Lowe had chosen to spend the night. Mr. James had two manservants. The senior, having lighted the parson to his bed and closed the house for the night, went home to his own wife in the village. The junior was an "innocent," that is to say, mentally retarded. He slept in the room next to his master's.

At some time in that stormy night the curate smothered the parson. Characteristically, he was not immediately successful, and the servant heard a commotion through the wooden wall:

The parson's voice, "What doe you meane, do you come to murther me?"

The little girl's, "Good sweet master Lowe kill not my deere father!"

"Peace, Moll, holde thy tongue, thy father hath no harm."

"Pray God he hath none," said Moll. "Father, father, how do you father?"

"Hold your tongue brat I charge you for waking your father." Moll was making Lowe cross, but he had finished now. He smoothed the bed clothes so there were no signs of struggle, left the room, and went to his own bed. Moll quietly hugged her father and fell asleep.

The servant lay perplexed all night, waiting for his senior to come in the morning and decide what to do. The senior led him and Mrs. James' maid into the master's room, bringing Mrs. James's maid as well. There they found Moll asleep, her arms still wrapt round her cooling father. The maid ran to tell her mistress through the door that her husband was murdered. Mrs. James made no answer at all, but Lowe ran downstairs "like a man halfe distraught," crying out, "Marry God forbid where are the murtherers?" All but Mrs. James then rushed back to the master bedroom. By now Moll was awake and crying. The maid took her up and started to carry her to Lowe's bed, but Moll was afraid to go. He had killed her father, she whimpered. The maid said nothing but carried her downstairs to her mother. She found Mrs. James taking the news, she said, "very impatiently." Moll kept repeating that Lowe had killed her father.

"Peace, foole," replied her mother, "hold thy tongue, he loved us all too well to hurt thy Father." The maid left the room, and Mrs. James came out just in time to hear the junior servant telling the maid his story.

"Peace wretch," she told him, "doest thou know what thou said? Wilt thou cast away the man?" She joined Lowe in the entry alcove and they began whispering. The maid overheard him say something like "I have devisde a course for him, and for the rest, I way not a pinn, not one of them all can detect me."

Mrs. James had the church bell rung, and told the assembled villagers that her husband had died a natural death in the night. She then arranged with a poor woman to wrap up the corpse for burial, giving her extra money not to remove its shirt: concealing a bruise, probably. The late parson was duly buried, only a little sooner than usual, the Reverend Mr. Lowe performing the funeral ceremony with an appropriately dejected countenance.

Lowe had told Mrs. James in the alcove that the simpleminded servant was his only problem. This was a lie. Moll presented a more serious threat, but of course Lowe was not likely to tell Mrs. James so. He might go through one of his lethal soul-searches and find himself forced to do something best not shared with Moll's mother. For the present, he had to deal with the servant, so he told him a story. Lowe's rich and childless uncle, he said, was near death at this very time in a far off place. That lonely old man needed company and would leave a fortune to the person who provided it. Lowe of course would go himself if he could, but... Instead, Lowe had recommended him, lucky servant, and now here was a little money for his journey to the distant uncle. The next day villagers were telling each other the servant had left before dawn without telling anybody he was leaving. Lowe had created a suspect if foul play came to light.

Even as they gossiped, the servant was chatting with a man he met not far out of Rockland. The man knew him, and got him to tell his story of Twelfth Night. This time he could add his good news about Lowe's rich dying uncle. It was such a nice story that the man took him to the justice of the peace and he got to tell it all over again, under oath.

The justice grasped what was going on, but he had a legal problem. The two main witnesses against Lowe would be a simpleton and a child. A little dissimulation, he told himself, might bring the truth nearer. He put the servant in jail. Hearing of this, Lowe decided that his scheme was working. To drive it home, he visited the justice and shared his dark suspicions that the runaway had murdered his master. The justice treated Lowe cordially. He confided to Lowe the story the servant had told him, leaving out the part about Lowe's fictitious uncle. The justice bound them both over to trial, leaving the servant in jail but treating Lowe with singular courtesy and asking him to await trial as a guest in the justice's own house. Lowe was reassured by the obvious favoritism.

Soon an unknown gentleman dropped in on Lowe. He exuded prestige, dropping names and referring casually to the court of King James. Of course, he said, nobody wanted a man of the cloth like Lowe to get into trouble, as the justice himself had shown by his hospitality. Now if Lowe did happen to have a problem, well, the gentleman thought it highly advisable that Lowe should tell him in time for him to use his influence at court to obtain a pardon for Lowe.

Lowe was unprepared for this approach. He did not answer for some time, and when he did it was in a broken manner, with many pauses. "If I should trust my life in your hands," he finally got out, "would you prove faithful?"

"I would," replied the gentleman, "and deal with you as affectionately as with mine owne sonne." The fatuous Lowe then sought to bind the gentleman to secrecy by "ceremonious conjuring" ("Cross your heart," perhaps?) Reassured, he confessed James's murder, with much therapeutic regret and cursing of his hands. (It was really his hands that had done it.) Very good, said the friendly gentleman, now if we are to prevail at court I shall need to have all this in writing, or what would there be for the king to pardon? And if you want to help Mrs. James, be sure to include her in your confession so his majesty can pardon her too. Have money ready—as an educated man you know what it's like at court. And oh, of course, just your signature at the bottom, and we'll all be shipshape, won't we?

Yet when the justice read the confession he saw that Lowe had said nothing about Mrs. James, so the gentleman was set to work on her. He let her in on a secret: Lowe wanted to meet her and discuss a matter very close to them both. As she sat nursing her child, the woman was beyond artifice.

"Out upon him, hath hee not brought mee to shame enough but he would draw my life likewise in question? I know your policye better than you imagine, but you both are and shall be deceived in me, and as for master Lowe, pray returne this, I have nothing to doe with him neither will I stir over the threshold to meete or speake with him (being guilty of my husbands death) would it save his life."

She was arrested and locked in the justice's gatehouse, and Lowe was moved to jail. The move did not trouble him. He was certain of his royal pardon. When the justice called him in for further examination, Lowe was not worried, and when the august gentleman came in and laid a paper on the justice's table, he was so sure it was his pardon that he relaxed and indulged in a few pleasantries. Then the justice read the paper to him, and he heard his own signed confession. He was struck dumb. For minutes he "seemed in a traunce." When at last he could speak, he said only, "Villaine hast thou betrayed mee?" He seemed to lose all interest in his case, though he did try to break out of jail, and would have liberated himself and all his fellow inmates if the jailer had not made an unscheduled night visit to help a poor prisoner. Because the law was harsh on any jailer who lost a prisoner, this one clapped Lowe in irons and kept him thereafter in the dungeon.

At Thetford, Lowe was found guilty of murder, and Mrs. James of petty treason. She was burnt at the stake in his sight on the prehistoric earthwork called Castle Hill, and he was then hanged. She confessed only to covering up for the murderer. Standing on the ladder he told the spectators all about the infanticide. It was the first time anybody knew that there had been a baby and that he had killed it.[3]

The Collector from Hell (1641)

A popular Coventry musician named Thomas Holt had 19 children. He had been taught from the Psalms that "Loe children the fruit of the wombe are a blessing, and an inheritance that comes from the Lord." For a while he felt that, if they were all that desirable, the Lord might be providing for his 19 better than He had done so far, but, as time went on, Thomas did do better, very well, for a musician.

He grew somewhat miserly, keeping a locked chest that even his wife said she never saw open. So matters went until 16 February, 1641. All day long a tempest raged over Coventry. Some lost their haystacks, some had their houses blown over. Mrs. Holt was to tell people that, as the day roared on, Thomas felt weak and took to his bed, which to her surprise he regarded as his death bed. He asked for paper, pen, and ink so he could write his will. She thought he was joking, but he insisted. If a man comes to the door asking for me, he added, tell him I'm not at home. At last she brought the supplies, but before he could begin writing his will, they heard a knocking at the front door.

I'm afraid I'm not going to get this done, said the musician, hold him off if you can. Mrs. Holt thought the man at the door was handsome.

"Woeman where is thy husband?"

"Sir he is not now at home."

"Nay woeman ... deney him not for that is in vaine, for I know that he is now in bed, and I must and will speake with him."

The woman was uncomfortable telling a lie, so she led the man to her husband's bed. Holt and the visitor had a short exchange that she did not overhear. Then, before her eyes, the handsome man took the form of the Devil. The wife ran downstairs to get her neighbors. When they returned, they found Thomas dead, his neck broken. Soon after, she opened the forbidden chest. It was filled to the brim with what looked like gold, but at her touch it fell to dust.

There the story ends. It could have been generated in some fertile environment like Coventry market, where everybody knew you could sell your soul to the Devil for gold, and that the Devil is a cheat in the end. Simplicity urges another scenario: Suppose the handsome man was not the Devil, but the wife's lover. (The 19 children need not have been hers). They could have broken Holt's neck, appropriated the gold, and explained its absence to a gullible reporter.[4]

A Note on Ratsbane

Even learned Elizabethans shared quarters with the rather tame black rat, unaware of its connection with plague, but they naturally tried to keep rats from biting their children, spoiling their food, and stealing their tallow candles. They used ferrets, rat terriers, and poison, which they called ratsbane. This could be anything that worked, such as arsenic, but commonly it was mercuric perchloride, also known as corrosive sublimate of mercury. One penny at the neighboring apothecary bought enough to bring a miserable death to a human.

Of course, a pennyworth may be insufficient if it is not all administered. A London maid named Burs was beaten by her master and mistress for no better reason, she complained, than stealing their ale. Her plan for revenge seemed quite clever to her. She fed the wife some ratsbane, but saved enough to show her while she was suffering from the poison, so she could tell her mistress that she had found it in the master's clothing, and therefore he must be the poisoner. If all worked well, the wife would die accusing her husband, and he would hang, and the maid would be elegantly avenged on both of them. Withholding the sample, however, had reduced the wife's dose below the fatal level. Nobody believed the maid anyway, but as there seemed to be inadequate cause to hang her, she was carted about the city in disgrace, and must have had a problem ever after with employment references.[5]

Another servant, Peter Moore, also sought revenge against his employers. He too was attracted by the cheapness of this poison, but he knew a lot more about it than Miss Burs, because he was apprenticed to an Exeter apothecary named Humphrey Bidgood, who provided him schooling and introductory training in the trade. When Bidgood married, however, his bride kept Peter much busier than he liked, so Peter put "powdered white mercury" into his master's pottage for dinner. Bidgood swelled up and died. At his own parents' urging, Peter confessed, and was hanged, without having explained why he poisoned his master instead of his mistress.[6]

Ann Hamton, like her rowdy Westminster neighborhood, was convivial but not well governed. While her husband worked, she spent his money drinking with various men and women, including the Hamtons' landlady, Margaret Harwood. Life was never better than when she was tippling with her friends, and never worse than when she was cooped up with her laborious and sober husband. When he finally did complain, Anne ran straight to her landlady confidante. It's your own fault, said Margaret, for letting somebody like that live. Hang him. Cut his throat. He is not fit to live on earth among good fellows. Poison him. So Anne bought five drams of poison, enough, it was said, to put down ten men. She poured the lot into her husband's food. He immediately started to swell, and eventually died bloated and losing his nails. A surgeon opened him up, but we encounter the limitations of the forensic science of the day when we read that the surgeon found the poison "lying about his heart," and that he discovered the poison by putting it in a Venetian glass. It was believed that Venetian glass would break if it came in contact with poison. The glass broke. The silly pair confessed, and that was that.[7]

The Chattel Fights Back (1635)

With the possible exception of young White, her first lover, Alice's life was a progressive disaster. When her employer got her pregnant, he gave her some money. He also promised to find her a husband and send her some support money from time to time, as long as she continued to "condescend unto his desiers, which were most unlawfull, dishonest, and unchaste." He never sent her a penny, but he did find her a husband, named Fortune Clarke. Fortune was old, mad, and sadistic, drunk or sober. By the time Alice realized it would have been better to be the mother of a bastard than the wife of Fortune, it was too late to choose.

Alice did not try to sweeten her husband's character, continuing to make love with White at every opportunity. She ran off for a fortnight with a sailor named Hillinden. His advice about Fortune was "to pop him up with white bread and milke, and to put something else into it." As an alternative, he offered to take her overseas with him. She did not go, though Fortune was worse than even America would have been. He would strip her, tie her to the bedpost, and beat her, sometimes because that was his mood and sometimes because he had just caught her with White again.

One Ascension day, Fortune caught them together in his house, and got to beat them both. White whined that he had rather hang than to go on living this way. Later that day, he gave Alice a penny's worth of farthing tokens and told her to buy "mercury" from an apothecary in Uxbridge.

The rest of the story comes from Alice, foggy with contradictions: Alice bought the poison, if one chooses to believe her, after saving Fortune when he tried to drown himself in one of his drunken spells. She was not sure (she said) what she would do with the poison; perhaps kill Fortune and herself. If she really did save Fortune from drowning so that he might experience ratsbane, we might think she had a sadistic bent of her own; but it is better just to follow her tale and not get bogged down in analysis. Alice said that when she arrived home from the apothecary, a drunken Fortune searched her, as he did routinely in the barren hope of finding money. Now he found the mercury. His immediate reaction (said Alice) was to gulp the lot then and there. Shortly he became very ill; this at least we can believe. Alice says she begged her husband to take an antidote and thus save both their lives. Egg white in large and timely doses is the classic antidote to corrosive sublimate poisoning. Did Alice know that? Would she have cared? Her husband refused to take any antidote (she said) saying he wanted to die; he especially wanted to die if he could do so in the sure and certain hope that his wife would be burnt at the stake. In this state of spiritual preparation Fortune died. White was hanged and Alice burnt, Wednesday, 10 May, 1635.

The reverend Henry Goodcole allows her a little compassion:

"Her injuries, and harsh and unmanly usage spurred on by the instigations of the devil, almost compeld her to what she did."[8]

Our authors often mention a marked or grotesque swelling as a symptom, before and after death, of "mercury" poisoning. We cannot be sure that they are reporting at first hand. Such swelling is not mentioned in modern references.[9]

Oatcakes for All (1604)

God gave Mr. Duncalffe a daughter instead of a son, and he set about making his little Elizabeth into a prize for some substantial county family. He set up an income of ten pounds a year for her future husband and his heirs. He even brought in a good tutor and had her educated. This plan was so successful that she was still an adolescent when he was able to bestow her on the young scion of a good family, Thomas Caldwell. Thomas's only known fault was an adolescent hankering to see distant lands, and as soon as he was married and had the means to indulge it, he took to traveling abroad much of the time, leaving Elizabeth at home. As his cash dwindled, he left her "often times verie bare," lonely, and angry. The girl had the sympathy of all, even the Caldwells.

Nobody was more sympathetic than a wealthy young neighbor named Jefferey Bownd. Although he got nowhere with his first straightforward proposition to bed her, he hired an old widow, Isabel Hall, to befriend the lonely girl and assist in her seduction. After much time and effort, Isabel succeeded. Jefferey and Elizabeth became lovers, meeting in Isabel's house as opportunity offered.

Jefferey was not finished with Isabel's services. What he had in mind was marriage, attainable of course only by eliminating Thomas. First Isabel and Jefferey worked on Elizabeth to get her to accept the general principle. It took a long time, but eventually they wore her down and won her terrified and doubtful acquiescence. Then Isabel and Jefferey planned the murder. Elizabeth, who irritated them with constant entreaties to give up the project entirely, was spared the details. They decided to give five pounds to George Fernley, a needy brother of Isabel's, to do away with Thomas. George agreed straight away, took the five pounds, and assured Jefferey he would manage everything. Later on he reassured him, and still later he reassured him again, and still Thomas lived. It finally became obvious that George had no intention of earning his five pounds. Jefferey was angry, but all his effort settled down to trying to get his five pounds back. Thomas lived on.

Time was against the conspirators. Thomas was at home now, but given his wanderlust he might go abroad again. To break the impasse, Isabel sent Jefferey to Knutsforth to buy some ratsbane. Jefferey took it to Elizabeth, who did not want it, so Isabel sent her maid to Elizabeth with instructions to get "the spice." Isabel baked a batch of oatcakes, something Thomas was known to relish. She spiced them with ratsbane and sent them to Elizabeth, who left them on the bedroom window sill in the evening when she came to join her husband in bed. Early in the morning, Thomas arose, and Elizabeth stayed in bed. Ah, oatcakes! Thomas asked if he might take any of them.

"Yea, all of them if you like," she answered from under the covers. He took several and strode out, calling to the maid for butter. Elizabeth lay in an agony, not knowing how to stop the nightmare that she thought was about to unfold.

The nightmare that did unfold was not the one she expected. Thomas expansively shared his treats with the servants and children, even a little neighbor girl who was recovering from an illness and had dropped in for fire. Isabel's recipe must have had some flaw, for soon the household staff were vomiting instead of dying. Later that day two not very fastidious dogs and a cat died. Still later, word came that the little neighbor girl, weakened by her illness, had died. Thomas lived on.

Elizabeth was arrested. Tormented already with guilt, she was so burdened by the death of the girl that she could not wait to confess everything to the justices of the peace. Of course she implicated Jefferey and Isabel, and though they denied everything, all three were locked up behind the gloomy purple stones of Chester Castle, isolated from each other to await the assizes. Hilary term was upon them, so the trials were postponed to Easter. By then, Elizabeth was found to be pregnant, so their trials were postponed to Michaelmas term, nearly nine months after the arrests. Elizabeth spent this time concentrating on her spiritual state, meditating and conversing on religious subjects. With her education, she proved eloquent, and soon people were coming to the castle to hear her, sometimes 300 on a good day. Her material needs in prison were taken care of by two pious benefactors, John Battie and Lady Mary Cholmsly.

At last Michaelmas came, and Elizabeth received her sentence. Jefferey Bowndes was arraigned on a Saturday. Protecting his estate from forfeiture, he refused to plead, and the justices ordered him pressed the following Monday. He died about nine Monday morning.

That night, Elizabeth gave birth to a boy, her second. Her death warrant was set for 13 days after her delivery, more than the usual time allowed. Some said it had been at her husband's request that the execution was scheduled in this way. The constable of Chester Castle muddled his part and neglected to deliver the warrant to the sheriff until after that date, so there was nothing to do but hold her until the next assizes for resentencing. When the assizes came around again, Isabel too was tried and condemned and the two were hanged together. Lady Mary Cholmsly had tried unsuccessfully to get a reprieve and pardon from the new king. The infant boy joined his older brother in his father's care.

Elizabeth left a letter to her husband. In part it expressed repentance for having tried to kill him, but on balance it was much more a plea for him to mend his ways. Her warning that he must keep the Sabbath suggests that the youthful survivor liked to hunt and play games on Sundays.[10]

Sir Francis Bacon, during one of the trials stemming from the Overbury murder, mentions similar miscarriages by poisoners. A poisoned apple meant for a mother killed her daughter instead. More famously, an attempt to poison the Bishop of Rochester killed 17 of his household and an unknown number of the paupers who regularly came around for his table scraps.[11]

V

Robbery on Land

The more primitive and simple-minded robberies seldom merited a pamphlet. One pamphlet listed a great many ingenious ways in which shoplifting was carried out. Most shops were stalls on the ground floor of a residence, and opened out onto the street. Transactions took place where stall and street met, so that goods were vulnerable to theft. Robberies with or without murder might be lifted from obscurity by a narrator's sense of some unusual working of providence, such as collaborative detection by a mute and a dog, or of an engaging yarn.

Home Fires Burning (1608)

The thrice-widowed Mrs. Killingworth was sometimes an excellent seamstress, but cyclically she would pass out drunk in her house in Creechurch parish near Aldgate, or in the street in front of it. She had cheated and beaten so many maids that she could not find any more, so easygoing neighbors would lug her up to bed, lock her door, and throw the key into her house. Her hangovers were equally gargantuan. Nobody expected to see her again for a day or two. Mrs. Killingworth accused neighbors of stealing and snooping, until eventually they stopped helping her. In January, 1608, she finally found a new maid, Elizabeth Abbot. I don't know much about Elizabeth, she told a crony in nearby Cornhill. The girl might be pregnant, but she says she has a husband, a tailor in the Strand. Besides, the widow said, I am amused by the girl's quaint north country accent.

By Friday, 23 January, she had been out of sight longer than any hangover would explain. Her maid went to Mrs. Sutton's shop next door on

Wednesday to fetch bread and beer—much more than usual, Mrs. Sutton told everybody. Mrs. Sutton's maid remembered that on the last Wednesday evening she had heard complaining sounds through the wall, but the Suttons supposed it was "her old desease" again. The maid kept hearing odd sounds, like the moving of furniture, until she fell asleep. The maid in the Dutchman's house across the street recalled hearing Mrs. Killingworth about midnight, groaning, "O Lord shal I die thus and never a neighbor come at me?" Upper stories leaned out over the street, so their windows were often quite close to those on the other side. The Dutchman's maid had opened her casement and asked Mrs. Killingworth, Are you all right? Elizabeth Abbot had answered, saying, God help her, she is not well, but it is her old disease and she will be better after some sleep. One more oddity: The Dutchman's maid could usually see all of the widow's bedroom, but now for the first time a heavy cloth was stretched across the window, giving an unprecedented privacy.

The neighbors sent for the constable, who went up a ladder and looked in. The fireplace had burnt so hot that the mantelpiece had caught fire. There was still water on the floor in front of the hearth, spilled when somebody put it out. The constable sent the beadle to fetch the alderman's deputy, and at last it seemed legal to break into the house. Everything valuable and portable had been removed. In the fireplace they found some small bones and took them to the lord mayor. A surgeon declared them human. In the meantime, searchers had looked behind the fireback, and found a lock of hair tied in a lace attached to a chin band.

The authorities began a search for Elizabeth Abbot. All London was talking about the murder. It was the favorite subject at the nearby drinking places. A girl from Brentwood was seized and brought back to London, where the constable had difficulty protecting her from "the ruder sort" who saw no reason why so wicked a person should be accorded a trial. A gown in her possession looked like one that Mrs. Killingworth had owned. The authorities put it on display for identification, but soon satisfied themselves that the girl from "Burnt Wood" was not Elizabeth Abbot. They were about to give the girl a little money for her trouble and send her back home, when a citizen identified the gown as his wife's. They had been nearly ruined by a burglary in Whitechapel. The girl went to Newgate, but Elizabeth Abbot remained at large.

She surfaced in a little town in Surrey a mile or two from Nonesuch Palace when she and her husband tried to burglarize a yeoman's house. They chopped a hole in his garden wall, but in that quiet town the noise aroused the owner. He ran out armed with a pitchfork, and Elizabeth's husban ran off into the dark. The owner's mastiff insisted on barking at the saw pit, so its master poked the pile of sawdust with his pitchfork and sent a prong through Elizabeth's arm. She screamed, he called for help, and Elizabeth the fugitive was a prisoner, though nobody knew who she was. She was held to await examination by Sir Edward Sanders, the justice of the peace.

Sunday morning at the inn men were still milling about with pitchforks and staves, and savoring the story of the clever mastiff and the woman in the sawdust. The innkeeper's sister, a Mrs. Cox, had come the day before just to be merry with her brother. She was especially curious about the hubbub because she lived in Creechurch parish, near Mrs. Killingworth's house. We do not know what was in the back of Mrs. Cox's mind, whether a hunch or idle curiosity, but she wanted to talk with the prisoner. Her brother promised to arrange it. Sir Edward could have sent Elizabeth to speedy trial, but to get more information he committed her to the White Lion prison in Southwark. To help his sister with her investigation, the innkeeper invited the guards and their prisoner to have a drink. Mrs. Cox was allowed to sit in a separate room with the prisoner so they could talk more freely, though others stayed in ear shot.

Mrs. Cox asked, "how shee beeing a woman could bee so hardy to attempt to break open a house, to rob and undoe an honest countryman, that lives faithfully by his labours."

"Why, as I did before with my handes; and were it to doe I could as resolutely attempt it againe."

"Woman, if I mistake not, I have seene you somewhere in London."

"It might be so in the Strand perhaps."

"No, about Aldgate if I be not deceived."

Elizabeth overreacted to this, a slip so fatal that the author commented at this point, "heere note the power of the Divell."

"O I sound your meaning: you goe about to intrap mee about the woman that was burnt by Aldgate, but you are deceived in that in faith, as they that did it were deceived of their expectation."

"Why, of what were they deceived?"

"Why, I tell you, of their expectation, they lookt for much and had little, she was a good old gentlewoman, and she had beene a proper young gentlewoman: but if you thinke to insnare or intrappe mee you are deceived."

Here a bystander chimed in, "Surely you were much interested in the villany, that knew so well what profitte they made by their murther, and what manner of person the murthered was, and can so rapidly deliver it."

"Lord, how you are deceived, for I tell you, I heard it of a woman of Luttruge some three or four miles off, and about three or foure days since." But Elizabeth could not say who that woman was.

Elizabeth was lodged in the White Lion later that Sunday. The news of Mrs. Cox and her interview spread fast: to Sir Edward, to the dwellers about Aldgate and Creechurch, to the lord mayor. So far only Elizabeth knew that she was wearing a certain petticoat: a petticoat stolen from Mrs. Killingworth, a petticoat that would hang her when she was searched. She turned to an old woman in the prison, a widow Barthelmew, saying, I'll trade petticoats with you; mine's twice as dear as yours but I won't charge you anything for the trade. But the widow Barthelmew was marching to some drummer of her own, and immediately told the keeper, who prevented any such trade. Elizabeth had to content herself with tearing off the lace to disguise the garment. What she did with the lace she never told.

Monday morning the authorities placed Elizabeth among some other women in an identification lineup. Mrs. Cox, Mrs. Sutton, Mrs. Sutton's maid, and other women all picked her out. Later in the day, she was taken for a preliminary hearing before the lord mayor, the sheriffs, the recorder, and a justice, who had all gathered for another case. Again she denied ever having known Mrs. Killingworth. They sent her below while they discussed the evidence.

Downstairs it was Mrs. Sutton's turn to play detective. Mrs. Sutton asked Elizabeth, don't you have a husband?

"Yes."

"Is he not a Tailor?"

"I graunt he is."

"Did hee not work in the Strand?"

"Yes."

"And did not you tell mistresse Killingworth so much."

"I confesse I did."

There it was. The crude trap had caught the woman who denied ever knowing Mrs. Killingworth, and a surgeon and stationer were present as witnesses. Elizabeth Abbot went to trial on Friday, 8 April, 1608, before Sir Edward Coke. She was carted, probably on the Monday, from Newgate to execution in Creechurch parish where the crime had been committed. Because she still denied everything, the sheriffs unbound her and led her into the parish church, where she was urged to confess for the good of her soul. She refused. The witnesses confirmed their testimony in the church, and Elizabeth was led from the church and hanged. She presumably saved her elusive husband, so he could go on tailoring and thieving.[1]

The Maid in the Garden (1612)

Elizabeth James's husband, being a gamekeeper, spent much time away from their home near Windsor. Each time he came home, there would be some bit of news. On one visit, he learned that Elizabeth was employing a maid who had come around looking for work. Elizabeth told him how sorry she had felt for the shy, simple girl at the door. He left feeling rather satisfied with matters at home.

A later visit was less pleasant. The maid came to him in tears. Elizabeth had been borrowing from her and now she had borrowed every penny the maid had saved in the world, and even a dress of hers. James was cross with his wife, and made her give it all back. If you can't get along with her, send her away, he told her.

The next time he came home, the maid was gone and the house was peaceful. After a couple of quiet days James proposed going out for a pleasant dig in the garden. Oh, no, please, said his wife, not after all the time and money I've just spent putting in seeds there.

The village had news. A dumb woman had apparently gone mad. She would mime a charade for anybody who would watch, dragging herself by the hair, wringing her hands, stabbing herself, and slitting her throat. She did not seem to be enjoying her own good act, but the placid villagers were slow to grow suspicious. At this point, a dog intervened. It was sent, explained the author, by the Almighty, pursuant to Genesis 21: "He that smites a man that he die, shall die for it."

The dog dug in the James's garden. Encouraged by finding collops of maidservant here and there, it did not give up until it found her head. Proudly the dog carried it back by the hair, to show to the dense humans. This was a gratifying moment for the dumb woman, who repeated her charade. This time she could also point from the severed head to the flustered and now equally speechless Elizabeth James. Elizabeth went off to the White Lion prison in Southwark. At her sentencing, she pleaded her belly. At the time of writing, she was awaiting delivery.[2]

The King's Chapel (1612)

For Christmas, 1612, King James attended the royal chapel in Whitehall Palace. English subjects liked to see their monarch. James appreciated this curiosity so little that he once threatened to moon them, but he let his court see him at various activities such as dinner, drinking, and prayers. The courtiers were numerous, and each had servants, so that in practice any well dressed person might wander unchallenged over much of the palace. In the royal chapel an attendant named Edmond Doubleday grew suspicious of a stranger standing by Leonard Barry. As the stranger turned to leave, Doubleday asked Barry if he had his purse. Why no, said Barry, and it had 40 shillings in it. They caught the stranger just outside the chapel, Doubleday holding his wrists while Barry searched him and recovered his purse. Word was immediately sent to the king, at prayers with the queen, Prince Charles, and Princess Elizabeth. Services were only briefly disrupted while the king ordered the stranger held, and then the royal family received the sacrament.

Household officers took the prisoner before the clerk of the green cloth, Sir Robert Banister. The prisoner was John Selman, living in Shoe Lane. Despite his fine black cloak lined and laced with velvet, he had no honest means of living, and admitted entering Whitehall just to steal a purse. Selman's clothing was exchanged for something more suitable to his class. He observed New Year's Eve by pleading guilty and being sentenced to death. On his knees he asked the prosecutor, Sir Francis Bacon, for a Christian burial and for his goods to go to his widow. Sir Francis agreed in return for the names of several other thieves whom Selman knew. He was hanged nearby at Charing Cross the day after Twelfth Night. In his final speech he admitted to having corrupted several promising youths. He was ashamed, he said, and "ready to be spewed out of the Commonwealth." A pickpocket who had not absorbed Selman's lesson was seized operating among the spectators.[3]

Tom and Bess (1635)

Parts of London changed completely with the setting of the sun. Daytime business receding, the underworld flowed in. Henry Goodcole, minister at Newgate prison, had good reason to know where these parts were. First on his warning list was West Smithfield and the adjacent end of Duck

Lane. Smithfield was a railed lot where livestock was traded by day, as well as being an execution site. Most of the other dangerous places were nearby: Smithfield's pond, sheep pens, taverns, and the cook shops that clustered about Cloth Fair and Pie Corner, and Cow Cross. Yet even Cheapside, one of London's broadest and busiest streets, was risky at night around the smaller of the two water conduits that stood in its center. There were other dangerous places, such as London bridge and the suburban St. Pancras and Bloomsbury. Goodcole, if anything, understated the situation around Smithfield. This area was taken over each August by the notorious Bartholomew Fair. It drew, says another writer,

> Knaves and fools, Cuckolds and Cuckoldmakers, Bauds, and Whores, Pimpes and Panders, Rogues and Rascalls, the little Loudone and the witty wanton.... Saint Bartholomew's hospitall ... appears to me a fucking Exchange ... for there many a handsome wench exchanges her maidenhead for a small favour.... The Faire is full of gold and silver drawers: Just as Lent is to Fishmongers, so is Bartholomew Faire to the Pickpocket.[4]

Goodcole learned some of these dangerous places from Canberry Bess, and Bess was an expert because she as much as anyone made them dangerous. Her routine was simple. If, in the course of turning tricks, she noticed a certain kind of victim, she would pick him up for special treatment: Don't I know you? Well, you are a handsome gentleman in any case. Don't think I'm one of these whores, that would charge you money. I know a nice quiet place where we can be alone and I'll do this and I'll do that, and nobody will know but me and you. But I hope I can trust you, a girl like me all alone.

On a January night in 1635, she trusted Rowland Holt, a merchant and citizen of London, and let him take her to Clerkenwall fields near Smithfield. Mr. Holt was found there the next morning, robbed and beaten to death. After meeting Bess, Holt had met her partner, Country Tom Sherwood. Tom was always in view of Bess as she plied the streets. They had agreed on the victim's profile: clearly prosperous, a little drunk, and not carrying a cudgel or wearing a sword. Tom wore a special shirt in which he carried an invention of his own, a wooden handle cased in knobby iron. He would arrive at the dark and lonely rendezvous, and attack while the victim was concentrating on Bess. The rest was easy.

Holt's body was displayed in Turnbull street for identification. Out of bravado or curiosity, Tom went to view it. If Tom believed, with his contemporaries, that a corpse gives witness against its murderer by bleeding in his presence, he was taking a great risk. In the event, it was not Holt's wounds but Tom's nose that began bleeding, not a supernatural but a psychosomatic phenomenon. He left the scene quickly, fearing that his nosebleed might betray him. It was a shaken Tom who confessed to Bess, "I have suffered such a thing this day about Master Holt, wee must of necessity, leave of this course of life."

They planned to leave the country as soon as they could afford the trip, but this required stealing a little more money. At Easter, the battered corpse of Lieutenant Thomas Claxton, a soldier, was found in Gray's Inn Fields. He had been flashily dressed in a new red suit when Bess picked him up in Bloomsbury; when he was found, he was completely naked until a passing maid charitably dropped a towel on him.

After the Claxton job, the pair were ready to take ship abroad and start a new life. Tom bought Bess a new petticoat. The lieutenant's bright red new suit was an extra bonus. Tom decided to sell it to a shop in Houndsditch, but for a little extra filip, to be a peacock for an hour or so, he wore it himself. As he went to meet Bess in Moor Fields, somebody recognized the suit. Tom was arrested and lodged in Newgate. He had no subtlety, no second line of defense, and he confessed the murder of Holt and Claxton, as well as of a Mr. Long who had lingered three months after being found, bloody and groaning, against Lady Hatton's garden wall in Holborn. Tom also confessed to numerous other robberies. He explained that he was not a bad sort at heart, and would have done much better if whores like Bess had not misled him. Bess too ended up in Newgate, loudly blaming Tom for leading her astray. Tom hated whores like Bess, and Bess hated thieves like Tom. Their companionship may have produced a fatal *folie a deux,* wherein they turned murderers who would otherwise have been hanged only for theft.

Even while preparing to face divine judgment, Bess disagreed with Tom on one point. He said she helped undress Claxton while he was dying. She swore Claxton had taken off his own clothes that April Fool's night. Goodcole was tactful enough to say that he believed none of her aspersions on the late lieutenant, but Claxton had after all followed Bess voluntarily, and for only one imaginable purpose. On the other hand, Londoners who completed these transactions with streetwalkers would have been adept at doing it without much undressing, especially in the chill of an English early April.

Tom was hanged in chains at the scene of Claxton's murder in Gray's Inn Fields, but the government's plan to leave him there proved so obnoxious to pedestrians in the normal course of their business that he was moved near St. Pancras, where arriving travelers would see him at a little distance. As this was a place favored by highway robbers, it was not long before two of them attempted to rob a butcher there. The butcher had no money, and they were so annoyed that they gagged him and bound him for the night to Tom's gibbet. So Tom was moved again, out to Ring Cross, Islington. These moves prompted Goodcole, and probably other Londoners, to make a feeble little joke about *"habeas corpus."* Unlike Tom, Canberry Bess was no trouble at all. The college of barber surgeons begged her body, and in their stately hall by Cripplegate her skeleton instructed students indefinitely.[5]

Picaresque Characters

In spite of their preachers (or because of them), people enjoyed unedifying accounts written from the criminal's viewpoint, a popular genre inspired perhaps by picaresque tales from Spain, and sometimes termed "rogue biography."

Citizens have sometimes taken a sneaking pride in the rascality of their cities: New York and Chicago, for instance. In London, a prideful literature entertained readers with the titillating underworld of London. In a sort of travel guide, Henry Pecham professed to warn visitors to stay out of alehouses, dice and card games, and crowds, especially in playhouses, but his purpose was entertainment. He tells of a country wife coming back from a playhouse, missing her four gold pieces, six shillings, and silver toothpick. Where was it? her husband asked. Under my petticoat.

"What, did you feel no bodies hand there?"

"Yes, I felt ones hand there; but I did not thinke hee had come for that."[6]

In Thomas Harman's *Caveat*, London vagabonds went by such names as Wel Arayd Richard, Core the Cuckolde, and Wylliam Cooper with the Harelyp, or descriptions such as "Thomas Gray his toes be gonne ... Harry Smith he drivelleth when he speaketh ... Robert Brownswerde, he weareth his hair longe." Richard Horwood won something of an accolade: "wel nere lxxx yeres olde, he wyl byte a vi penny nayle asunder in his teeth, and a bawdy drunkard."[7]

Picaresques: You Know the Way (1609)

To these names we can add Double Diligence and his woman, named Old Doublets for the second-hand vests and jackets she bought and sold in her shop. Double Diligence, *alias* Tendance, was an extortionist who offered protection to a variety of thieves and streetwalkers in exchange for information. Tell me where and when you are going to operate, he would propose, and I'll see that nobody peaches on you. Then for the dividend: Give me a share of what you bring in, and I'll keep protecting you. Protecting from whom? From Double Diligence, who knew enough to terminate many a criminal career, and would do so now and then when it seemed sound business.

By a curious coincidence, Double Diligence's less fortunate clients might meet him one more time, busily tying knots here and there at Tyburn, for Double Diligence was the assistant to Derrick the hangman. As part of their compensation, the hangman and his assistant received the clothing of their victims. Shakespeare in this very year took note of this custom in a metaphor for worthlessness: "doublets that hangmen would bury with those that wore them."[8] Double Diligence marketed his share at his special outlet, Old Doublets' shop. This elegantly balanced economy promised to go on and on, but Old Doublets thought that, because her shop was also a place to fence stolen goods, she and her Double Diligence would make a closer couple if he would do a little of the dirty work himself, go out there and pick pockets. This was professionally a retrograde step for him, but either from greed or to please the old girl he joined the ranks of those he had been managing, and got down to picking pockets. He neglected his managerial duties, and before long, in Leadenhall, Cheapside, Westminster Hall, all the haunts of pickpockets, his underlings noticed a loosening of supervision. Then, as might be expected of a self-taught amateur, he was caught and lodged in Newgate.

Old Doublets, whatever else she may have been, was loyal. With some of their money she bought permission to move in as Double Diligence's cellmate in Newgate. As luck would have it, prison yawned for her too, and her purchased residence in the cell made her all the handier when she was arrested for dealing in stolen goods. The assistant hangman and his faithful, disastrous mistress "both lovingly ended in a hempen friendship." The author did not tell us what conversation Double Diligence had with his old master Derrick on this final visit to his familiar work place.[9]

A more typical rogue of the genre was Ned Browne, partly invented by Shakespeare's rival Robert Greene, though Greene's modern editor says there was a real Ned Browne. Ned wants us to understand that he is not one of those sorry wretches found in ministers' didactic accounts; his tale belongs with the rogue biographies, intended for entertainment:

> If you think (Gentlemen) to heare a repentant man speake, or to tel a large tale of his penitent sorrowes, ye are deceived: for as I have ever lived lewdly, so I meane to end my life as resolutely, and not by a cowardly confession to attempt the hope of a pardon. Yet, in that I was famous in my life for villainies, I will at my death professe myselfe as notable, by discoursing to you merrely, the manner and methode of my knaveries, which if you hear without laughing, then after my death call me base knave, and never have me in remembrance.

Greene introduced Ned by describing his swaggering end:
"But at last hee leapt at a daysie for his loose kind of life, and therefore imagine you now see him in his owne person, standing in a great bay windowe with a halter about his necke ready to be hanged, desperately pronounsing this his whole course of life and confesseth as followeth."

Ned cheated, robbed, traded wives, fled to Europe, and ended hanging from a French church from which he had stolen a pyx. His relation is less candid, after being polished and manipulated by a professional like Greene, than those provided by amateur writers.[10]

Picaresques: Ratsey (1605)

Nobody would have believed that condemned prisoners in the ratty cells of Newgate had penned the sentiments ascribed to them in the pamphlets. One hundred twenty lines of doggerel were fathered on the gentleman thief, Gamaliel Ratsey, on the eve of his execution. The first verse ran:

> The silent night that shadoweth every tree,
> And Phoebus in the West was shrowded low,
> Each hive had home her labouring Bee,
> And Birds their nightly harbour gan to know,
> And all things did from weary labour linne,
> And I began to weigh my state and sinne.

Even so, the account of Ratsey's adventures is probably furnished by him, for it shows much self-flattery.

Ratsey's father had wanted him to be a scholar, but he went off instead with the Earl of Essex to fight in Ireland. He returned in 1603, an unemployed exsoldier who had learned mostly antisocial skills. Heading homeward to Market Deeping he stopped at an inn in nearby Spalding. One of the maids instantly fell in love with him, and saw that he got special favors about the place. Even the landlady took him into her confidence, and proudly showed him the bag holding £40 that a farmer had just left with her for safety. The farmer was to pay off a bond with it the next day. Ratsey, with the freedom of the house, picked the landlady's lock, and traveled on to his mother's garden to bury the farmer's bag.

After the farmer and the landlady discovered the loss the next morning, a constable jailed Ratsey. Ratsey denied everything, and despite his having had means, motive, and opportunity there was no conclusive evidence against him. The jail system, however, put him under pressure. He needed money just to subsist there, and none was offered by his father. Somehow he had to get into his cache in the orchard. Whom to trust? He chose his mother, and told her where to find the buried money.

With this confidence he put her "in a great perplexitie what to doe, whether she should prove unnaturall in revealing the same, or by concealing it, hazard her reputation in the Countrey." She could not bring herself to do either, and sought the advice of her husband. He too sought advice, and soon the secret was no secret. The news even came around to Ratsey in jail, and being a slim youth he wriggled free and escaped in his shirt.

Once at large, he conned some poor servant out of his master's best gelding and took to the road. He looked up an old friend named Shorthose, who had never been in trouble before but was short of cash. They recruited one Snell, twice branded in the hand at Newgate. This punishment was a method of penal record-keeping. If caught again, Snell would not get a third branding.

The trio began a series of highway robberies. One example shows their method. Ratsey had Snell and Shorthose hide behind a hedge on the highway and come only if he called them. Ratsey lay lounging under the hedge, cracking nuts as nine men came riding down the road. One of them recognized Ratsey and warned the others, but Ratsey jumped on his horse and met them before they could escape.

I have come for money, he said, and money I must have. "Therefore dispatch ... for one of your companie heere knows me, and knowes I will not be trifled with."

"On our faythes ... maister Ratsey, wee are no better provided than will be our charges to London, and that at the most is not twentie shillings a man, if you will have that, you shall have it with all our hearts."

"Nay," said Ratsey, "that will doe me no good, for it is well knowne I robbe not for trifles. But what have you ... in your Portmangle?"

"Fayth ... I have a little money that I am to pay uppon bond by a day, and wee are two or three of us heere bound to pay it, if you take it from us wee are undone."

"How much is it?"

"Two hundred poounds."

"I Marrie ... such a lumpe I looke for. And seeing there are so many to pay it, it will not hurt you much if all of you loose it. Therefore be briefe, deliver it, for if you stand uppon tearmes, or delayes with mee, I have Whelpes within the inside of the Hedge, that upon a Watchworde will presently come foorth, and they never barke till they bite: if they stirre, it is all things to nothing, but some of you loose your lives, and your limmes." For Ratsey, "hee thought it the best cracking of Nuttes that ever he made, that yeelded such shelles," which was slang for coins.

And so they haunted the highways, robbing here a Cambridge scholar, there a conjuror. They took £80 from two wool merchants, and in a festive mood Ratsey knighted them (Sir Walter Woolsack and Sir Samuell Sheepskinne). They came across an old couple tottering toward a fair. I lack money, Ratsey told them. It is a hard time for us soldiers. Without wars we have no employment.

The old man, shaking, "told him that in all the world hee had but five nobles and that he was fain to make hard shift for, and sell some of his household stoffe to make it up, and if he should die hee left not one penny at home to helpe him, and my wife (saies he) hath but one Edward shilling and a Mill sixpence, which hath seene no sunne these seaven yeares ... and all this we have pacht upp together (maister) to buye us one cow to keepe me and my wife now we are old. If you take it from us wee are utterly undone."

"You are an old dissembler, Sirra," scoffed Ratsey. "I have met with such as you that have said as much as you doe, and yet I have found more silver and gold in a russet hose than in velvet breeches."

"It may be so ... but on my faith and hollidome I deale truly with you sir," said the old man, pouring out all their coins. Ratsey told them to put them back. He gave them forty shillings and suggested they buy two cows.

"For," said Ratsey, "I hold it worse than Sacriledge to rob the spittle [hospital], and while I live the Sermon in the wood must teach me to favour and pitie them that are poore, and helpe them, for the rich can helpe themselves."

"Sermon in the wood": alluding to Robin Hood?

Flexibility was Ratsey's signature. He started to rob a farmer of £250 that he was taking to pay off a mortgage for £300 that had come due. The farmer still lacked £50 and was afraid the creditor might take advantage of him and foreclose. Ratsey's businesslike solution was to make up the £50 for the farmer and then rob the creditor of the £300 he had just collected.

Not everybody found Ratsey's humor benign. He came across a footpost, or messenger, and in the course of drinking wine with him, discovered his other calling. His leather bag, which Ratsey took care to investigate professionally, held the best collection of lockpicks he had ever seen. After Ratsey and the picklock footpost and Shorthose and Snell had all enjoyed each other's company, Ratsey asked the footpost to carry a letter to the chief jailer in Cambridge to ease a friend's imprisonment, he said. In fact, Ratsey forged a writ as if from a magistrate, ordering the messenger to be imprisoned for theft. Of course in Cambridge the jailer would have searched the messenger and found the lockpicks.

The robbers met their match in two brothers in Bedfordshire. Snell kept one of the gentlemen from escaping with the money while Ratsey and the brother fenced. The gentleman wounded Ratsey dangerously and was getting the better of it when his sword broke. Snell rode up and wounded the gentleman in the leg, so that at last the brothers gave up their money. They gave the alarm and a hue and cry was raised. The three split up and made rendezvous later at an inn in Southwark. They split the money four ways, Ratsey getting two shares because of his wound.

Snell, back in London, rode his stolen horse up Duck Lane. This short street led to the Smithfield market, where Snell would have meant to trade his horse. Unfortunately, this was just the area where people were most likely to recognize familiar horses or horsebrands, and Snell (himself twice branded) was arrested as a horse thief. Hoping to save his life, Snell gave up Ratsey's location. Ratsey was seized in Doctors Commons and jailed in Newgate with Snell, where the two remained without trial for two or three sessions. This delay in trying Snell and Ratsey caused great anxiety to Shorthose, still at liberty. He finally grew so anxious that he confided in an old friend named Walter Skellington, asking what to do. Skellington told the authorities, and Shorthose too was arrested.

Snell, afraid for his life in Newgate for having betrayed Ratsey, asked to be lodged in the King's Bench jail; but all three were taken to Bedford, the site of the last robbery. In Bedford jail Ratsey tried one more trick. He got some acid and managed to free himself of his iron shackles, but the keeper caught him before he could escape. At the Bedford assizes, says the writer, "they shewed themselves so valiant that they thrust twelve men in a corner, who found them all guiltie for the Robberie committed in Bedfordshire upon the Gentleman and his Brother." Snell's bargaining did him no good, and all three died on 20 March, 1605.[11]

Picaresques: Courtney (1612)

By a statistically stunning coincidence, seven years after Ratsey's execution, another condemned thief, Charles Courtney, penned 120 lines that were, word for word, identical to Ratsey's. In spite of this suspect opening, Courtney left a narrative in which he claimed to speak for himself. It contrasts strongly with Henry Goodcole's focus on the salvation of the prisoner and of others who might err. His prisoners' narratives are thickly interspersed with their regrets, and with the role of the Devil in their misfortunes. By the time Goodcole edited his interviews, any initial rationalizations, boasts, or justifications—and the convicts must have aired a lot of them—have been washed out. This sort of editing has diminished our knowledge of the felons' minds in their sinful days. Fortunately, some of Courtney's worldly thoughts survived his repentance, to show us his egotism and other unwashed snippets of his personality.

Courtney's origins resembled Ratsey's. He was a gentleman who led a quiet, honest life until he lost his father and young wife, and with them his moral compass. Dice and whores in London followed, then robbery to pay for them. Along the highways feeding into London he formed a network of crooked ostlers, who skillfully assessed the probable wealth carried by travelers, and would tip him off. He boasted of his efficient method.

"I never stood upon the way to watch for any passengers, nor never undertake any Robberie, but what was appoynted and certaine notice given which way they would passe, and what store of Coyne they carried...."

From this sound business practice Courtney extracted a certain self-righteousness. "I never tooke from the needy, or those whose povertie might cause them to complaine, but all my aime either at house or highway, were at such Curmugions, who care not who starve so themselves bee Cornefed." The philosophy of his gang was, "he that is borne must be kept."

Courtney teasingly states that two innocent men were hanged for one of his robberies, but he never gives their names. He says that he did not hear of the case until after the execution. "Had I known thereof before the execution, I should have yeelded my owne life, and have thought it chiefe meanes to obtain remission of God, for my manifold transgressions to save the Innocents."

Having been thwarted by poor communications from easing his importunate conscience, Courtney returned to carouse with his cronies in London and plan a major burglary. Near Temple Bar stood a house, familiar to Courtney because he often went there to borrow money until his next robbery. It belonged to an old pawnbroker named Gardner. Courtney of course calls him a usurer. Courtney the con man grew familiar with Gardner and took him out for wine from time to time. Eventually Courtney got the key he needed, and his gang cleaned out most of the money and pawned silver in the house. Neither Gardner nor any other man had insurance, and probably the old man was ruined.

The gang hid the loot in a nearby house while the constabulary notified every goldsmith and jeweller to watch for the goods. Courtney had an old pirate friend living on the channel coast, who made a living smuggling fugitives to France. While Courtney made arrangements with the pirate, his confederates were growing anxious. Go on and stay with the pirate then, Courtney told them, and I'll join you soon. A few days later, he sent a message warning them that things were getting hot and they had better set sail while they could. And so they did, with the help of the pirate friend, who was in on the scam. Courtney now possessed all the loot and his jolly comrades stood penniless on the French coast.

After more adventures, he was captured. He tells us no details, probably because he could not brag about them. He was sentenced to death, but because he might be useful in helping his victims recover some of their losses, he was reprieved for a little while. In Newgate prison he fell in with Clement Slie, a fencer who performed at sword matches. The men were of like character, and spent their time planning an escape. Paying prisoners had little supervision and could wander about within the rambling, thick-walled building. Courtney and Slie climbed a rope they had taken off a pulley, and found a locked door that barred their way onto the leaded roof. Courtney with his fingernails scraped a hole through the wooden door until he could insert two fingers and slide the bolt on the other side. They were nearly free when the keeper happened to drop in after his supper. He missed Courtney, and the other prisoners gave evasive answers. (He was just here a minute ago!) The jailer launched a search that extended through several adjacent private houses, while Courtney huddled under a covered table in the garret of Newgate. Finally he found Courtney, who says he knelt and asked forgiveness.

"There is no hurt done, Master Courtney, for I am the gladdest to see you of any man alive." He would have been glad, because losing a prisoner could be disastrously expensive for a jailer.

Courtney talked to a fellow prisoner who had some contacts with influential men on the outside. He persuaded the prisoner and his outside connection that with four days' reprieve he could recover several hundred pounds, and they would get some of it. Somehow the outsider managed to get him this reprieve. Courtney had been studying his surroundings, and felt sure that he and Slie could escape if they only had time. In the days left to them, they stole enough rope and sticks to make a ladder, climbing to the top of a high hall in Newgate and exiting through a hole they punched in the roof tiles. On the night of the escape, they disembarrassed themselves of a companion named Woodward, a coiner, by getting him so drunk he had to be carried to bed. From the roof they descended by a pulley that lowered beer barrels into the tap house. The jailer's nightmare had begun anew.

Once free, they hid for a day in a pig sty in Hyde Park. They robbed a gentleman in Layton, and then, taking a boat from Temple Stairs, committed several more robberies the same day at St. Katherine's by the Tower. On returning to Temple Stairs they were seized, not knowing who had betrayed them.

On Friday, 30 March, 1612, Sir Henry Montague, the lord chief justice, had Courtney brought over to his house in Aldersgate. Sir Henry told Courtney that the next day he would be hanged, and now would be a good time for him to get his soul in order. The next day Slie was hanged in front of Newgate, and Courtney in Warwick Lane behind it. Slie, who had only killed another fencer, got a decent burial across the street in Christ Church. Courtney's body was given to the barber surgeons.[12]

VI

Robbery at Sea

Pirates at Work (1608)

Historians crisply distinguish the legal privateer, who was an instrument of state policy in wartime, from the illegal pirate, by definition a robber at sea. Queen Elizabeth on the other hand preferred to keep such things indefinite.[1] She might be formally at war or at peace with Spain, but in practice much of the time she hovered vaguely in between. In this twilight labored privateers, pirates, and adventurers. Elizabeth habitually played ambiguity like a Stradivarius, and never more than in her relations with her seagoing subjects. Her successor, on the other hand, besides being by nature less tolerant of ambiguity, had a dislike for war, privateering, and piracy. King James made peace with Spain and prohibited further raids by his Scots, English, and Irish subjects on Spanish and Portuguese commerce. An unintended result of the king's proclamation was a sudden economic depression among privateers and a reciprocal increase in pure piracy, which he then moved vigorously to extirpate.[2] In the last days of 1609, 19 English pirates were conspicuously punished. Some were small fry, but these stories of the captains among them give a picture of sea rovers long before the classic age of Blood and Teach, who color the modern image of pirates.[3]

Captain Harris

The middle class in the port of Bristol were largely merchants and sea captains trading in the Mediterranean, Africa, India, and the New World. James Harris came from this background, and when he grew up it was only natural for him to go to sea as his father had done before. He began in the reign of Elizabeth as purser aboard a "man of war," which did not yet connote "Royal Navy." It raided Spanish and Portuguese shipping and brought back the spoils to the Bristol merchants who had invested in the venture. After gaining wealth and reputation in this position of trust, James became master of his own ship, and fed such wealth to his backers that his ailing father wept with pride while his fellow aldermen discussed James at the city council.

Fortune's wheel, an emblem that haunted Elizabethans, abruptly turned against Captain Harris in the straits of Gibraltar. A "Turkish" ship approached to attack him, and he counterattacked.[4] In the melee he was captured and taken to Tunis. His head and beard were shaved and he was sold as a galley slave. A slow year passed, filled with toil, flogging, and hunger; then another year, and another. Depression had numbed him when, after three years of this, Harris had the surreal experience of being visited in Tunis by an English Captain Bishop, whom he had never met.

Bishop knew about him from friends in Bristol, and when Bishop's business called him to Tunis, he sought out this brown, bald, beardless bag of bones from prosperous Bristol. Bishop was a friendly sort, bringing news from home, and weeping to see where the wheel of fortune had put Harris. He left the slave with a few gold pieces. Soon after, Harris learned that Bishop had bought him for 300 ducats. Free, but something of a wreck, he stayed in Tunis with his benefactor, who paid all his expenses while he recuperated.

To understand why some Englishmen were galley slaves in Tunis while others came and went in comfort, we must look beyond ideas of a holy war, Cross versus Crescent. On the lawless seas, Muslims and Christians robbed each others' ships. That was one relationship. Another was for Muslims and Christians to rob in consort, and do business with each other. On English ships and in the ports of the Barbary coast there were pragmatists aplenty. Bishop and his like sold their loot and resided in Tunis, and its governor enjoyed his bribes.

Captain Bishop brought Harris up to date on events he might have missed during his slavery. The political news was that Queen Elizabeth had died and James was now king. The economic news was that, in his great wisdom, and for reasons that it was not for subjects to know or enquire, the new king had made peace with Spain and revoked all permits for his subjects to raid Spanish and Portuguese shipping. The old privateering game is up, said Bishop, and Harris might consider his future. He could go back to Bristol and be welcomed home by relatives and old friends, and try to find employment in a shrunken market. If Harris wanted to do that, Bishop was ready to carry him to Bristol without charge.

"But," said Bishop, "if with me and my love to thee, thou wilt fasten thy fortunes, I will call thee my brother, and in the riches I have gayned I will make thee a sharer." He was offering the risks and rewards of a pirate's career.

Harris asked time to consider, but his decision was easy. He owed his life to Bishop. In the meantime, a friend of Bishop's, a Captain Roup, came ashore to celebrate his successes, and Harris saw what great wealth lay in piracy as Bishop and Roup conducted it. Harris joined them, and Bishop gave him a ship. For a time, the three took great loot in the Mediterranean, but Bishop was not feeling well, perhaps from excessive celebration at Tunis, and returned there, for recuperation and probably more celebration. A Captain Jennings joined them, and then Harris sailed off on his own from Tunis. Bishop deducted nothing from Harris's share to compensate for the ship he had given Harris. Storms frustrated Harris's expedition, damaging rigging, killing some of the crew, and making many seasick. He made for Ireland and found refuge in Baltimore Bay on the coast of County Cork.

Baltimore Bay, dotted with islets and surrounded by wild and sparsely populated hills and heath, made a good hiding place for pirates. Piracy made Baltimore a little boom town. Semiautonomous lords ruled the coast. The natives, known at the time as kerns, sold pirates supplies, food, and water. Exotic booty was traded in this bucolic area: wines, jewels, ivory tusks.[5] The balance between confidence and betrayal was a fragile one. A pirate who left the lawless sea for the lawless heath left his own element for the element of the kerns. Still, Harris completed his business, repairing the ship and taking on supplies and some fresh crew members.

He returned to the Mediterranean coast of Spain, and captured a French ship, the *Margaret*, carrying sugar from Lisbon to Southern France. Stowed below the sugar lay 8,000 French crowns. After taking some of the sugar and all of the crowns, Harris let the *Margaret* proceed to France. Next he stopped a Dutch ship larger than his own and made the Dutch trade ships. With this, after a brief fight, he boarded the *Mary*, a French wine ship out of St. Malo. While Harris was on the deck of the *Mary*, his lieutenant Jerome Lockey went below and beat the wine merchant with cables until he revealed a well-hidden 800 silver dollars. When Lockey dutifully delivered them to him, he scolded Lockey for his cruelty; but he took the money just the same.

Harris now had a cargo to sell, and his ship needed repairs. It was time, he felt, to go back to Baltimore Bay. This decision struck his officers and crew as stupid. The Dutch and French captains were both bound for England and would by now have reported Harris's name and description to the admiralty. By now it would also be known that he had been using Baltimore Bay. Harris however insisted, and back to Baltimore Bay they sailed.

In London, the privy council examined the French and Dutch reports and sent a king's ship to Ireland under Sir William Saint John. His mission was not to chase Harris, but to clear pirates out of the coast of Cork and deny them a base. Sir William placed observers on the mountains over Baltimore Bay, with instructions to signal him if they saw any ship coming in. He hid his ship behind one of the islets, and was able to suprise and corner Harris. Harris and his crew had just time, as they gloomily watched Sir William approach in his longboat, to agree on a story.

Their story was that Harris was bound to obey his rescuer Captain Bishop, and that in everything he had done he was only following Bishop's orders. In fact, the tale went, Bishop had been in Baltimore Bay with them before their last departure. Luckily, a storm had allowed them to escape from Bishop's control, and of course the very first thing Harris and his crew did was to rush back to Baltimore, like the dutiful subjects they were, to yield themselves to the king's mercy. Sir William politely told Harris that if this were true he would be his friend, but to have the truth sifted he must send him and his crew as prisoners to Dublin.

From Dublin they were taken to Bristol, a touching homecoming for Harris. His sympathetic friends gave him enough money to live as a gentleman prisoner. When admiralty officials in Bristol examined him, his story fell apart. He was sent in December, 1609, to Newgate, handed along the way from sheriff to sheriff, but accompanied for comfort and support by his loyal brother. From Newgate he was carted to the Marshalsea prison, where he found a familiar prisoner, Captain Jennings of Barbary Coast days. Jennings was throwing snowballs in the prison yard, and when he had finished with this pastime he greeted his old acquaintance. That eccentric captain brought Jennings up to date from their farewell at Tunis.

Captain Jennings

Captain Harris, being educated, wrote his own narrative. Captain Jennings could not read or write, and his tale was taken from his dictation.

From early childhood, the martial life and the manly resolution of seafarers had totally engaged him. He went young to sea, never "disanimated" by stories of danger, and never fearing any tempest. He developed a valuable specialty. It was generally allowed that nobody could repair an underwater leak as fast as Jennings. As an ordinary seaman he loved to see how everybody obeyed the captain—not that he liked being obedient, but he was determined to be one of those captains. Having no money to become a legitimate captain, he scraped together a reckless crew who enjoyed riot as much as he did, and somehow got a ship. Using Dunkirk as a shelter, he robbed Spanish and Dutch coastal traffic. He was proclaimed a pirate, and the English authorities captured him. In London awaiting trial, the buoyant adventurer expected nothing but a speedy execution.

He had not reckoned on his loving and enterprising sister. She visited the various merchants who had suffered from her brother's piracies, telling them one by one that her brother was a reformed man. They were particularly persuaded of his moral stature by her argument "that not a man in Christendom could stop a leake under water better." They petitioned Queen Elizabeth, who pardoned him. Because he suddenly showed himself eager to fight for England, some of his English victims bought him a flyboat to command, and in this flat-bottom coastal vessel they sent him forth to join the navy.

Jennings set out with good intentions, but he had no patience, and chafed at being under orders. He also found that he was not making much money this way. With his like-minded crew, he sailed southward on his own in his awkward craft, seizing a Spanish caravel and taking his prize to Tunis for disposal. He had an unpleasant surprise there. Some of the English adventurers had just cheated the governor, who in his pique threw several Englishmen and now Jennings into prison; but when the governor examined the loot and saw how productive Jennings could be, he freed him. Jennings wintered in Tunis, and this is when he met Captains Bishop, Roup, and Harris. By spring they were ready to campaign together, having in their cups made Bishop their admiral, Roup vice admiral, and Jennings rear admiral. Their forays brought them great loot, which they were careful to sell only to the governor of Tunis.

Back in Tunis, the three disagreed on the distribution of profits, the often generous Admiral Bishop claiming half, and the other two claiming thirds. Whatever came of this dispute, Roup and Jennings set sail, leaving Bishop in Tunis. Seven days out, Roup's ship suddenly sprang a great leak, and Roup barely had time to transfer with his crew to Jennings's ship before his own sank. For Roup it was perhaps humiliating to be the guest of Christendom's greatest underwater leak expert. In this crowded condition they made for the treacherous Scilly Islands off Land's End and took merchandise off a ship called the *John Evangelist*. They turned toward Baltimore, seizing a cargo of brass from a French ship on the way.

Jennings describes how pirates conducted business with their victims and with the Irish. When a pirate captain boarded a merchant ship, he got the bill of lading from its master. With this information, he seized the portion belonging to the merchant, as far as it was identifiable, leaving the ship and their portion to the captain and crew. His reasons will appear later. In Baltimore Bay, the pirates' purser went ashore in a longboat to show the Irish the bills of lading and negotiate trades with them. The kerns bartered pigs and other essentials for various sorts of loot. While Captain Jennings was ashore, he took a fancy to a local woman. When he was ready to sail, he prevailed upon her to keep him company at sea. A certain amount of gold helped the woman decide on this radical change in her life.

Offsetting the natural advantages of the bay was its notoriety as a resort of pirates. Jennings having been again proclaimed a pirate, a king's ship was sent to capture him as he left. When they met, Jennings saw that he would lose a battle, so with his speedier ship he escaped into the ocean. This experience undermined the morale of the crew. Ashamed of having retreated, the captains agreed that henceforth they would attack any ship they found, even with uncertain odds.

Off Spain they found two large Spanish ships sailing together and drew within gunshot of the first. Without warning, they opened fire on the Spaniard, who instantly understood the message and put up a strong resistance. Jennings was slightly wounded, close to a dozen of his crew were killed, and a score seriously wounded. His ship was damaged. The pirates turned and fled unpursued.

Now the crew had leisure to treat their wounds, make emergency repairs on the ship, and discuss their last two fruitless and damaging encounters. The sailors knew that these were God's judgment on them for ever "suffering their Captaine to bring his whore aboard." The captain, instead of planning profitable attacks, spent his time wallowing in lust in his cabin. As the crew imagined the details of this lust, they inconsistently, but naturally, began to ask, Why can't we have whores too, like the captain? Captain Roup, normally more gruff and impersonal than Captain Jennings, turned out to be surprisingly sympathetic. Quietly planting thoughts in the sailors' heads, he reflected "that successe in their condition was never found, when a woman was more Maister of the Captaine, than the Captaine of his men." Just wait until the loot is divided, she will get the cream despite all the sweat and blood you have expended getting it. Roup's old crew members were already loyal to him, and now Jennings's own men were angry.

A mutiny broke out. Roaring sailors broke in Jennings' cabin door to find him toying with his Sheila on his lap. Jennings did not take kindly to this insolence in front of his mistress. He knocked one man out with a truncheon and chased the rest from his cabin, calling to Roup for help. No help came, of course, and Jennings ran to the gun room, slamming the door just as somebody fired a musket through it. The shot missed Jennings, but he was in a rage and quite ready to fight to the death. Roup slowly calmed him, and arranged a compact which recognized the realities of the situation. Jennings was to be captain no more, and confined in the gun room without his wench. Roup was to be his keeper, and captain of the ship.

In time, Jennings persuaded Roup to allow him the freedom of the ship. The deposed captain began to have friendly chats with leaders among his old crew. With Roup's accession had come subtle changes in what we would call the corporate culture. Roup lacked Jennings's interpersonal skills. He was also showing favoritism toward his own crew members, while those who had enjoyed influence under Jennings observed their own decline with silent resentment.

Roup had been heading steadily southward, until the ship reached the southern cape of Africa. A French pink, with its narrow stern, hove into sight, bringing home riches from the Indies. Roup attacked. The French resisted, and a grappling and boarding followed. Here the clash in corporate cultures became plain. Roup and his men were hot to show themselves more mettlesome than Jennings's men. In the heat of the fray they did not pause to wonder why Jennings was cheering them on from the deck of their own ship. Roup's men took the French ship and immediately busied themselves with ransacking it. While they were away enjoying themselves on the pink, Jennings talked to his old crew. He reminded them how fair he had always been, and built on their growing fears that they would not get a fair deal from Roup. They made him captain again. Jennings sent a message to Roup: I am captain now, and you had better keep the French ship, because I'm not going to let you on board mine. Roup quickly grasped this stark reality. The captains agreed on sharing the loot. Everybody became friends again, and the two ships turned north for Ireland.

VI. Robbery at Sea

Jennings's experiences set him on a new train of thought. Piracy seemed to have grown riskier lately. Worse, his own crew had been inconstant, to say the least. Here was love betrayed. The expansive captain could not trust anyone again. At the same time, his feat in lifting himself from close prisoner to captain again had given him high confidence in his own powers of persuasion. By the time the grey hills of Cork broke the horizon, Jennings had decided to get out of the game.

Baltimore Bay and all about lay within the partly feudal, partly tribal, rule of the Catholic but powerful Richard de Burgh, Earl of Clanricard. Jennings had bargained with powerful men before. If he could buy the protection of the sultan's representative, surely he could buy the earl's help in getting him a royal pardon. Once in the bay, he meant to approach the earl. It is not clear whether his crew guessed his intentions, but for some reason they would not let their captain leave his ship. Instead they sent the longboat ashore with four sailors, including a Frenchman who was the ship's trumpeter. The crew who did not trust their captain found in a few days that they could not trust their four mates. They absconded and went their separate ways. The French trumpeter trusted a kern and hired him as a guide: a mistake, for the guide cut his throat. Clanricarde's men arrested the other three and sent them off to Dublin Castle.

Sensing something amiss, Jennings and Roup took their ships around the Irish coast to Limerick, out of Clanricarde territory. The magnate to deal with here was Donough O'Brien, Earl of Thomond. Jennings knew little of him and approached him gingerly. He and Roup left their ships anchored far down the Shannon from the earl's great castle, poised for a quick getaway, and Jennings, no longer hindered by his sailors, took the longboat to a safe distance from the shore. He called for a parley, and a mistrustful dance began. From the castle the earl sent one of his sons and several attendants to learn what Jennings had to say. Jennings wanted a private conference with the earl, and would be happy to meet him in the castle. Of course, he explained, that would put him wholly at the earl's mercy, so during the conference he would like the earl to give two hostages. Of course, agreed the earl, and he sent two of his kinsmen. Jennings spent that night in Limerick castle, and in the morning he had his conference with O'Brien himself.

Jennings told his life story, and offered to put his ship, his crew, and all his property under Lord Thomond's protection if he would mediate for the king's mercy and get him a pardon. The earl weighed the situation. He granted Jennings and the two crews his protection for two weeks, and promised to do everything consistent with honor to procure the pardon. Our anonymous author tactfully explains that the earl made this deal because he had two kinsmen aboard the pirate ships, which were too far down the river to catch. This is nonsense, for the earl had willingly provided these hostages. The true explanation, which the author would not have dared to utter, is that the earl would get a lot of money from the captain for arranging his pardon.

Jennings's reaction to this fragile deal was to celebrate. He made great revel, entertaining one of the earl's sons and several neighboring lords not only in Limerick town but aboard his ship. In euphoria, he told Roup and the crews of both ships about the prospects for a pardon. They were skeptical, and Roup saw to it that no more than three of his men were in town at any one time to fetch necessities. Above all, he insisted, the hostages must be kept on board.

But poor Roup simply did not understand good fellowship. Jennings liked to drink with his two hostages, and one day when he had drunk more than usual he announced that for a really jolly time they all three ought to adjourn to Limerick. His officers advised against it, but he would not listen and the longboat took the trio into town.

When Roup learned of this, he sent his longboat to Jennings's ship and "borrowed" most of its gunpowder and shot, unloading it through one of the gun ports in the night. Then he weighed anchor and stole off. The master of Jennings's ship awoke to find neither Roup's pink, nor Jennings, nor the hostages. Fearing some treachery, the master set sail without Captain Jennings. From the castle, the earl saw that both ships were gone. He had his hostages back, and Jennings was in town, probably hung over. By coincidence, the two weeks' promised protection had just expired. The earl tightened the leash, so gradually that we cannot know just when Jennings realized he was a prisoner. He was given comfortable lodging in a more secure place, true, but still he was treated with kindness and hospitality. Lord Thomond sent a letter to Sir Arthur Chichester, the lord deputy in Dublin, laying out the story. The council in Dublin gave Thomond a warrant to send Jennings to Dublin. Jennings proceeded comfortably to Dublin, the earl hospitably sending him off with £100.

Jennings spent the next three months in Dublin. Business brought Lords Clanricard and Thomond there, too. Their influence enabled Jennings to hunt and hawk in a ten-mile radius, with no attendant but one of Clanricard's musicians, subject only to the requirement that he return to his lodging in Dublin Castle each night. In the meantime, the authorities were learning more and more of Jennings's past. Unkown to him, his fate was sealed. The earls would normally have succeeded in getting the captain his pardon, "had not his former life been so contemptible." They chose an oddly oblique way to get him to England for trial. They released him from custody and entrusted him to cross the Irish Sea as a passenger, a special messenger, carrying a sealed letter from Sir Arthur to the Mayor of Chester. The letter directed the mayor to send Jennings to the Marshalsea prison in London. Sir Arthur or one of his officials may well have seen this trick played in a performance of Hamlet. In the prison, Jennings met not only old acquaintances like Harris, but the notorious William Longcastle.

Captain Longcastle

William Longcastle had been active so long as a sea rover that at the trial he was called an arch-pirate; but only one last case brought him to the Marshalsea. This last chapter began in London, where a merchant named Mr. Hal invested £1,000 in a venture to the West Indies, sending a ship of his, the *Ulisses*, with one of his employees aboard as master or factor of the voyage. Factors had great discretion to change plans and earn the venture whatever money they could. The *Ulisses* was still in sight of England when she began to develop serious troubles. She put in for repairs at Plymouth, where the factor hired three mariners experienced in long voyages, William Longcastle as captain, William Taverner, and John Moore. From Plymouth the *Ulisses* sailed to Safi, in Morocco, to take on fresh water.

At this Barbary port the *Ulisses* met another English ship, the Susan, out of Bristol under Captain Anthony Wye. The compatriots traded greetings and at Longcastle's invitation the *Susan* pulled alongside. Her captain and officers stepped aboard the *Ulisses* for a banquet. During the festivities, Captain Longcastle, with Taverner and Moore, hijacked the *Susan*, clapped the crew below, and sailed off before either Captain Wye or the factor of the *Ulisses* knew what was happening. Longcastle had acted with such speed that he left some of his own property on the *Ulisses*, including a black man he had just bought a few weeks before and already converted to Christianity. Longcastle appeared to head the *Susan* for the West Indies. The *Ulisses* returned to London, where Captain Wye lodged a complaint with the admiralty against Longcastle, Taverner, and Moore. The factor handed the black man over to Mr. Hal, the ship's owner. The factor having cleared himself of complicity, Mr. Hal sent him out on another voyage.

Longcastle, Taverner, and Moore were proclaimed pirates, and the admiralty awaited their next deed somewhere in the Atlantic.

Actually, they were hiding ashore in a Cornish bay west of Plymouth, conducting a piece of urgent business. We have seen that it was a common practice for English pirates to seize only the goods of a merchant. This was not magnanimity or social awareness; it helped reduce the number of witnesses who were willing to give evidence against the pirates. Captains and crews tended to settle because they would rather get money than hang somebody. On the other hand, pirates could afford to offend the merchant, because he was usually not at the scene of the piracy and could not be a witness against them. Longcastle was eager to settle accounts with Wye, but he could not hide long, even in Cornwall. The gossip of neighbors soon reached the local justice of the peace, who haled the trio before him. Asked to account for the past four months, their replies were not at all persuasive, so they were bundled off to the Marshalsea.

At their trial, matters seemed to take a favorable turn for the defendants when Captain Wye failed to appear to testify against them. He was all the more important as a witness because the crew of the *Ulisses* were scattered and her factor had gone off to sea again. The judges readily guessed that Longcastle had somehow paid off Wye. Without this witness, the spectators and the defendants began to see an acquittal looming. But the judges had been hiding a trump card, which they now played by producing Longcastle's black man. He was a clear and damning witness to the seizure of the *Susan*, throwing the three pirates into confusion. Longcastle argued that the word of a pagan should not be taken against a Christian, but there was ample evidence that, thanks to Longcastle himself, the black was a Christian. If Longcastle had not indulged in his missionary work, he and his two mates might have been acquitted. Longcastle and Moore took their sentences stoically, but Taverner, revealing some folk notion of the law, screamed to be brought "a book" on which to swear his innocence.

Captain Downes

Downes had started as a merchant near Colchester, Essex. Though not ostentatious, he fell into debt, and fear of debtors' prison led him into piracy. Beneath a bland demeanor, "he was more violent, cruell and merciles, than any of the rest." In midsummer, 1605, he entered the port of Fowey, Cornwall, on a Portuguese caravel he had taken in Madeira. It was laden with various goods including sugar and wine, which he sold openly in Fowey, explaining that it was all legal because he had a commission from the States of the Netherlands, a country at war with Spain and Portugal.

Subsequently he was arrested for a piracy closer to home. John Shipman and his brother Thomas, Bristol merchants, had gone to Portugal and loaded a Scottish ship, the *Royal* out of Leith, with 50 tons of salt, a hundred pounds of silver, a "pack" of calico, 200 pounds of tobacco, and 500 pounds of cordage. As the *Royal* made for Bristol, it was intercepted off St. Ives, Cornwall, and boarded by Downes and ten of his men. The pirates put the whole crew, except for a couple of boys, into one boat and abandoned them over 20 miles from shore. Overloaded as the boat was, the Shipman brothers, the Scots master Matthewson, and the crew had no chance of reaching shore as their stolen ship receded to the horizon. Then it occurred to Downes that the rascals in the boat might still be carrying money which in their haste the pirates had neglected to pilfer. Downes hastily sailed back to the boat. As the victims watched his approach, they must have felt themselves truly between the Devil and the deep blue sea. They were all taken back on board and imprisoned below.

Little money was found when they were stripped, but Downes had developed an obsession: There was money somewhere, cleverly hidden. He began torturing his victims. First the two boys were strung up and whipped. Where is the money? he demanded after every lash. The boys knew of some, but they did not reveal its location until the torture was changed, and ropes were tightened about their heads. This discovery only strengthened Downes's belief that there must be more. He bound John Shipman to the foremast and had him whipped with ropes while his brother pleaded for mercy. Then he had John hanged, cutting him down poised between life and death. Downes ransacked some sea chests, finding, among coral bracelets and other valuables, some clothing, diamonds, and tobacco, all worth 100 marks, belonging to Anthony Wye, whom we have met already as the captain of the *Susan*. Downes and the pirates finally returned to their own ship and left the victims to take the *Royal* and its cargo of salt to Bristol as best they could.

Later we find Downes leaving Plymouth on a ship bound for the Guinea coast, but transferring around the Scilly islands to a pink under a pirate Captain Tomkins. Under Tomkins they headed toward the Severn and the rich shipping lane off Bristol. An October storm, however, drove them ashore on the Welsh side at Swansea. They were a rough and riotous lot, instantly suspected to be pirates. Far worse for Downes, Thomas Shipton, a survivor of the *Royal's* ordeal, happened to be in Swansea too. He recognized Downes and enthusiastically reported him to the authorities. Tomkins, Downes, and another man were clapped into Cardiff Castle and examined. They did not give a convincing account of themselves, and suspicion was increased by the fact that Downes had on him 20 Barbary gold ducats, jewelry, and some small wedges of gold bullion. Tomkins's purse held similar evidence. You win all sorts of things at dice, they explained, but on the basis of Shipton's evidence, they were sent to London for trial. The way they were sent was to be taken by one constable to the jurisdiction of the next constable, and so on a great many transfers.

There is a parlor game in which one person whispers a sentence to the next; the entertainment comes from the garbled message that emerges from the end of the line. By the time the prisoners reached Reading, the latest constable had very little idea of what he was supposed to do, and the three escaped. Downes was recaptured in Cornwall. The Shipmans' evidence regarding the Royal was deadly, and Downes's argument that he had a Dutch commission to legalize his seizure of the Portuguese galleon collapsed because King James's proclamation prohibited his subjects from taking such commissions.

Down to Wapping (1609)

All in all, counting these and smaller fry, 20 men accumulated at the Marshalsea prison in Southwark and were tried in quick succession before a London jury in admiralty court. Captain Jennings, as was his buoyant nature, at first expected a pardon; but at the trial, the voluble illiterate labored to save not himself but his men. In his somewhat disorderly way he kept intervening for them and trying to take all the blame.

He did score one success, the only acquittal among the 20. This was a shoemaker from Cork whom Jennings had asked aboard at Baltimore to fit him with new boots. Sensing opportunity, the enterprising craftsman brought along his two apprentices and all the shoe leather he owned. As he had hoped, he found many customers among the pirates. At the end of the day he sent the boys ashore and stayed for a drink with the captain. It was impossible to do business with Captain Jennings and stay sober. The Irish cobbler passed out. So did his luck, for when he awoke the next day the ship had weighed anchor and departed. When the pirates were captured, so was he. Thanks to Jennings, the jury acquitted him alone.

On the Friday before Christmas, the 19 pirates were taken by boat down the Thames to Wapping, their departure watched by the tenants of the apartments that clung to London bridge. The riverborne procession was preceded ceremoniously by the symbol of admiralty authority, the silver oar. Wapping executions were popular spectacles, watched from ships, shore, and boats, because pirates customarily dressed in their flamboyant finest for the occasion. Today they were quiet enough, and only the bloody-minded Downes continued to the last half hour to boast of the crimes at which he had never been caught.

Wapping is a short walk downriver from the Tower of London. Seamen lived there, and merchants who sold ships' supplies. A little back from the river rose the parish church; houses and a tavern stood by the river. At its edge, the tides crept up and down Wapping Old Stairs and a grim mossy stone sea wall. Here was Execution Dock, all the more convenient for hanging pirates because of its visibility to every mariner passing in and out of London. The custom was to leave the bodies hanging until three tides had washed over them, ruining any finery that the late owners had not torn off and given away at the last moment. The spectacle of 19 in a row conveyed a message: King James hates pirates.

Captain Jennings, the first up the ladder, made a speech. At first he was rather inarticulate, but soon he found a theme to comfort his men:

> My friends, you see that we are brought to take our earthly farwell the one of the other, and I am to conduct you, the way I have heretofore lead you on in place of danger, more induring then when bullets like haile have falne about our eares, yet you fearelesly and venterously have followed me, your Captaine, who have as bravely brought you of[f] as I have bouldly brought you on: do not be dismaid now to do the like, for where heertofore I have driven you through the footsteps of transgression on earth, I now wish you all be resolv'd as I goe before you the highway to my salvation in heaven, where we shall meete amongst the fellowship of Angels....

An optimist to the end, was Jennings.

When his turn came, Captain Harris mounted the ladder with pious dignity, but in his crew were two brothers, John and Thomas Spencer. After the elder was turned off, the younger did not go gentle as he hung beside him. Apparently furious with his big brother for bringing him to this pass, the younger brother kept beating on the other until he too lost consciousness.

Captain Jennings forgot to tell us what happened to his Irish mistress. We may wonder too what became of the black man that Longcastle bought in Morocco. What did Mr. Hal do with him? It is unrewarding to ask whether he was "free" or not because the system of indentures created a shading from bond to free, rather than a clear dichotomy. In 1772, the lord chief justice would decide that a black slave named Somerset, brought over by his master from the West Indies, became free the moment he stepped on British soil; but that clarification lay far in the future. Even though there were some blacks in London, Longcastle's convert would have been a curiosity to strangers. In six more years, Pocahontas just might have stared at him, as he would surely have stared at her.

VII
Fraud and Blackmail

Fraud attracted much attention in the form of cony-catching, or cheating oafs. There is considerable literature on card cheating and crooked dice, and on the timeless theme of innocent country folk being gulled in the big city. These however were not the only frauds.

Chancery (1616)

Judges held court in the morning, and at noon they went to their respective inns of court, which were the law schools of the day. A long dinner began the daily process by which senior lawyers, including the highest judges in the land, taught students the law. As usual at noon, Sir John Tyndal, a master in chancery, stepped down from his coach at Lincoln's Inn. An elderly man of Tyndal's own age stopped him and asked if he might not arrange a compromise in his case. Sir John recognized John Bartram: another tiresome litigant who had just lost.

"What, a Compremise now?" he asked, and turned to go into dinner. In a moment he was dead, shot in the back by Bartram with a pistol loaded with two balls.

The intricacies of his wife's inheritance ranked high among the remaining pastimes of John Bartram, who was over 75 in 1616, an advanced age for the year in which Shakespeare died at barely 52. During the inevitable litigation, a chancery clerk had mistakenly recorded £200 as an unpaid debt to Bartram. This false windfall so unhinged Bartram that he fought hard to collect it, and even had his wife's brother arrested for debt. Sir John found against Bartram. Fully aware that he had never had a case, Bartram shot him, and then stabbed himself.

In prison, Bartram's wound was treated. His prosecutor was the philosopher Sir Francis Bacon, but King James himself briefly intervened, as he tended to do when anything roused his roving curiosity. Roving, but not aimless: The king thought it just possible that so strange a murder by so old a man might be the tip of some corruption, but he was satisfied when Bartram swore that he had never bribed Tyndal.

Bartram sent his jailer out to fetch a biblical concordance, and the jailer quickly returned with one. Wrong translation, said Bartram, get me another, and some ale and a toast as well. This longer errand gave Bartram time to hang himself from a hook in the wall, and avoid the disgrace of a public execution. To the narrator, this was mere vanity: "hee that had no sence of preserving his life and soule, yet had an apprehension and care of his senceless Carcase."[1]

Worldly Possessions (1599)

A Nottingham musician named William Somers said he should have given the old woman what she asked for when the two of them found a hat lying in the road outside Bramsgrove market. He gave her the hat, but kept the copper band, because he thought it was gold. She wanted it for the same reason, but all she could do was threaten, saying it would have been better for him if he had given her the band. Her meaning began to appear that very night, when a strange light in his bedchamber put him in an inexplicable terror.

In time, Somers developed spectacular symptoms, including

> such strange and idle kinde of gesture, in laughing, dauncing, and such like light behaviour, that he was suspected to be mad.... His behaviour generally towards all that came was most impudent also and shamelesse, with much uncleannesse. His speeches were usually vaine, delivered in very scoffing manner, and many time filthy and uncleane, very unfit to be named, or blasphemous, swearing most fearfully, using one bloody oath after another: sometimes saying, I am God, and sometimes, There is no GOD.

This was plainly a case for the reverend John Darrel, famed exorcist. In 1596 he had driven a devil out of Thomas Darling of Burton, a boy of 14, incidentally getting Alice Goodrich convicted of bewitching him. The next year he won further fame by exorcising seven members of Nicholas

Starkie's household in Lancashire. These feats nearly eclipsed his first achievement, the newsworthy expulsion of nine demons from young Katherine Wright.

Darrel, after some hesitation, came the 14 miles from his home, to be told on arrival that Somers was black in the face, cold as ice, and not breathing. By the time he saw him, Somers had revived, but was having one of his fits. That evening, the boy gave a lively one-hour charade of several evils: brawling, swearing, highway robbery, cutting purses, whoredom, dicing, card playing, dancing. He even performed difficult charades such as "sluggishnesse in hearing the Word," and "pride both in men and women," such as to challenge the best parlor expert.

The next day, Sunday, Darrel began praying in earnest, in preparation for the climax planned for the following day. He asked other ministers to join him, to imply modestly that he had no special gift greater than his brethren. Somers swallowed his tongue that day, and could say only something that sounded like "Corne, corne." Monday was an exhausting climax. Somers foamed profusely like a horse, roared like a bear, squealed like a pig. The spectators had fallen into silent wonder as five men tried to hold him down on his back in bed. Somers flew into the air, landing face down with his feet at the head of the bed. For a time he lay as if dead, but the demon had departed.

"Thus," concludes the exorcist in triumph, "we have heard not only how it went with Somers in the time of his possession ..., but also how and by what meanes I came unto him, and being there, carried my selfe in the present action." For this victory over the Devil, Darrel was appointed preacher at St. Mary's in Nottingham, and his sermons on his specialty drew rapt audiences.

But Darrel was under surveillance. In March, the Archbishop of York launched an enquiry, and stopped his preaching. William Somers, Mary Wright, and Mary Cooper all confessed that Darrel had coached them on faking a possession. He had built on his experience with Katherine Wright's nine demons 13 years before. Katherine's demons had been her own and not Darrel's, but he foresaw that if his fame waned he could revive it with a possession of his own invention. Somers admitted that Darrel had recruited him in an alehouse in Ashby de la Zouche, picking him out as the most musical of a group of tippling boys. Darrel tutored him in the gestures, faces, and sounds of spiritual torment.

Darrel was deprived of his ministry and imprisoned in the Archbishop of Canterbury's gatehouse at Lambeth for a year. Thereafter we hear of him only in a furious pamphlet war over his case. Darrel kept selling pamphlets about his exorcisms, and one of the investigators, Samuel Harsnett, attacked him with a pamphlet called *Discovery of the Fraudulent Practices of John Darrel*. In the polemical style of the day, Darrell responded with a pamphlet called *A Detection of That Sinful, Shamful, Lying, and Ridiculous Discourse of Samuel Harshnet*. The pamphlet war did not end until Darrel's death in 1602. By then, Thomas Darling, the demon-haunted boy of Burton, had grown up to attend Oxford, where he had his ears cut off for libelling the vice-chancellor.[2]

Freed from the Iron Gate (1608)

The commuters who walked the paths of Peckham every morning paused to gather around an unknown corpse they had just found, and to play detective. They knew the dead man had not been lying there the day before. Accident? His throat was slit. Robbery? He had a knife in his hand, gold rings on his fingers, and 40 shillings in his pockets. Suicide then? No. Judging from his condition, especially the maggots in the throat wound, the man had been dead more than one day. He hadn't been here yesterday, so he must have been moved. Rummaging in the man's pockets, they found papers that identified him as Anthony Ferneseede, a London tailor with a shop in Addle Hill and a house in Duck Lane.

Some of the citizens of Peckham hurried the four miles to Duck Lane, where they found Anthony's wife Margaret. She turned out to be an odd character, a physical wreck, impatient, emotionally flat. Before any of the Peckham delegation could say anything, she broke in with a comment. Some said she asked if Anthony's throat had been slit. Others thought she told them he had slit his own throat. Her ravaged face and harsh voice conveyed no emotion as she and her servant boy set out for Peckham to identify the body. Twice on the way she met friends of her husband. Having already heard the news by the grapevine, they offered their condolences. Her coolness offended one of them.

"For mine owne part, had such a mischance falne to my fortune, I should ere this have wept out mine eyes with true sorrow."

"Tut, sir, mine eyes are ill alreadye and I must now preserve them to mend my cloathes not to mourne for a husband," was all she had to say to that. When Margaret and the boy viewed the body in the presence of a magistrate, she put on some show of sorrow but produced no tears. The suspicious magistrate took her servant boy aside for separate examination and learned much more.

Today the Tower of London is bounded on three sides by a deep grassy ditch wide enough for garrison sports. In 1608 this was water, the moat of the castle. On the far side to the east stood a few tenements, overlooking the moat as the tides sluggishly fetched seaward the sewage of garrison and prisoners. At ebbtide, the bloated cats and other debris would float downstream past the moored wherries, some returning hesitantly upstream with the next tide for a last visit. Near what was then the Iron Gate of the Tower, only a few yards from the riverbank, the row of houses ended with one owned and operated by Mrs. Ferneseede.

Margaret, promiscuous since "knowledge" (Elizabethan for puberty), had become a prostitute early on. After years of not caring "into what bed of lust her lascivious bodie was transported," she saw that disease, ugliness, and age were breeding "a loath in her ordinarie customers." It was time for prudent diversification, so she set up as a bawd. Her house by the Iron Gate had room for about ten women and their clients at a time. Some girls were supplied from wagon drivers bringing them into London from the country, but Margaret also had a system for recruiting and retaining London wives. She persuaded them deftly: Is your husband stingy? It is easy to make money while he's at work, and nobody will ever know. Margaret charged them ten shillings a week, for finding customers and for the use of the house. These arrangements would soon cease to be voluntary. As Margaret boasted, once the wives discovered she might expose them, they had to come to her house whenever she summoned. For any of them, a knock at the door and a look from a familiar messenger boy meant that she had to meet another client at the Iron Gate. This regime made them reliable employees. Margaret also received stolen goods there, but in retrospect she concluded that that operation had never been profitable.

She had probably married Anthony not long before the murder. Her motive for the marriage was the same as her motive for the murder. Some witnesses testified that she had tried unsuccessfully to poison Anthony with a powder she dumped in his broth, though he had never noticed the attempt. Her boy testified that she had a young lover who left London at the time of the murder, and that she was planning to follow him. She had started selling some of her husband's goods even before the arrival of the visitors from Peckham. She could run off with the youth if she pillaged enough to compensate for leaving her business.

The testimony of two barge men offers a curious vignette of life at the

Iron Gate. They were clients at the house one evening, and shared a room next to Margaret's own bedroom. That evening may have been the unique occasion when Anthony stayed with his wife at her house. Through the thin wall, the men heard him lecturing Margaret on her wicked life. Margaret loudly told him to mind his own business, and stamped out of the bedroom. A little later, Anthony heard one of the barge men cough, and investigated. He was scandalized to find them in what he called his house, though it is not clear why, after lecturing Margaret on her wickedness, he would be surprised by this evidence of it. He preached to them about the physical and spiritual perils of frequenting such places. He complained that he could do nothing to correct the use of the house because of that "devilish woman" his wife. Though this was not the entertainment they had envisaged, the men left cheerfully enough (or so they testified). When they later asked Margaret about this strange encounter, she said, "Hang him slave and villaine: I will before God bee revenged of him (nay ere long) by one means or other, so worke, that I will bee rid of him."

On a Saturday Margaret was sentenced to be burnt for petty treason the following Monday, 22 February, 1608. High treason was committed by a subject against the king, petty treason by a servant against a master or by a woman against her husband. The punishment of women, burning, differed from that of men. Among the mutilations constituting the public punishment of a male traitor was one that for anatomical reasons could not be carried out on a female, but a lawyer of the 18th century has provided another explanation for the distinction:

"For the public exhibition of their bodies, and dismembering them, in the same manner as is practised to the men, would be a violation of that natural decency and delicacy inherent, and at all times to be cherished in the sex."[3]

In the White Lion prison in Southwark, she was as crusty as ever, until three young gentlemen visited her cell. Robert Throgmorton, William Porter, and John Bishop were scions of prosperous stock who had found it stimulating to rob merchants on the approaches to London. Bishop, the swaggerer of the three, had stabbed a merchant to death during one of these robberies. Now they were waiting to be hanged on Friday. They were feeling guilty, and they coaxed her into joining in their prayers. To these young men, and to no one else, she told the story of her life. She never confessed to her husband's murder, which of course she may well not have committed with her own hands. The rest was silence, even on that Monday when two women dressed her in a girdle of canvas saturated with pitch, under a white sheet, and, with the sheriff of Surrey, led her to a stake in St. George's Fields near where her husband's corpse had been found. She had said all she would say; the rushes were piled high about her and lit, and she died (we are told) "presently," which then meant "immediately."

This story has its loose ends. We do not know whether her lover was apprehended. We may guess that it was caution that kept him from appropriating his victim's rings, but why did he leave the 40 shillings in cash? Where was the murder committed, and how and why was the body taken to Peckham? Yet the loosest end of all must surely be, Why did the moralistic tailor wed the poxy bawd? The barge men show Anthony could be a bit quixotic.

Anthony was obviously not the only naive man in town. Many a husband probably never found out about his wife's alternative career at the Iron Gate. None of them would have noticed that look of liberation and relief on his wife's face as she watched over the Thames for Margaret's smoke to rise against the winter sky.[4]

Proud Rascal (1623)

Griffin Flood's biographer concluded, "Never was there (I thinke) the like audacious and shameless fellow living in this Citie, nor any with a more impudent carriage before his betters." That would have delighted Flood. As a boy apprenticed to a leather-dresser, all he had was a gift for plausibility, which he used to get the other shop boys in trouble. When he outgrew his apprenticeship, he eked out a living by shaking down boys he caught in forbidden places, such as alehouses, bowling greens, playhouses, or, on Sunday, anywhere in the puritanical City other than home or church. He extorted a penny here, a penny there.

As apprentices did not have many pennies, Flood graduated to better extortions. The City aldermen prohibited outside competition. The oath of every freeman of London included a promise to hire only the sons of freemen as apprentices. All others were barred from practicing their trades. Informers reporting violations were given a set reward. Though violators were fined and banished from London, illegal workers lurked up and down the miles of dark and winding alleys.

Tapsters, vintners, and innkeepers were especially beset with regulations. Carrying a supply of petty rules in his head, Flood found them out and shook them down. A quart had to be an exact quart. Drunks could be fined five shillings (or six hours in the pillory), and the bartenders who served them 20 shillings. There were times (such as the Sabbath) when people were not to tipple in public. There were places (such as the publican's living quarters) where customers were not to be allowed. There were standards for the quality, strength, and price of beer and ale. Compliance was fitful. Some were too drunk to know they were being cheated. Poor children sent with pails by their parents could not argue about quantity or quality. There were said to be three or four thousand bars in and around London, making enforcement of any kind random. The city clerks got fees for registering tippling houses, and fees for annually testing the ale, but no fees for closing a place. Informers reporting alehouses for violations did not get the usual share of fines, because most alehouse fines went to the parish poor. An informer had to swear before a magistrate, and this required the informer to pay a fee, as well as make himself unpopular, all for little reward. Even so, anybody willing to go to the trouble could make things costly for a publican. This was Flood's leverage, though he assured his victims, "I am an enemy to all such knaves whose purpose is to wrong such honest meaning men as you are."

He was universally belligerent. To anyone attracting his attention he would eventually manage to cause mischief, such as getting a builder fined for an improper mixture of lime and hair in his plaster. London must have had other blackmailers, but Flood earned extra enmity. When a flax maid hanged herself in her own girdle, neighbors immediately blamed Flood, who had driven her out of her job. Once he went to prison for debt, but such was his reign of terror that an illegal Dutch candle maker helped pay his release, which Flood celebrated by prosecuting the Dutchman.

Where so many lived by their wits, some could turn the tables on Flood. On one of his officious raids on an alewife he had persecuted before, he discovered a foreign tailor working for her to pay off a lodging bill. During this discussion, she went into the cellar to fill a tankard of ale. Detecting a non-regulation tankard, he followed her into the cellar to charge her with that too. She bloodied his head with a pewter mug, and cried Rape! Flood went to jail to await trial, where he was visited and shaken down by the alewife.

Eventually Flood got a regular job, keeping people off the grass in Moor Fields, where people liked to spread their laundry to dry, practice their archery, and stroll about in the flats by the City wall. Flood happily patrolled his walks with a heavy club, put people in the stocks for walking on the grass, and fixed hooks on the railings to rip their clothing.

Then in one of his obscure quarrels he stabbed a vintner and a constable. The vintner died, and Flood went to Newgate, where of course he set the prisoners fighting. By day he was loud and blasphemous, and by night his bad dreams kept everybody up. On the other hand, his bartender victims visited him for the sport of drinking in front of him.

When Flood was arraigned for his homicide, he refused to plead, a characteristically pretentious choice, because he had no property. To the set question, "How will you be tried?" the formal response was, "By God and my country," country meaning a jury of the defendant's peers. Flood believed he had neither peers nor God. Sometime during 18 January, 1623, he suffocated in the pressing yard. He had composed his own obituary:

Here lyeth Griffin Flood full low in his grave,
Which lived a Rascall and died a Knave.[5]

VIII

From Sex to Disaster

Tight censorship inhibited descriptions of sex in the English language, but they were more overt than we readily perceive as we cope with 11 or 12 generations of linguistic change. Playwrights, especially Shakespeare, romped with sexual allusions at plural depths of meaning.[1] Other writers, however, made their sex lurk in a world of metaphor, where hills, sweet meadows, and bogs spread for swains to graze, or fortifications ambivalently awaited breaching. The authorities faced the classic frustration of moral censors: the ease with which any term can be conscripted into the service of the dirty mind. Less literary accounts seem more candid. An unlucky lad has left us some hint of his lustful desires, even though it has been strained through a Puritan sieve.

The Wish List of Youth (1643)

A cavalier of 21, Thomas Browne has told us what lust meant to him. He also loved good food and drink. Worse yet, he had a damnable weakness for music, just when the godly people were ripping the pipe organs out of churches. A Puritan has told us the trouble with Browne:

> The often enjoying of women ... he esteemed to be the top branch of this tree of pleasure, so that he was amorous wanton, luxious, gluttonous, and in all things a meere Epicure in pursuing sensual delights, soft and effeminate in all his waies, and a man wholly sold unto sin, and sought onely to compasse his voluptuous satisfaction, thinking all the women in the Turkes Seraylio were not enough to satisfie his greedy appetite, and was indeed a slave unto the Divell and his owne lusts.

To us this womanizer does not seem effeminate, much less soft.

The civil war disrupted Thomas's income, and a local truce barred him from a chance at the spoils of war, so he lacked money to sustain his lifestyle. As money dwindled, so did the supply of women. His demand grew in inverse proportion, until he could think of nothing else. Far into the night he would stamp about in lonely places, with his hat pulled down and his eyes fixed on the ground. His favorite place was the marshes of Redriff (that is, the later docklands of Rotherhithe), ignored by the busy butchers who found it convenient to slaughter and gut their beasts there, where nobody minded the environmental impact.

In the eerie thick fogs of this wild and lonely fen, so uncannily near to London, Thomas gradually became aware of a companion. He never got a good view of him, but the voice was clear. It was the Devil. Gradually on their walks the two worked out a deal. Thomas would have an assured 40 years of life, with an income of £2,000 a year plus £40 each holiday. If he ever married, he would get a dowry proportional to his income. Any woman he wanted, whether widow, wife, or maid, would reciprocate and "answer his desires in carnall copulation." The richest clothing and the daintiest foods would be his, and the choicest music. Finally, Thomas was to stay young for the whole 40 years. In return, of course, Thomas would sign over his soul to the Devil.

Thomas went home shaking and awed, but he spread out a clean parchment, and neatly wrote out the contract. He signed it with his blood. Early next morning, he headed back to Redriff with his contract in his pocket. He was so early that the roundhead night watch was still on duty. These were tense times. What the watch saw was a jittery young cavalier type who could not explain to them why he would be going, before others were astir, into the soggy shambles of Redriff. They searched him, and found the contract.

He was sent to Newgate to await trial. We do not know the outcome, or even the charge, only his timeless wants.[2]

The Mad Squire (1605)

Just as the aging Mr. and Mrs. Fitz were despairing of progeny, John was born to them, a welcome miracle. In time, John stepped into an enviable estate near Winstock, Devonshire. His father had wedded John to a lady from the influential Courtney family, which had held Devonshire for the Lancastrians in the Wars of the Roses a century and a half earlier. A broad and green plateau stretched before him in 1602, from which Fitz descended precipitously, out of lust and hubris. Mere whoring was his first step. The male who wrote his story applauded the wife for her patience. Lust had not finished with John Fitz, but it was hubris that was to get him into greater trouble.

Fitz and his neighbor Slanning both attended a friendly dinner one noon. As the tippling stretched on, Fitz expansively brought up a peculiarity in the tenure of his lands, which he said were all held directly from the queen. Fitz's boast hinted at both antiquity and nearness to the crown, without quite establishing either. Tact might have suggested letting the matter pass, but friend Slanning chose to puncture his balloon with the reminder that there was, in fact, a parcel of Fitz's land held of the Slannings rather than the queen. A public slight! Fitz drew his sword at the dinner table. Slanning grabbed a knife, but the host separated them and arranged an uneasy peace. Slanning, not sensing what fury he had stirred, gave his horse to a servant and started to walk the rest of the way alone. Fitz and three of his servants rode after him, and while one servant pinned his arms another ran him through and left him dead in a field.

Fitz fled to France, leaving his mother and wife in a quandary. After nearly a year, the wife was able, through her family, to obtain a pardon conditional on Fitz's leading a lawful life. Fitz returned from France, appearing sober and chastened. Slanning's son was still a minor and in no position to avenge his father's death. Before long Fitz went back to his old ways. His whoring grew more notorious, and he was heard to brag about having killed Slanning. As his reputation in Devonshire plummeted, he incongruously became Sir John Fitz. King James, having succeeded the frugal Queen Elizabeth in 1603, sought to pay for his generosities with revenue enhancements of various sorts, including knights' fees. He did not so much sell knighthoods as impose them on more or less unwilling gentry of appropriate means, so they had to pay the resulting fees. To hedge his venture, the king also levied a lesser but substantial fine on subjects who declined the knighthood. His majesty's net landed Fitz among many fish of like size. The honor did not inhibit Sir John.

His quest for more and lower company turned up a new henchman, known only as Lusty Jack. Lusty Jack and other rascals did as they wished in the neighborhood and always found asylum in Sir John's house. So did several whores in permanent residence with Sir John. Although Lady Fitz bore these affronts with the dignity society expected of ladies, her husband finally expelled her from their home, and made her live on the charity of her family.

Sir John took this provocative step about the time that Slanning's son reached his majority. With his estate, young Slanning inherited a vague traditional duty to avenge his father. He prudently chose to begin proceedings to revoke Sir John's conditional pardon, in light of his openly scandalous behavior. It was all utterly predictable that young Slanning would grow up, seek revenge, and go for Fitz's weak point, but the tidings shook Fitz profoundly, as if he now saw, for the first time, how "by his inordinate disorders he had impaired his estate, sever'd himselfe from his wife, wedded himself to wilfull obstinacie, abused his neighbours, furthered his freends, consorted himself with villaines, and caused himself to be so odious, as his life was now in new danger...."

In a kind of psychological fugue he set out for London, with a muddled hope of mending his fences with the mighty, and somehow deflecting the mortal threat posed by any reconsideration of his all too conditional pardon. On his journey, in the company of one servant, his fears grew spontaneously: Maybe his father in law, after so much humiliation and abuse of Lady Fitz, would give him no support in London, or even be a foe. Fitz reached a Kingston inn with "a dispersed and molested mind." In the dead of night he awoke the innkeeper, raving that Sir William Courtney was after him. The landlord gave Fitz a bed, but he jumped up and had his gelding saddled again. On the way out of Kingston, Sir John and his footman encountered the night watch, who had trouble persuading him that they were not Sir William's men. The two strayed on into the night. Coming upon a large house, Fitz aroused the inhabitants and asked to spend the rest of the night there, but they would not open their gates to him. More miserable riding in the dead of night took them to Twickenham. There he found a house displaying a sign of an Anchor. Thinking it might be an inn, he had his footman hammer at the door; in his rising panic, he even hammered at it with his own hands.

The owner, Daniel Alley, explained that it was only a food shop, and quite inadequate for a gentleman. Fitz swore that the worst bed in the house would suit him, and out of pity Alley took them in, put up the gelding, roused his wife, maid, and children out of their single bedroom, and changed the sheets on its only bed. Fitz sent his footman on to find the best road to London, make lodging arrangements for the next day, and then walk back to rejoin him in Twickenham. The footman was of course unhappy, but as there was no room for him in the house anyway he plodded

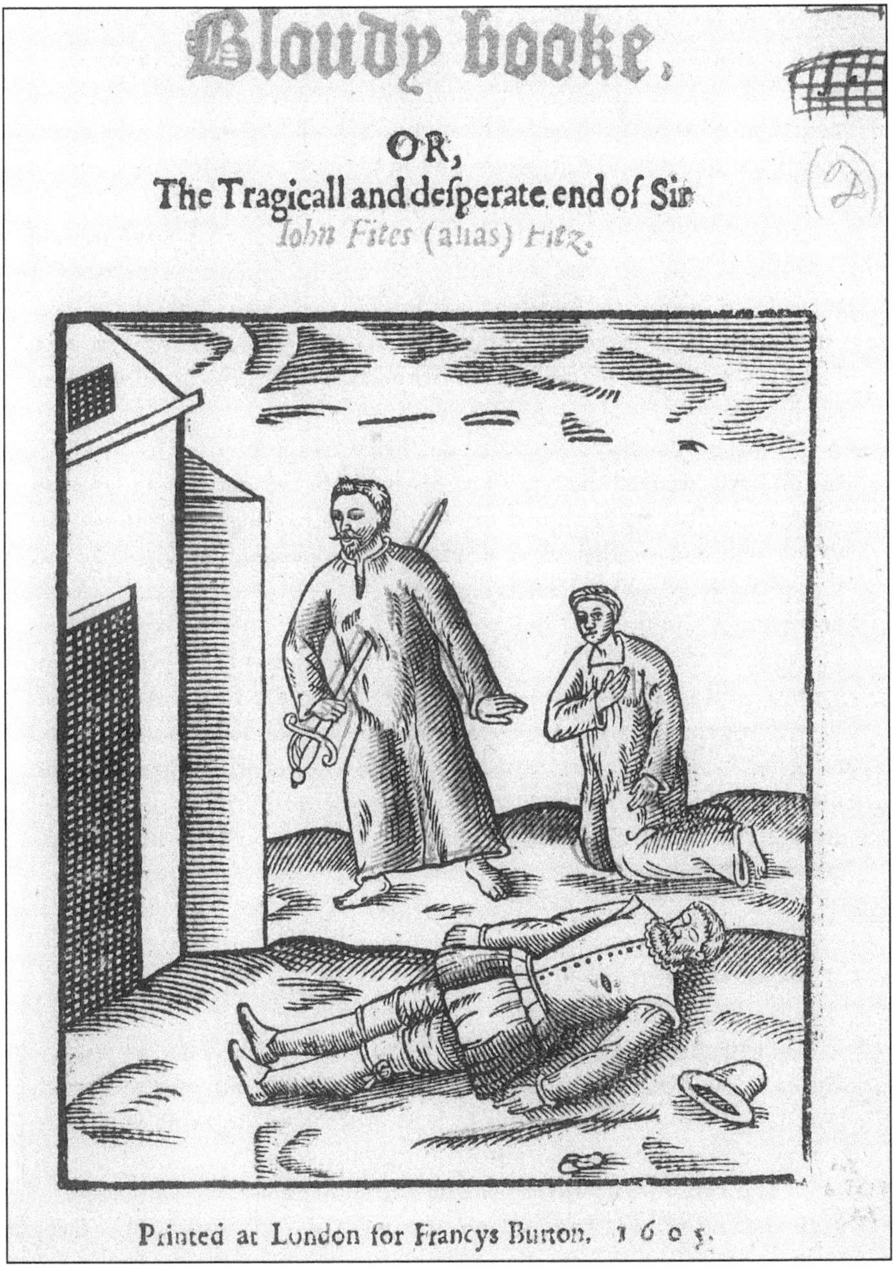
Bloudy booke.

OR,

The Tragicall and desperate end of Sir John Fites (alias) Fitz.

Printed at London for Francys Burton, 1605.

The Mad Squire: Sir John Fitz commits suicide after murdering his host, as the victim's widow prays. Reproduced by permission of the Huntington Library, San Marino, California.

on, at about two in the morning. As soon as Fitz was in bed, he called in Alley again, with "a certain wild and stearne looke," begging, "I pray thee mine host sit by me a while." I have slept in better beds, he said. Alley apologized. So went the wretched, fitful night till about four or five in the morning. It was time for Alley to go to work in his fields, but Mrs. Alley refused to be left alone with the frantic knight. Before this problem could be resolved, Sir John appeared in his shirt, waving his sword. He ran straight for his host, who slammed the garden gate behind him just as the attacker lunged with his sword. As fate would have it, there was a hole in the gate. Alley called out, "I am kild," and fell dead. Mrs. Alley knelt before Fitz, begging for mercy. He stabbed her in the arm but she escaped back into the house.

What to do next? Where to go? More to the point, why live? Fitz methodically wedged the handle of his sword in the garden wall, and ran upon the point. He examined his wound with his finger, rearranged the sword, and had another go at it. He finally collapsed, cursing and "wallowing in his owne bloud, like a Pigge that had been latelie sticked." Neighbors picked him up, put him in bed, and tried to bind his wounds, but Fitz tore off the bindings. He wanted no surgeon, but the neighbors sent for one anyway. Over the next 48 hours he weakened from loss of blood.

How wrong he had been about the surgeon! That learned man proved to be his best friend. He treated Fitz by bleeding him. So died the murderer and suicide, who might normally have been buried in unhallowed ground; but hospitable Twickenham buried frantic Sir John in the chancel of the church.[3]

Instead of Abortion (1614)

Martha Scambler was relieved when nobody noticed her pregnancy. She especially wanted it kept from the sister she lived with next to Bedlam hospital. Sister would be furious to learn Martha was working as an amateur prostitute. Sister would put her out in the street.

"The harlot (delighting in shame and sinne) makes no conscience to be the butcher of her owne seed, nay the Image of God created in her owne body, and now and then in the conception makes spoyle of the bed of creation before it can receive true forme." That is, abortion, and so Martha chose. Getting one sounded easy, if you could believe the London quacks, who would claim expertise in anything. Medications thought to terminate pregnancy included more than 20 herbs mentioned by the herbalist Gerard alone.[4] Many more herbal and non-herbal reputed abortifacients were available, but from all these a woman had to know enough to choose not only one that would work, but one that would not kill her. The odds were great that the potions one bought would be mysterious but useless. It was Martha's bad luck, in her secrecy and solitude, to find only these, so that the clock that ticked on through her several attempts to abort brought her to full term. She gave birth all alone, and immediately strangled her infant, throwing its body into a privy:

"The loathsome Jakes receav'd my child ...," a ballad-monger makes her sing.

The next door neighbor had at some time constructed a convenient chute into this privy, a sneaky practice that had been going on in London since at least 1347.[5] It would have caused Martha no problem had it not been for an untoward boy who lived there. Wrestling with boredom a day or two after Martha's delivery, he caught one of the mongrels that roamed the streets around Bishopsgate and conducted an experiment to resolve the question, What happens when you throw a dog down a chute into a privy?

The answer turned out to be, it barks and howls for three days and nights until a sleepless neighbor steels himself to the nauseous task of rescuing the dog, and discovers a dead infant. A magistrate selected some matrons and had them inspect those local women thought to be promiscuous. His screening caught Martha. To be a murder victim, an infant had only to have taken its first breath, and even the physicians of those days knew how to tell, from the color of the lungs, whether this first breath had been taken. Martha naively admitted the infant had been born alive, and she was hanged at Tyburn alongside the crippled beggar John Arthur.[6]

In the Warmth of the Kilns (1614)

John Arthur's cloud was that he was a crippled dwarf. Its silver lining was that he owned a little scroll licensing him to beg in London. He collected enough money to have a good drunk each night and the society of fellow beggars—even the company of a certain woman. Lacking Arthur's asset of pitiable deformity, her begging was probably illegal. At her suggestion, they worked as a team.

In his burdensome frame important functions remained mercifully intact. Homeless, he "obtained the daily use of her bodie" in the fields and byways. They slept in a favorite haunt of vagabonds, among the warm brick kilns of Islington. In the rubble and perils of this underworld life, a domesticity blossomed. The woman early on wanted them to get married, and early on he promised they would do so. As time went by, she grew more importunate. He grew cooler. Doubt fed on doubt. What was becoming of the freedom he once had? Worse yet, what if she told the lads everything he and she did in those fields and byways? The hilarity would never subside, and he would be ridiculous. One night by a brick kiln, after she had dozed off, he strangled her with the girdle she had laid aside.

How could John Arthur have overcome his physical disability to strangle anyone? With the help of the Devil, explains the author, to whom John Arthur's handicap was an inseparable part of his sin:

> Is it not a marvell, that fire fals not from heaven to consume an infinite number of worse than savage natur'd people in this land, when vile wretches, whom God hath markt with his secret brand of secret purpose, so impiously attempt things against nature, as for example ... a deformed creature, an unperfect wretch wanting the right shape and limbes of a man though in forme and visage like unto one of us....

The story ended quickly. The woman's body was discovered the next morning and many had seen them together. Arthur was tried on 18 July, 1614, and hanged at Tyburn three days later, before a curious crowd of several hundred, come to view the end of an unperfect wretch.[7]

"The Seed of a Varlet" (1631)

Carpenters having finished putting up a dais and canopy beneath the lofty beams of Westminster Hall, for this one day, 25 April 1631, its vast spaces had a different look. King's bench, common pleas, exchequer, and chancery, the four courts occupying each stony corner, sat silent because the whole hall had become the court of the lord high steward.

Such metamorphoses are made partly in writing, partly by ceremony. By eight in the morning, 15 earls, four viscounts, and eight barons took their places on both sides of a long table covered with green cloth. Below them sat eight justices and four crown lawyers. About nine, Lord Coventry entered, preceded by seven sergeants at arms bearing maces. He took his place on the dais under the canopy of state, attended by the chief herald, garter king of arms. The gentleman usher of the black rod, the royal messenger, knelt and presented him with a slender white wand, by virtue of which he became the lord high steward, though one of the sergeants would actually hold it throughout the trial. Then the lords, judges, and privy councillors put on their hats, while all others remained uncovered. The court was ready for its single task, to sit in judgment on a fellow nobleman.

Mervyn Touchet stood indicted on three counts of felony and would stand trial as twelfth Baron Audley rather than under his Irish title, second Earl of Castlehaven. Had parliament been in session, his trial would have been held in the house of lords, with every member sitting in judgment on him, but now precedent calls this court into being for him alone. He had considered foregoing all this privilege to take his chances with an ordinary trial before a jury, but being tried by one's own peers, he had learned, is not only a right but an obligation.

He entered with the lieutenant of the Tower of London and a detail of yeomen of the guard. He and the lieutenant took their places in two velvet-covered pews. The steward had the charges read, addressed a few formal words to the prisoner, and asked him to say whatever he could to refute the charges, but not to dishonor God and the king by denying any true charge. The earl replied that because he had been held in isolation from friends and counsel for six months he was not in a good condition to make his case. He asked for an attorney for consultation. The steward told him that his time in prison had been a special favor, considering that most felony defendants have only a few days before trial. These months had given him all the more opportunity to gather his thoughts and make his case. His request for a lawyer, a legal question, was referred to the justices, who ruled that a defendant in a criminal case has no right to a lawyer, unless on some specific question of law. Then the clerk of the crown read out to the echoing walls the three counts of the indictment, one for rape and two for sodomy. The indictment was in Latin. One English word, "buggery," floated up past the frozen smiles of the oaken angels holding up the roof. The earl pleaded not guilty.

"How wilt thou be tried?"

"By God and my Peers."

The steward instructed the peers. Some may feel pity for the prisoner, he said, others may be revolted by the allegations, but reason alone must rule their affections.

To a modern writer the assembled peers have seemed a somewhat monolithic aristocracy. None present at the trial would have thought so.

THE ARRAIGNMENT AND CONVICTION

OF

MERVIN Lord *AVDLEY*,

Earle of Caſtlehaven, (who was by 26. Peers of the Realm found guilty for committing Rapine and Sodomy) at Weſtminſter, on Monday, April 25. 1631.

By vertue of a Commiſsion of Oyer and Terminer, directed to Sir *Thomas Coventry*, Lord Keeper of the Great Seale of England, Lord high Steward for that day, accompanied with the Iudges.

As alſo the beheading of the ſaid Earle ſhortly after on Tower Hill.

LONDON,
Printed for *Tho: Thomas*. 1642.

The trial of the Earl of Castlehaven in 1631 was at least as interesting in the politically charged year 1642. As a part-time Catholic and spectacularly indulgent aristocrat, his case would have been a perpetual feast for the Puritans. Reproduced by permission of the Huntington Library, San Marino, California.

Thomas Howard, Earl of Arundel, had angered his king and twice undergone arrest for marrying off his son without the king's permission. Henry Danvers, Earl of Danby, had killed Henry Long 36 years earlier, and was alive now only because of a pardon which dubiously assumed self defense. Edward Sackville, Earl of Dorset, had killed a Scots lord in a duel in Holland 27 years earlier. Henry Montagu, Earl of Manchester, was a lawyer and had been lord chief justice. Lord Arundel was England's first art collector; Lord Dudley was a musician and poet. George, Lord Goring, and Robert Devereux, third Earl of Essex, were soldiers. The Earls of Holland and Carlisle had served jointly in 1627 as ambassadors to France. Richard, Lord Weston, was a strong supporter of the king's favorite Buckingham, Lord North an active member of the faction intriguing against Buckingham.

Their careers after this trial emphasized their diversity. Thomas, Viscount Wentworth became Earl of Strafford and was beheaded in 1641 at the insistence of a parliament so powerful that his king could not save him. In the civil war that followed, the Earls of Dorset and Worcester took the king's side, Lord North the other side. The royalist general Lord Goring fought the more aristocratic parliamentarian general the Earl of Essex.

Sir Robert Heath, the attorney general, had his witnesses called in: some of the prisoner's servants, his wife, and his stepdaughter of 13. The story unfolded.

The defendant had recently married Anne, daughter of Ferdinando, the short-lived fifth Earl of Derby. Since Ferdinando had no sons, his title went to his brother William, the sixth earl, but Anne and her two younger sisters claimed vast estates as co-heirs, and a ruinous litigation was dragging on. Anne was the widow of Lord Chandos, by whom she had had a daughter, Elizabeth Brydges, born about 1618.

The defendant had three sons by a previous marriage: James, George, and Mervin, and three daughters, including one named Frances. His estates, though mostly in Ireland, included property in Dorset and Audley house in Salisbury, and he had recently purchased from his mother's family the mansion at Fonthill Gifford, about 14 miles west of Salisbury.

He kept many servants. Of these, several males came to know the earl well and have sex with him: an unnamed boy, Giles Broadway, and Lawrence Fitzpatrick (some clerk wrote Florence for Lawrence in copying the indictment). The alleged offenses with Fitzpatrick took place on 1 June, 1630. Two pages also played important parts. One named Ampthill or Antil had been the earl's page for eight years. The earl was exceptionally generous to him, giving him the privilege of boarding horses on the earl's lands, a concession from which the page had so far made £2,000.

At Fonthill Giffard, a day or two after marrying Anne, the earl called Antil into their bed and tried to persuade her to have sex with Antil there and then. If she loved her husband, he argued, she must love Antil. Any sin involved would be his and not hers: Had she not just vowed to obey him? His argument failed on this occasion, but eventually the bride did lie with Antil while her husband watched them. The countess said she cried out, but the servant Fitzpatrick testified that later he had often seen her making love with Antil. The earl would amuse himself as a spectator, and occasionally introduce variety by parading his male servants nude before his wife while he commented on their various features and dimensions. The earl finally married his page off to one of his daughters. On this occasion he gave the page £7,000. From then on, Antil sat at table with the family.

Then one morning the earl had his eldest son James, who was about 13, married by a Catholic priest to Elizabeth, his stepdaughter of 12. That evening they went through a second ceremony with a Protestant clergyman from his estates in Kilkenny, Ireland.

To serve as a page for the countess, the earl brought over from his Irish estates a servant named Henry Skipwith. Unlike many pages, Henry came of mean parentage, but in the earl's eyes he outshone all other men. Henry regularly lay with the earl, but he was also kept busy elsewhere. His master ordered him to have sex with the countess. She later testified that on the first occasion Henry merely faked a performance for the earl's benefit, but later they became regular sex partners. From his doting master Henry got lands worth £1,000 a year and another £500 a year in cash. The earl stopped all money and resources to his wife and stepdaughter, leaving it to Henry Skipwith to dole out to them from his own allowance whatever it suited him to give. Mother and daughter became totally dependent on Henry, even for food. Henry and the countess regularly had sex at the earl's behest, with the earl and the servant Fitzpatrick as audience. She became pregnant. Despite Antil's earlier involvement, Skipwith believed himself to be the father. Though the earl had begotten six children, nobody who knew him considered him a candidate for this paternity.

The earl arranged for Anne to send the infant away. This dismissive act offended Henry and estranged him from the countess. As a result, Henry's attention swerved to her daughter Elizabeth. The earl encouraged him to seduce this still-virgin bride of his son James. To support Henry in his courtship, the stepfather told Elizabeth he would turn her out of the house if she did not comply. Her husband James did not love her, he said, and if she did not consent he would tell James that she had consented anyway. Henry testified that there was love between him and Elizabeth before and after this seduction. They did indeed become regular bedmates, and were observed in the act from time to time by her stepfather, her adolescent husband, and nine servants in the exhibitionist menage. Skipwith, for all his professed love, suggested sharing her with two servants named Paulet and Green, but did not press the plan when she refused. The girl's testimony was that, despite a painful initiation (supervised and facilitated in clinical detail by her stepfather), she was tempted and seduced, but not raped. She confirmed, however, that she was totally dependent on Skipwith, even for food.

It was no ordinary seduction, reminding the attorney general of passages in Suetonius. The earl was so infatuated with Henry Skipwith that, in a turn of fancy reminiscent of Caligula, he wanted to have an heir by him. Because he could still grasp the impracticability of this ambition, he delegated it, so to speak, to his stepdaughter. And that is why the earl stood by the horizontal couple urging them to give him a boy.

This inward manor house was not wholly isolated. From the village, the earl brought in a trull named Blandina. Blandina lay with the earl and others, and even with the busy Skipwith, a feat witnessed by the earl, Fitzpatrick, and four other servants. All but the earl testified that Blandina stayed six months. He told the court she stayed two weeks, and was warned that it only damaged his credibility to lie about little things. Blandina was eventually turned out, blamed by every participant for spreading a disease.

The rape indictment arose from an incident on the night of 20 June, 1630. The earl woke Giles Broadway, who usually slept at the foot of the bed. He had intended to send the servant for a light for his pipe, but on one of his sudden whims he invited Broadway to come into bed and enjoy his sleeping wife. When she awoke and resisted, the earl held her hands and one of her feet, and Broadway overcame her despite her cries. Immediately afterwards, Anne seized a knife and tried to kill herself, but Broadway broke it. This was the basis for the indictment. Practically, the earl had raped his wife by proxy. At law, Broadway had raped the countess, and the earl, as an accomplice, was equally guilty.

In November, 1630, when he was about 14, the earl's eldest son James sent a crucial letter to his father complaining of his "monstrous change from a father to an enemy." Even if estates were partially protected by entail, a hostile or besotted father could do his son a great deal of economic damage. The son appealed for protection from this kind of father to the father of his country, King Charles, by sending the king a copy of his letter. Any one of several parties could have put James up to this. When the king read the letter, the whole story came out, leading to this trial.

A few days before the trial, the judges had met twice at one of the law inns, Sergeant's, at the corner of Fleet Street and Chancery Lane, to dispose of certain threshold questions:

1. Could the defendant claim benefit of clergy? In many capital crimes, a person in holy orders committing his first felony was technically handed over to the bishop's ordinary, in effect being given a second chance in society. Many Oxford and Cambridge students qualified by having taken minor orders to matriculate. Eventually other persons could take a test for "holy orders," which consisted merely of being able to read a page of the Bible. That university wit, playwright, and brawler, Ben Jonson, had once killed a man and escaped punishment in this way. Castlehaven might have qualified where the benefit was applicable. The judges agreed that the benefit was applicable to the rape charge, a common law offense from which benefit of clergy had not been expressly removed by statute. But it was not applicable to buggery, an offense unknown to the common law, created in Henry VIII's time by a statute that did not expressly grant benefit of clergy.

2. If the defendant refused to plead, he would suffer the *peine forte et dure*, pressing to death. Would his silence keep the whole matter quiet? Not necessarily, said the judges. If the court wished to go ahead and call witnesses and otherwise enquire into the indictment, it could do so.

3. Was penetration essential to rape? Although at the time there was some dubious precedent to the effect that it was emission rather than penetration that made a rape, the judges held that penetration was essential.

With these matters settled, the attorney general opened his case. Because the countess was reputed to have been first Antil's and then Skipwith's voluntary lover, the attorney general was careful not to let the lords get bogged down in legally irrelevant questions about the lady's virtue. He explained that, according to the medieval authority Bracton, the law says that an unchaste woman can be the victim of rape. This law went back at least as early as King Athelstan's reign, 700 years before.

The lords had a few legal questions of their own. Can a wife testify against her husband? Yes, said the judges: though she could not have testified in a civil case against him, she can do so in a criminal case, especially in which she is the alleged victim. Can a man of no worth be sufficient proof against a baron? Yes, any man can be a witness in a felony case. Because the countess let a long time pass without reporting the rape, can there still be a charge of rape? It is indeed too late for her to lodge a personal appeal of rape, said the judges, but here it is not the woman but the king who is the accuser, and against the king time runneth not out. Another question: Because both the alleged homosexual acts had been interfemoral rather than anal, were they still sodomy? Yes, said the judges, possibly stretching the definition of "penetration."

Before the verdict, the defendant was allowed to speak, and gave his peers three warnings, which he called "woes":

> 1. Woe to that man, whose Wife should be a witness against him!
> 2. Woe to that man, whose Son should persecute him, and conspire his death!
> 3. Woe to that man, whose Servants should be allowed Witnesses to take away his life!

Beyond that, the earl said only that his wife had "been naught" and had an illegitimate child whom he concealed to save her honor. He said that he was getting old (he was about 39) and now she would be able to marry a younger man. His son was 21 (he was actually about 15) and would get the estate. Therefore, he argued, his son and the countess had plotted to cause his death in this way. He courteously asked their lordships' pardon, and was led out while the lords withdrew to deliberate. Two hours later all were back. They found the defendant guilty, unanimously on the rape count, 15 to 12 as to the buggery.[8]

The lord high steward passed the sentence required by law. Just what this was had become somewhat muddied over the centuries. One medieval legal authority said that sodomites, like sorcerers, are burnt. Another less reliable authority had said, don't kill them, just bury them alive.[9] The court resolved some ambiguity about whether convicted sodomites forfeited their estates, and passed sentence of hanging and forfeiture. He asked the lords to pray the king to banish him instead of executing him; but if he would not do that, to give him some time for repentance. Then the lord high steward ended the court and his own commission by breaking the white wand.[10]

As was customary when lords were sentenced to death, the king commuted hanging to beheading. His majesty, feeling that Castlehaven had more spiritual disarray to compose than most culprits, gave him 19 days, much better than the usual weekend. His execution was set for Saturday, 14 May, 1631. About a week before that, his coffin was brought into his room in the Tower of London, to help him focus his attention on his situation. The Dean of St. Paul's visited him daily. In shifting back and forth between Rome and the Church of England the earl had shown fickleness. In the Tower, the earl wrote a letter to his son, urging him to settle down to the church of England. "Then are you come from fearfull blowes unto a quiet and smooth sea."

As he stood on the scaffold on Tower Hill, attended by clergymen and 12 of his servants, it was important politically that he die a Protestant, and so he did after a courteous speech and appropriate public and private prayers, pulling a handkerchief over his face and laying his neck on the block for a single neat stroke. His titles and estates were forfeited to the crown. After some two years' difficulty, the king restored the titles and some of the estate to his son James, though by then much of the English property had been given away to courtiers and was lost forever to the Touchet family.

Disgust is said to have led James to turn in his father for trial and execution. James's wife and stepsister Elizabeth must also have found life traumatic in that household. The two adolescents shared grotesque memories. She and her sisters had a prospect, though bitterly contested, of immense wealth, including the Isle of Man. Materially, her marriage would have been reckoned a good one, but according to his great aunt Lady Eleanor, Elizabeth and James never lived together after the execution.[11]

James pursued a successful if tumultuous military career in Ireland. Like his father, he was a rather ambiguous Protestant, never fully trusted by the government. He died childless in 1684. Elizabeth, his stepsister and wife, lived to 1679 and is buried in St. Martin's in the Fields, London.

On the 27th of June, 1631, Westminster Hall was in its normal mode, and in the corner that was the court of king's bench the two indicted servants stood trial: Giles Broadway for rape, and Lawrence Fitzpatrick for sodomy. For Broadway's trial, the widowed countess arrived to testify against her rapist. The justice asked her if she still swore, as she had done at her husband's trial, that Broadway had actually penetrated her, and she repeated her testimony. In both trials, Broadway unsuccessfully maintained that he had experienced a premature gratification before matters could reach that stage. The countess said that though she felt indignation and shame at the mere sight of him, her testimony was not affected by malice, and she hoped that she would be believed.

Fitzpatrick, who was next, felt wronged. He had given evidence in the earl's sodomy trial, and now that testimony was turned against him. He argued that he was not "bound to be the destruction of himself." True, replied the justice, no man is obliged to be his own accuser, but where his testimony, that served to take away another's life, shows him to be guilty of the same crime, "it should serve to cut him off also." Toward the end of the trial, the jurors still had a question that reflects the layman's view of buggery as a one-way street. If it was the earl who did it to Fitzpatrick, they asked, why is Fitzpatrick a sodomist? Because, explained the justice, he was an accomplice, and felons' accomplices are equally felons. He was old enough to know what he was doing, and physically able to resist his master.

Both Broadway and Fitzpatrick were found guilty. The king had ordered sentencing to be delayed ten days until he could have a report of the cases. At Tyburn they stood on separate carts, and were given ample time to tell their stories. Broadway told the crowd that he had come over from Ireland only because Skipwith wanted some company. He had intended to return, but, from day to day and month to month, the earl's unexpected generosities kept him postponing his return to Ireland. He said the earl had talked him into his misdeeds. He admitted that the countess strongly disliked him, but rather unchivalrously added that he might eventually have bedded her because she commonly slept with Antill and Skipwith. As a Protestant, Broadway was attended by that aging perennial gallows pastor, Henry Goodcole. Fitzpatrick simply asked any Catholics in the crowd to pray for him. First Broadway's cart, then Fitzpatrick's, drew away as the Protestant and Catholic raised their unbound hands—perhaps in prayer, as the minister believed, or perhaps to grab the rope.

The indictments had said nothing about Elizabeth's abuse: "Though you dye not for it," the lord high steward told Castlehaven, "yet you have abused your daughter." Concluding the trial, he looked beyond the technicalities. The defendant, he said, had offended not only against nature but "the rage of a man, jealousie." He was most unnaturally not jealous when he ought to have been. And though sodomy was regarded as the crime against nature, the earl had committed another crime beyond nature, even though he could not be indicted for it. This crime was, the steward told him, that "having honour and fortune to leave behind, you would have had the spurious seed of a varlet to inherit both." The thought cannot have been far from the minds of anyone in this most aristocratic of courts.[12]

VIII. From Sex to Disaster

Downfall in Dublin (1640)

Brilliance, scholarship, and ambition put John Atherton on the fast track of ecclesiastical promotion. By 1640, at the age of 42, he was the Protestant Bishop of Waterford and Lismore in Ireland, and in deep trouble. These were dangerous times for religion and politics, not least in Ireland, but this bishop's problems were of his own making. His aggressiveness was inordinate, his greed was ruthless, and his great lust was magnified by a sort of stubborn exhibitionism. He did not hide his trespasses because he would rather defend them, and in this way display his skill in argument. Some men he persecuted, some he ruined, and some he cuckolded, rapidly accumulating enemies; those he counted friends were toadies and spies whose revelations led to his fall.

This bishop, husband, and father deflowered virgins, and wherever he was a guest he might attempt the virtue of his host's wife. If he was not invited he might appear anyway. At least one Waterford gentleman, desperate to borrow a hundred pounds, left his wife with the bishop as security. It was said that the bishop could not even blame the pressures of ordinary lust for his deeds, because he dosed himself with cantharides, or Spanish fly, to keep up his ardor. His adventures included going to bed with his wife's sister, committing incest in canon law.

The bishop's own sister came to him to warn him that the ghost of her late mother in law had been pestering her lately to tell Atherton that if he did not mend his ways he would hang.

"If I must, I must dye. Marriage, and hanging, come by destiny," the bishop told his sister.

Even so, he admitted later, there had come a time of dangerous illness, when he vowed to mend his ways if he recovered. The very Sabbath that he had chosen for starting this new life, the justices of assize arrived in Waterford. It troubled Atherton to think that if he suddenly adopted a virtuous life on this day, people would say he feared the judges. The day thus passed without that promised first step to reform, and a like day never came again.

Then at last he was impeached before the Irish parliament for incest and "many other enormous crimes," including buggery with his proctor, John Childe. Seized in Cork, the proctor had confessed to having sex with Atherton. Childe was hanged at Bandon Bridges, Cork, confirming his confession. In his trial, Atherton was at first as arrogant and confident as ever, up to a point when his quick mind saw that he was doomed. From then on he made no further effort to save himself, turning with agility to the only business at hand, saving his soul.

He might, he said, have had Childe prosecuted for theft and, by thus making Childe a felon, have disqualified him as a witness, but he did not. When the Earl of Strafford, the Lord Lieutenant of Ireland, was himself imprisoned in the Tower of London in 1640, Atherton could have applied for a reprieve until a new lord lieutenant was appointed, but he did not. He probably would have been accorded the privilege of beheading instead of hanging, but he did not ask, saying that he deserved to die like a dog. Finally, he selected the meanest part of the churchyard for his burial, and forbade the chaplain to say anything good about him in his funeral sermon. His coffin was brought into his cell to focus his mind.

Atherton's case had many undercurrents and Irish contradictions. The Catholics had every reason to resent his harshness after the more tolerant regime of his predecessor, but, with the exception of the Catholic sheriff, they did not gloat or mistreat him. Atherton embodied the strict and conformist policies of his patron, William Laud, Archbishop of Canterbury, and his own downfall coincided with the imprisonment of that doomed prelate. Atherton blamed not events but himself for the pass to which he had come. His jury and judges had made an error here, an error there, he said; but after all, for all that he had done, detected and undetected, he was ready to die. In Dublin on a December morning, the dean of Ardagh rode with him in a coach to the gallows amid an emotional mob of both Protestants and Catholics. After a well-turned speech and prayers, Bishop Atherton was turned off the ladder. Then the dean sat with the dead bishop in the coach again, reflecting on human mortality as they rode together to the humblest corner of the churchyard. [13]

Vicar Is Showing Off Again (1641)

A public who were talking about the hanging of a bishop, and were awaiting the decapitation of an archbishop, would be attuned to scandal among the clergy. It was safe to print the proceedings of the court of ecclesiastical commission, and under this aegis to regale readers with the tale of a delectably disgraceful vicar, John Gwin, of Cople, Bedfordshire.

It took no dogged reporter to expose Gwin's transgressions; he so loved to expose them himself. The villagers could usually see him stagger and stumble into church, or consume beer and tobacco in the alehouse, where recently he had hurt his brother in a brawl. When he visited Robert Purser's house and had sex with Mrs. Purser in the hall while the unsuspecting Robert was sitting by the kitchen fire, Gwin advertised his exploit. When he did not show up for Sunday services, he explained that he had spent the whole sabbath in the next parish in bed with the sister of a Mr. Fowcks. He paid her, he said, with the money he had realized from farmer Brooks's tithe. Tithes were a sore subject, and connecting them publicly with a trollop shows Gwin's perverse genius in such matters.

At Bedford Fair, Gwin recognized John Davy's daughters Dorothy and Mary, and spent four or five shillings on wine for them in a room at an inn. He found some excuse to send Mary out, and had sex with Dorothy while she was gone. After a while, Mary came back and Gwin sent Dorothy out on an errand, hoping to have Mary too, but she disappointed him, crying out, "Ah, master, what will you doe, will you undoe me?"

The vicar had a wife. Once he had gone to the trouble of making up a story for Mrs. Gwin, to conceal the true source of the gonorrhea he had brought home to her, but later on he made her part of his exhibitionism. She and the vicar were about to rise from bed one morning when a gentleman arrived on business with the vicar. First, said Gwin, "I must have a bout with my wife," which he proceeded to do while the gentleman stood by in embarrassment. Gwin enjoyed retelling this bit of theatre.

Having an expansive nature, he sometimes invited others to have a bout with Mrs. Gwin. While one of these men was thus occupied, Gwin put on the man's red coat and colored hat and headed into the village. How do you like me in this? he asked a friend. The owner is back home with my wife, who is "giving him a posset."

And so the shows went on: Gwin and a drinking friend alternating dirty songs with stretches of liturgy; Gwin strolling out of his church during psalms to post some scurrilous verse of his own on the whipping post; Gwin whimsically altering the psalms during services, to the confusion of the parishioners.

That is where we leave him, the commission having concluded that "he hath been, and is a shame, and scandall to the Ministry."[14]

IX

Corruption

The Handsome Duke (1592-1628)

King James and his favorites created a court culture in which homosexual relationships gave rise directly or indirectly to a number of public scandals. The latest study leaves little doubt that his relations with his favorites were physical, widely known, and even more widely suspected, domestically and abroad. If we do not know the precise details of these physical contacts, we know enough to see an unbroken chain from the king and his minions to several events that offended the public.[1]

One of these was the most notorious poisoning case of the age. So much has been written about the murder of Sir Thomas Overbury that it needs only brief mention here.[2] Sir Thomas was the intimate friend and mentor of a Scots lad, Robert Carr, who was dangled by courtiers before King James and became his favorite and Earl of Somerset. Somerset and the teenage Countess of Essex desired to marry. Her husband, the Earl of Essex, had shown so little interest in her famous charms that she was able to win an annulment, though only after a trial in which the king overruled the Archbishop of Canterbury on scriptural interpretation. This marriage would bring a major shift in power at court, to the detriment of Overbury. Known for his blunt speech, he vigorously opposed the match. To get him out of the way, Somerset and the countess tried to send him abroad, persuading the king in 1613 to offer him a foreign embassy. When Overbury refused, they anonymously maneuvered him into a cell in the Tower of London, as punishment for his high contempt in refusing the honor of an embassy. To reassure Overbury of Somerset's and her own continued friendship, the countess with the help of a Mrs. Turner sent him pies and delicacies from time to time. They concealed messages of cheer and encouragement. The pies also contained poison, so that Overbury died a slow and nasty death in his cell. In 1614 the scandal broke. In 1615 Mrs. Turner was hanged. Somerset and his wife were tried and sentenced to death in 1616. After six years in the Tower, they were released into disgrace and rustication on their estates. By then, the discarded favorite had been well and truly replaced at court.

George Villiers was a youth of flawless beauty, when rotten teeth and noses put a premium on flawlessness. Planted by scheming courtiers, he soon captured the heart of King James, who raised him in 1616 and 1617 to royal favorite, then made him a duke, and finally the most powerful subject in the kingdom. The king called him "Steenie" and he called the king "Dad." His many enemies were quick to see his hand in several sinister events.

Spirits of the August (1626)

The Reverend Thomas Scott had never minced words in the pulpit, nor stopped lecturing the king on the evils of sodomy with his favorite. Nor had Scott concealed his opposition to Buckingham's and King James's intermittent attempts at friendship with Queen Elizabeth's old enemy, Catholic Spain. The keystone of this policy was negotiating a marriage of Prince Charles with a daughter of the King of Spain. In the days when diplomacy, and especially royal marriages, were regarded as exclusively royal prerogatives, Scott was a prolific, courageous, and effective critic with wide popularity. He was finally harried out of the land, finding refuge in 1623 as a chaplain in the Anglo-Scots-Dutch garrison in Utrecht. From then until his death three years later, his critical publications continued, some printed in London, some in Utrecht, incompletely suppressed by the authorities. Many of Scott's attacks were aimed at Gondomar, Spanish ambassador in London, and his "treacheries intended for the subversion of England."

One of the pamphlets, published in 1624, bore portraits of James, Charles, the "Winter Queen" Elizabeth of Bohemia, and her husband the Pfalzgraf. They caught the attention of a soldier in Utrecht, John Lambert. Lambert had visited countries where he could easily have learned that he was one of the elect of heaven. The son of a London shipmaster and a Warwickshire gentlewoman, he sailed with his father and grew fluent in French.

When his family fortunes declined, he became an expatriate, and like many young men in his situation went as a mercenary to that hungry employer, the Thirty Years War. In the phrase of the times, he trailed the puissant pike. During his travels, and especially at Utrecht, he would have heard Calvinist conversations on the subject of the elect of heaven. He also had ideas about the transmigration of the soul. These are harder to trace to their origins. Some vague folk beliefs may have survived on the continent, though in England transmigration notions mostly involved animals.

Lambert incorporated Scott's portraits into his delusional system. According to Lambert, when the late great Queen Elizabeth died 25 years before, her soul transmigrated to her namesake, the sister of King Charles I. This latter Elizabeth was now Queen of Bohemia. The old queen had considered Lambert to be one of the elect of heaven, and by transmigration so did Elizabeth of Bohemia (the same soul, after all). She was therefore going to look after him and take him into her service. Though the young queen was born seven years before the old queen died, this technicality did not intrude upon Lambert's system.[3]

There was nothing daft about wanting to enter the young queen's service. She was a famous beauty and charmer, courted by aristocrats of several nations. She and her German husband were colorful figures, a symbolic if rather ineffectual focus for the Protestant cause. They had actually reigned in Prague only one winter before being expelled by the Habsburgs, but she was ever after called romantically "the Winter Queen." For her effect on men she was called just as romantically "the Queen of Hearts." Without knowing it, she had occupied much of Lambert's brain. We do not know whether Lambert ever actually sought her patronage in any recognizable way, only that he expected it. Later, when he was allowed to write a letter to the Winter Queen, its language was gibberish to all but its writer. To Lambert, the road to preferment seemed slow; a sane person would have known that nothing at all was happening.

His troubled brain still had room for the sermons of Thomas Scott in the English church at Utrecht. He enjoyed these, but careful attention to them gradually revealed that Master Scott was somehow coming between him and the queen. So of course he had to sharpen his rapier and sit waiting for Scott just inside the churchyard gate. His project was interrupted by an evil spirit that came and carried him to the top of the city wall, and then led him to his home, but it was not long before good spirits visited him there. They reminded him that he would never get any preferment from the Queen of Bohemia as long as Scott lived. The good spirits promised to give him no ease night or day until he slew the minister. Now the Bible itself urged him on: an eye for an eye, it said.

The minister sailed to England to visit his brother, vexing Lambert's good spirits for some seven weeks. Finally Scott returned to Utrecht, and that Sunday Lambert returned to the churchyard and stabbed Scott as he walked to services, flanked by his nephew Thomas and his brother William. Why? asked the wounded minister.

When Lambert explained, Scott could only say, "I know thee not, God forgive thee and I doe from the bottom of my heart."

Several bystanders who felt less forgiving would have lynched Lambert if a Dutch official had not persuaded them to let the legal system run its course. Lambert was jailed and Scott died in a few hours. For a day or two, the prisoner cheerfully awaited some kind of rescue by the Queen of Bohemia. Though local authorities doubted any of the royal connections he claimed, just to be safe they sent off an enquiry to their prince, who simply replied that justice should take its normal course. Part of this normal course in Holland was to stretch Scott on the rack to see if he had any further information. Torture did not deter his visiting spirits, who kept reassuring him of his special place in heaven. The main object of this routine racking was to discover whether anyone had paid Lambert to assassinate Scott. Nothing came of this line of enquiry, but the rack extracted a few other truths from Lambert. As a mercenary, he had served with the Catholic enemy at the siege of Bergen op Zoom, and in garrison in Flanders. Lambert insisted he was not a Catholic, and the more his examiners learned of his unorthodox beliefs the more they would have agreed. Another fact he revealed on the rack was that several times, while he was weighing the strait commands of his spirits, he had considered having a talk with Scott to resolve the difficulty peacefully. But, he said, he was afraid that that would get out, and the soldiers would jeer at him and he would be the butt of jokes throughout the garrison.

As the end approached, Lambert tried some macabre bargaining with the court martial that had tried him. He suggested the officers content themselves with cutting off his right hand (the true culprit) and letting the innocent rest of him go. They showed no interest in the hand and sentenced him to the usual continental punishment: to be bound to a wheel and have his bones broken, after which the wheel and what was left of Lambert would be propped up indefinitely in some public place as a lesson. Lambert entreated that his body be buried. The officers modified the sentence so that, on the next day, he would have his right hand cut off and then he would be merely hanged, and his body laid on the wheel after death. In the remaining hours he was visited by several preachers, but they could not compete with the other callers he was receiving hourly: the late Queen Elizabeth, joined now by the late King James and the late Prince of Orange.

The many people who hated the Duke of Buckingham would not have been deterred by Lambert's insistence under torture that he acted alone. Scott's own life and writings made him a plausible target for assassination by agents, either of Spain or of the Duke of Buckingham. Both Buckingham and the Spanish had the means, motive, and opportunity to slay this stubborn and abrasive minister. The only clear evidence to the contrary is the statement of the mad soldier, John Lambert; but his mind obeyed various spirits, and might well have been malleable enough for skilled manipulation.[4]

Allegations of a Scot (1628)

Though they interpret them variously, modern historians are aware of allegations, made by one of the king's attendant physicians, that King James was murdered by the Duke of Buckingham. This physician, Dr. George Eglisham, a fellow Scot attending the king for ten years, fled to the continent, fearing that he knew too much about the king's last days. From an anonymous press, ostensibly in "Franckfort," he published his account:

King James was in declining health when, at the age of 59, he came down with an intermittent fever known as the tertian ague, debilitating but not fatal. On the Monday six days before his death, while the physicians were all at dinner, the Duke of Buckingham brought him a white powder to take. James, who from infancy had been the target of kidnappers and assassins, was suspicious of any such offers, even from his favorite. On the other hand, James had acquired the habit of letting Buckingham manage him, so he took the white powder, washing it down with wine. The king, said Dr. Eglisham, immediately grew worse. Suffering violent gastrointestinal pains, he cried out, "O this white powder! this white powder! would to God I had never taken it, it will cost me my liffe."

The following Friday, again while the physicians were at dinner, the duke's mother came in to James and placed a plaster on his chest, whereupon he grew short of breath and his pain increased. After their dinner, the physicians looked in on the king. They found him worse, and noticed a foul smell in the chamber. Tracing it, they discovered the plaster. Some of them exclaimed that the king was poisoned. This hubbub brought Buckingham into the sick room. He ordered all of the physicians out, confining one of them to his chamber and sending one of them away from court altogether. The duke's mother joined him and knelt by the king's bed.

"Justice, justice sir I demand justice of your Majestie."

"For what?" asked James.

"For that which there [their] lives is no sufficient satisfaction, for saying that my sonne and I have poysoned your Majestie."

"Poysoned me," gasped James, and fainted.

That Sunday he died, and Buckingham gave the physicians a paper to sign, declaring the white powder to have been "a goode and safe medicin." The physicians refused. The duke's supporters spread a story across the kingdom that his grief for his beloved master had nearly led him to suicide. The duke warned the physicians to watch their tongues if they knew what was good for them. There was a silent witness the duke could no longer reach: the late king. Dr. Eglisham wrote,

"But in the meane tyme the Kings body and head swelled above measure, his hair with the skin of his head stucke to the pillow his nayles became loos upon his fingers and toes."

So much for Buckingham. He had means and opportunity. He had motive too, according to Eglisham. While the duke and the Prince of Wales were in Spain trying to negotiate the prince's marriage, the duke's influence at home seemed to wane. His followers reported to him in Spain that King James was heard to complain about him from time to time, and that the Marquess of Hamilton, an old friend of the king's, was telling him in blunt Scots what a mistake it was to send the prince with somebody as inexperienced as Buckingham.

The duke hastened home to preserve his influence. He settled into his room, which controlled the entrance to the king's bedchamber. There "he so caryed him selfe that whatsoever the King commanded in his bedchamber he controlled in the next chamber." Now he had started intercepting foreign dispatches and answering them without involving the king. The king was highly offended by this arrogation. It did not take jealous courtiers long to judge the royal climate, and pile onto the duke criticisms they would never have dared make before. They suggested to James that France would be a good place to send Buckingham for a while, and James seemed to like the idea. Buckingham's absence in Spain had been liberating for the king, and his return felt more oppressive than ever. It was just at this point that the tertian ague sent James to bed. Thus Buckingham had ample motive to kill his master.

Motive, means, opportunity: Now Eglisham argued a pattern as well. The Marquess of Hamilton, the friend of the king and harsh critic of Buckingham, had met his death just 25 days before the king. They had a personal enmity. The duke was an upstart, raised from obscurity solely by the king's personal attraction to him. The marquess too had some claim on the king's affections, and he represented an old aristocratic family. When the duke tried to marry his niece to the son of the marquess, Hamilton refused. This aristocratic haughtiness deeply offended the haughty upstart duke. They quarreled; were pressed into a reconciliation, quarreled again, four or five times, according to the doctor.

Suddenly, the marquess fell ill at his town house near Bishopsgate. Sick persons were customarily sent various foods, such as cakes. Immediately, Hamilton refused to eat any of these if they came from the duke. Hamilton was an old patron of Dr. Eglisham's family, and had raised Eglisham to his present position as king's physician. He was still also Hamilton's physician. Hamilton begged him, he said, not to let the duke near his sick bed. The duke did indeed try to see Hamilton, and persised in his efforts until Eglisham could no longer put him off. Hamilton had Eglisham stay with them and cut off the duke's visit as quickly as possible on medical grounds. These precautions did no good. Two of Hamilton's servants died with symptoms of poisoning. One had worked in the kitchen, one in the wine cellar. Two days later, the marquess died. The duke had been able to delay the arrival of Hamilton's son at his father's death bed. His purpose was to keep the father from exacting a death bed promise from his son not to wed the duke's niece. His scheme worked, for at the age of 14 the new marquess married the niece.

As soon as Hamilton died, the doctor saw to it that no one touched the body until he could hold an autopsy. Buckingham's men soon appeared, intending to bury the marquess that very night in Westminster Abbey, but the marquess's fast gathering family and friends were able to keep control of the corpse. Deciding that they could not keep the duke's physicians from viewing the body, they invited several London physicians, to make it more difficult for anyone to suppress evidence. The corpse of the late marquess was surely evidence of something untoward, having swollen grotesquely, disconcerting even the most experienced physicians. Eglisham said he led one of them, Dr. Moore, to the corpse, and drew back the sheet, saying, "Looke yow here upon this pitifull spectacle."

"Jesus blisse me," said Moore, "I never saw the like. I cannot know him. I cannot distinguish a face upon him."

IX. Corruption

The ghosts of Dr. Eglisham, the Marquess of Hamilton, and King James confront the ghost of their alleged poisoner, the Duke of Buckingham. All are wearing the shrouds that were fashionable at the time. Visitors to St. Paul's Catherdral can still see the monument of poet John Donne wearing just such a shroud. The victims bear the palm of salvation, but not Buckingham, who consequently must perch his ducal coronet on his topknot. Reproduced by permission of the Huntington Library, San Marino, California.

Others made similar comments. They had not seen the like—except, said some, the late Earl of Southampton, another enemy of Buckingham's. They began talking openly of poison. At this point one of the duke's physicians whispered first in Moore's ear, then to other doctors. Several left the scene in silence. Those that remained hedged a little: they did not see how anything but poison could have such an effect, but they could not imagine how any poison so strange could show up in England. Eglisham told them that money could bring the art and the artist into England from the farthest part of the world. The Hamiltons, with much pomp and show of clan solidarity, bore their chief from London to rest with his ancestors in the Hamilton chapel in Scotland. The Duke of Buckingham professed grief at his enemy's death. In case he had not quite squelched talk of poison, he let slip a hint that King James had been highly displeased with the marquess, implying, displeased enough to have him poisoned.

Eglisham spoke of a list, supposedly found in King Street by the daughter of a Hamilton kinsman. This list bore the names of Buckingham's enemies: the late Duke of Richmond, the late Earl of Southampton, the late Marquess of Hamilton, and others. By the names of some was written the word "embawme." Dr. Eglisham's own name, he said, was on the list, and he too had earned an "embawme" by his name. The doctor went into hiding in Europe, publishing his allegations abroad in the form of a petition to parliament and King Charles to bring Buckingham to justice.

Eglisham's pamphlet appeared in 1626. Some English Catholic's correspondence to a priest in Spain describes Buckingham's unpopularity, and mentions "a kind of mad Scottish poet and physician, called George Eglesham, accusing the Duke of having poisoned the late King and various other persons." We possess this little observation because it was intercepted by the English intelligence of the day.

There are tales in Dr. Eglisham's past that we ought to include with his allegations. In 1617 he married Elizabeth Downes in the Bishop of Winchester's jail, the Clink, which has lent its name to numberless jails throughout the English-speaking world. Eglisham and Elizabeth Downes went there to be married by Father Preston, a Catholic priest and prisoner.

This fact surfaced at Mrs. Eglisham's death 13 years later. For some reason, perhaps connected with their only daughter, Dr. Eglisham, now in Brussels, needed proof of his marriage. He had not asked Father Preston for a marriage document for two reasons. First, some noblemen had saved Father Preston on his promising not to exercise any priestly functions, so that any certificate, if discovered, would get them all in trouble. Second, as King James's personal physician, Eglisham was most concerned that his royal master never learn that he had been married by a Catholic priest. To get his certificate, Eglisham wrote to a senior Catholic cleric to seek out Father Preston if possible.

The fact that his letter ended up among the English state papers shows that it was intercepted by the government. Either English intelligence officials were keeping a watch on its Catholic recipient, or they had Eglisham under surveillance in Brussels, or both.

There were also rumors of Eglisham's living with a mountebank and pirate called Captain Herriott. The writer, another Herriott named Andrew, says that they had been counterfeiting double pistoles, a large gold Spanish coin worth about 36 shillings. Andrew commented regretfully that the pair were still unhanged. In fact, Eglisham survived Buckingham by a decade, dying naturally in 1642.

By then with civil war in the air, Londoners were happy enough to beat King Charles with the Buckingham stick. One of them printed a skit in which the shrouded ghosts of Eglisham, Hamilton, and King James meet. An illustration shows each of them bearing a palm signifying salvation. They encounter Buckingham, pointedly portrayed without a palm. They accuse him of poisoning Hamilton and the king. The ghost of Buckingham (what has he to lose?) admits his crime and characteristically announces that now he is going off to weep for grief.[5]

Curing Doctor Lambe (1607–1628)

The duke was also blamed for elevating and protecting an egregious quack whose misdeeds exacerbated the popular hostility toward the favorite, and became a symbol of the corruption of the system. For a while, John Lambe taught English to the children of Welsh gentlemen, but, finding medicine more promising, he bestowed on himself the title of doctor. A Jacobean quack could easily drift into magic and wizardry. There was money in these mysteries. Clients were impatient to know the future: girls who could not wait to see what their future husbands looked like, women who had to know right now whether their husbands would return from the sea, men who wondered whether a commercial venture would prosper. Even questions about the present brought clients: Is there any gold buried in my cellar? Why do my joints ache? And the bread-and-butter parts of the trade: Where have I mislaid my little silver amulet? Is my spouse faithful?

Lambe's knowledge, he kept suggesting, sprang from his easy familiarity with dark and demonic powers. This was part of the showmanship that charlatans in the golden age of drama well understood. They risked prosecution for witchcraft, but were willing to take the chance because suggestions of traffic with the Devil awed and excited clients. Lambe once invited a stranger into his house with the promise of making an angel appear. Midspell, he revealed that there had been a change of billing and the apparition was going to be a demon named Benias—his favorite familiar, he confided. The stranger ran out and spread his tale, just as Lambe had intended. Again, during an eerie storm, when gawking people fancied prophetic scenes in the (probably baroque) clouds, Lambe made sure to be seen on a rooftop gesturing and "causing" it. He trod that narrow wizards' walk between gleaning money from the gullible and being hanged amid their execrations.

The best-certified of physicians did a lot of damage to patients, but they felt clearly superior to quacks, attacked by one doctor in this catalog:

> Thrasonicall and unlettered Chymists, shifting and outcast Pettifoggers, light-headed and triviall Druggers, and Apothecaries, Sun-shunning night birds, and Corner creepers, dull-pated and base Mechanickes, Stage-players, Juglers, Pedlers, prittle-pratling Barbers, curious Bath-keepers, common shifters, and cogging Caveliers, bragging Soldiers, Bankerupt marchants, lazy Clowns, one-eyed or lamed Fencers, toothlesse and tatling old wives, chattering Char-women, and Nurs-keepers, long-tongued Midwives, scape–Tibornes, Dog-leeches, and such like baggage and earth dung.

This is said by the printer to be a translation from a German's Latin treatise, though it must be a rather free translation. What, for example, is the Latin for "scape–Tibornes"? The writer goes on to sort good from bad. Physicians have a grounding in the liberal arts, a library of books that are opened now and then, and a knowledge of anatomy. Quacks have no books, or buy them for show and never open them. Quacks "know not whether Anatomy be a Man or Woman, an Horse, or a Cow. And yet it is as possible for him to be a Phisition, that never knew or sawe Dissection, as for him to be a good Carpenter, that never sawe an House, or a good Marriner, that never set eyes on a Ship, in his Life."[6]

Magicians and the like did not have to get into trouble with the law. They would not offend merely by prognosticating or giving advice on the basis of astrology, as long as they remembered always that it was high treason to prognosticate the death of the sovereign. Statutes and ordinances against jugglers and mountebanks were aimed rather at vagrants than the thriving clinical magician. An earnest astrologer like Simon Forman based his powers rather safely on laborious planetary calculations; his legal problems lay rather with the college of physicians, for selling a medication he invented.

Spells and charms probably succeeded through the unwitting cooperation of suggestible subjects. Lambe's tricks, coming to us only from uncritical witnesses, may have depended on subtle hypnotic suggestion. Once in a knot of men and women in Warwick he pointed out a woman about to cross the street, and told them he would make her hoist her skirts above her waist; and so she did, ignoring the shouts from indignant women. When they asked her why she had been so immodest, she said it was to cross the deep puddle in the street; but in fact the street was dry. To be sure, she might have been a confederate. A book of the time that lays out numerous tricks familiar to London mountebanks tells how to make a boy strip naked against his will, the boy of course being a confederate. On the other hand, Lambe might have had her as a client, and planted such a suggestion. Lambe regularly used a crystal ball, and no doubt got suggestible clients to fill it with visions.

Early in his career, in 1607, after some obscure falling out with Lord Windsor, a boy of 16, he was convicted of witchcraft, using "execrable arts to consume the body and strength" of the young peer. His sentence, which would have been death, was postponed and never pronounced. Lord Windsor could perhaps have had a sickly adolescence, which Lambe may have pretended to cause, just to advertise his black arts. A true prophet would have been amused by all this, knowing that the victim was going to outlive the wizard by 14 years. We do not know who put off Lambe's sentencing. King James I, who took a lively interest in witchcraft cases, may have mitigated the acts of the more zealous prosecutors against such persons as Lambe. Lambe's crystal ball and the accuracy of certain prophecies of death earned him another conviction in Worcestershire. Again his execution was stayed, and he was imprisoned in Worcester castle. Within two weeks, we are told, death came to the sheriff and several jurors including the foreman, and enough other persons connected with the case to make up a round 40. Worcestershire arranged to have its unwelcome guest moved to the King's Bench prison in Southwark.

Prisons placed their inhabitants in comfortable apartments or wet, verminous cells, according to how much the prisoner could keep paying the custodians, purveyors, and officials whose livelihood depended on the system.

In the King's Bench prison, money could buy a great deal. The main building adjoined a complex called the Rules, where affluent prisoners dwelt in comfort. When Lambe arrived here in 1608 he was able to settle into a Rules apartment and employ servants. Most important of all, he could carry on his business, receive clients, and keep making money.

London was the capital of quacks, astrologers, soothsayers, jugglers, and mountebanks. The market was broad, from the very rich and to the steady inflow of fresh maids and bumpkins. Convicted of capital crimes but still unsentenced, Dr. Lambe prospered as he plied his trade in his comfortable prison. He lived suspended in some sort of balance. The influential party who had been able to delay his sentencing apparently found it impolitic to seek an outright pardon for him. Lambe himself may have considered it dangerous to press for a resolution.

Fourteen years passed in this ambiguity, until 1622, when the busy prisoner hooked the biggest client of his career. The Duke of Buckingham and his mother, Lady Compton, called on Lambe for advice about the duke's insane brother. Whatever this advice may have been, the duke continued to consult Lambe, and became his protector as well. This connection was a mixed blessing, for the duke had fallen from popularity, to become easily the most detested man in England. In the eyes of the public he was silly, arrogant, ignorant, corrupt, dangerously incompetent, chief enemy of their liberties and the rule of law, treacherous to every supporter, and a poltroon who had hidden in a boat while his soldiers were slaughtered on the French coast. Historians may no longer credit all of these opinions, but at the time they were widely and vehemently held.

The reach of the mighty duke's protection was soon to appear. On Whitsun Friday in 1623, the busy Lambe had so many errands for his servants that all but one had gone. He sent a message to a maid's house telling her to deliver some herbs to him. She lived near the prison because her dying husband was a debtor there. The only person she could send to Lambe was her daughter of 11, Joan Seager. Lambe entertained the girl for a while by letting her play his virginals (only a small keyboard instrument, but not bad furniture as prisons go). Virginals! Lambe's opportunistic mind was at work. He sent his last remaining servant out on some errand, locked his door, and enticed Joan into his bedroom. As she grew more frightened by the unmistakable character of his kisses, he held her down on a joint stool and raped her. The author, "for modesty's sake," omits further details. Then Lambe sent her home.

At first the daughter said nothing, afraid her mother would beat her, but Lambe's maid Becke arrived with a bowl and according to his instructions "treated" Joan's genitals with its contents. In spite of this treatment, or because of it, a burning pain developed, and one way or another Joan told her mother what had happened. The mother ran to her neighbor, a bricklayer's wife named Mabell Swinnerton, tried to say what had happened, could not, and had Joan sob out her story. Mabell, who did not know Lambe, sought him out and found him tidily folding linens with his servants amidst several clients. In the privacy of Lambe's closet, Mabell gave him a piece of her mind.

"You have undone an honest mans child, for well shee may recover her health of body againe, but never her credit, for it will bee a staine to her reputation whil'st shee lives: so many strumpets in the towne and to seeke the ruine of a poore child."

Inconsequentially, Lambe replied by reverting 15 years to Lord Windsor, telling Mabell, I do more good deeds in a week than Lord Windsor in a year. Mabell was not to be put off.

"This one ill deede hath quite put out the light of all them good deedes."

Just send Joan to me, Lambe suggested, and I will see how she is.

Joan has been with you too long already, observed Mabell.

Lambe offered to have her examined by 12 women "to see if she bee torne."

"Shee is not so much torne, for I will wrong nobody for a thousand pound: but in plaine tearmes you have burnt her, eyther you have a foule body, or you have delt with some uncleane person."

Lambe was tried and found guilty of rape. This was not "statutory rape," as the age of consent was ten. He was then completely pardoned, with the result that he not only went unpunished for the rape but was released from the gentle confinement in which he had spent the past 15 years. He left the prison, where his victim's indebted father lay dying, and set up practice in a house in Westminster. None doubted that the royal pardon was the work of Buckingham. Lambe's practice continued unabated. In 1625 King James died. The change of reign took nothing from the duke's power, for King Charles was just as dependent on the duke, and less suspicious of him than the quirky but canny James was said to have become. As friction grew between crown and parliament in early 1628, popular ballads were sung in the streets of London about Lambe and the duke. Some ballads said that Lambe exercised an evil influence over the duke. That was perhaps bringing coals to Newcastle, but another ballad voiced the rumor that Lambe employed his magical spells to keep supplying chaste women to a supposedly insatiable Buckingham. Political tension was building, headed eventually for civil war. Buckingham was contributing mightily to this tension in 1628, and Lambe's pardon provided a highly visible demonstration of how far the duke could and would subvert justice.

On a Friday in June, Lambe went to see a play at the Fortune playhouse. The performance was, as always, in the afternoon, the theatres needing the daylight. Some apprentice boys in the cheap pit recognized him, and the word spread in the audience. When the play ended, Lambe stepped out of the theatre to face a knot of hostile playgoers. Then began his nightmare journey.

The Fortune stood between Golden Lane and Whitecross Street, its site now remembered as Fortune Street, next the modern Barbican. Between the Fortune and the Windmill Inn in Coleman Street, where Lambe often went for supper, lay a walk of about three quarters of a mile. To escape the spite of the puritanical London government, the Fortune like other theatres was built outside City jurisdiction. About half a mile of Lambe's way, mostly scattered houses and open fields, lay outside the reach of the City constabulary, such as it was. As he walked back to the City the sullen men and apprentices followed him. When Lambe came across some strolling sailors, he hired them on the spot to be his bodyguards. With this convoy he passed through Moorgate into the City, but the crowd did not turn back at the gate.

Accounts of what followed differ. The most circumstantial states that Lambe entered the Windmill, a famous tavern also frequented by Ben Jonson, who used it as a scene in his play, *Every Man in His Humour*. There he had supper. The anxious landlord, after trying to disguise him, put him out to face the waiting crowd. His sailor bodyguard had fled. Lambe tried to frighten the crowd away with threats of his dark powers, and his last recorded words were that he would make them dance naked. The men and boys, grown to a mob, pelted him with cobblestones as he ran down Old Jewry Street. He was stoned and clubbed until at last four constables appeared. A report a few days later says, "Dr. Lambe knocked on the head by the prentices against the Compter."

This was the Poultry compter, a holding jail where the constables were stationed. It certainly looks as if they had put off their appearance until they could no longer pretend ignorance. The mob dispersed, satiated, leaving Lambe speechless on the cobbles. No part of him was unbruised; his skull was crushed; and one eye hung from its socket. He died in the morning

Doctor Lambe meets his end: A mob of apprentices and adults lynch the charlatan outside the Windmill, an inn that both he and Ben Jonson frequented. It would not be surprising if Lambe usually affected gaudy clothing, but this suit might have been the disguise that the landlord of the Windmill gave Lambe to get him out of the inn. Bodleian Library, University of Oxford 4oR21 Art Seld (7).

with his crystal ball in his pocket, and was interred in a new burial ground just outside nearby Bishopsgate. That same day, the king's sister, Queen Elizabeth of Bohemia, was sent a report by her secretary that "Dr. Lambe, of whom her Majesty has heard so much, being at a play at the Fortune, was espied by certain prentices, who fell upon him at his going home, drove him from three several houses where he took shelter and so wounded him with clubs and stones, that he died the next day. The Lord Mayor and Sheriffs have been sharply reprehended and the City may chance to be fined."[7]

The Lambe story reflected so severely on Buckingham and the king that its London printer prudently chose anonymity, placing "Printed in Amsterdam" on the title page of the account. The king was incensed with the City of London for not protecting the protégé of his protégé the Duke of Buckingham. One report says that the king rode in person to London to rescue Lambe, arriving too late.[8] The hesitant constables were imprisoned. Charles demanded from the City a fine of £6,000, which the aldermen were able to bargain down to £1,000, in ways that London had learned over centuries of dealing with its kings. Not one member of the mob was ever apprehended. The king saw the murder as an affront to his minister and himself.

So did one of several ballad-makers commenting on the episode:

> Let George and Charles do what they can,
> The duke shall die like Doctor Lambe.[9]

The ballad-maker's skill at prophecy proved superior to his skill at riming, for within 80 days a man named Felton stood waiting behind a courtier about to greet Buckingham. Felton was counting on the courtier bowing low before the duke, and when he did just that, Felton reached over him and stabbed the duke in the heart. Felton might well have escaped with the help of the populace but for a false rumor that he was an agent of the French king, in public opinion probably the only man worse than Buckingham.[10]

X

Shades and Witches

Wraiths, green men, fairies, and other spirits abounded, seldom getting mortals in trouble with the authorities. Witchcraft on the other hand was dangerous. Its existence was attested by superstition and (thanks to the Bible) religion. The usual actual witch (the kind hauled into court) was some poor woman, steeped in local folklore and persecuted by neighbors with exactly the same lore in their background. Not only did both accusers and accused believe witches existed, but sometimes the accused believed themselves to be witches.

Nor were all witches innocent by modern standards. A witch might vent malevolence by sticking pins in a waxen image, firmly hoping to kill an enemy. What do we think today of a person who attempts murder thinking the unloaded gun was loaded, or the baking soda was arsenic? If we believed spells were potent, we too would attribute our random misfortunes to them, and the mischievous among us would use them as weapons.

A law of 1603 made some distinction between felonious and merely undesirable witchcraft. The *Mirror for Justices*, a guide used by justices of the peace, explains that

> Invocation, Conjuration, consultation, intertainment, employment, feeding, or rewarding any demon or spirit, taking up of dead bodies, or any part thereof, to be imployed in Witchcraft or Charmes, or using any manner Witchcraft, whereby any person shall be: killed, or any part of them wasted or lamed, and also accessaries, is felony without Clergy.

On the other hand, those who used these methods merely to discover buried treasure, to find lost goods, or "to provoke unlawfull love" would get by, once, with a year in prison and standing six hours in the pillory each quarter. A second such offense, however, would be capital.[1]

Public attitudes ranged from credulity to discreet doubt. Questioning witchcraft was a slippery and dangerous slope. To deny its existence altogether might offend King James, an authority on witches whose maturing skepticism was not as widely known among his subjects as his youthfully earnest volume, *Daemonologie*. Denial would also imply either that the Devil does not tempt humans and employ them for his nefarious ends, or (an even more perilous contradiction of scripture) that there is no Devil. Some argued that the Devil does not need witches, and that witches existed in biblical times but no longer. The more cautious, while too prudent to question the existence of witchcraft openly, required higher standards of evidence in specific cases. It was safer, of course, to expose impostures, as Harsnett did Darrell's fake possessions, because there was no need to question "real" witchcraft.

John Cotta, a physician, tried to bring discipline to the consideration of witchcraft, in his lengthy treatise, *The Triall of Witch-Craft*. Man cannot know everything, by the decree of God and nature, but an educated person can learn more than a lazy and ignorant one can, using the same means to investigate witchcraft as he uses to acquire other knowledge. Vulgar superstitions such as scratching, looking for marks, and throwing witches into the water are not valid tests. Water does not reject witches, for if it did, then why should not wine and bread, which are used in the Eucharist, reject witches? He also raises a legal argument, that the water test is an ordeal, a form of trial prohibited by statute ever since the 13th century. Finally, he warns that a confession alone is not sufficient proof of witchcraft. One reason impostors need to be carefully examined is that true witches might pretend to be impostors.[2]

It is mostly the believing writers who tell us that somebody else doubts witchcraft, an assertion safer for them to make than the doubters. One wrote in 1612:

"But as there are many, that remaine yet in doubt, whether there be any Witches, or no, or any such spirits, who offer their service unto them, or rather who by fained service do tyrannize over them: So to answere their doubts, would aske a greater labour, and perhaps more art, then I intend, or happily can shew."[3] Some doubters, he said, grant that witchcraft occurred in biblical times, but argue that it has disappeared, a dangerous opinion that he refutes easily thus: Even if these doubters ignore the example of the Druids (who were all witches), they cannot ignore the experience of the learned judges, who frequently try and condemn witches.

As nearly all witches were women, questioning whether they were capable of witchcraft would cast a skeptical cloud over most of the accusations. These skeptics are dealt with thus:

> Many are in a belief, that this silly sex of women can by no means attaine to that so vile and damned a practise of sorcery, and Witch-craft, in regard of their illiteratenesse and want of learning, which many men have by great learning done, *Adam* by temptation toucht and tasted the deceiving apple, so some high learned and read by the same temptor that deceived him hath bin insnared to contract with the Divel; as for example, in the instancing a few, as *English Bacon of Oxford* .... but how weake women should attain unto it many are incredible of the same, and many too are opposite in their opinion against the same, that... inveterate malice of a woman entirely devoted to her revengefull wrath frequenting desolate and desart places, and giving way unto their wished temptation, may have conversed with that world roaring lion, and convenant and contract upon condition, the like hath in sundry place... ben tried at the Assizes....[4]

Our witches and ministers, unlike King James, show no evidence that they had read the late mediaeval *Malleus Maleficarum*, which has led some to assume that black masses and diabolical sabbaths were central to witchcraft. We do not have to postulate a Protestant witchcraft to suppose that black masses might have become less interesting to a people who had rejected white masses.[5]

The Witches of Northamptonshire (1612)

Even though some believed themselves to be witches, others of course denied guilt to their last breath, for example Agnes Browne and her daughter Joan Vaughan, accused in 1612 of giving cramps to a Northamptonshire gentlewoman, Mrs. Belcher. (In this same year Shakespeare had Prospero inflicting cramps on Caliban.) Some class friction may have started this case. Joan spoke impudently to Mrs. Belcher in a way that "touched the modesty of this Gentlewoman," who slapped Joan down for her insolence. Joan and her mother made threats which Mrs. Belcher scorned. Three or four days later Mrs. Belcher was stricken with painful griping, and she felt strange terrors, crying, "Heere comes Joane Vaughan, away with Joane Vaughan." When Mrs. Belcher's brother, Mr. Avery, came to see her, he suspected witchcraft. He sought a simple and popular cure known to bring instant relief: draw blood from the witches. Joan and Agnes however had established some kind of invisible perimeter around their house, persistently thwarting him until he returned disconsolate to his home. There he came down with the same symptoms as his sister. He persuaded Sir William Saunders to commit Joan and Agnes to jail, where it was possible to scratch them.

Our hedging author writes:

> Which Art, whether it be but superstitiously observed by some, or that experience hath found any power for helpe in this kind of Action by others, I list not to enquire, onely this I understand that many have attempted the practising thereof, how successively I know not. But this Gentleman and his Sister being brought to the gaole where these Witches were detained, having once gotten sight of them, in their fits the Witches being held, by scratching they drew blood of them and were sodainely delivered of their paine.

Their cramps returned as soon as they left Joan and Agnes. The brother and sister painfully mounted their horses and headed home. On the way, a strangely gesticulating man on a black horse met them and cried out prophetically that either they or their horses were going to miscarry immediately. Their horses then dropped dead in the road. Mr. Avery put a positive interpretation on this seeming misfortune, picking himself up off the road and offering thanks to God, because the forces of evil must be weakening if all they could get at was the horses. The brother and sister were troubled no more.

Other information emerged about Agnes, suggesting that she had bewitched a child to death. Children dying of unknown causes were common, and all too readily available as instances of witchcraft. Besides, Agnes and two other local witches had ridden on a sow's back to visit a very old witch, who died before they arrived, but left a message saying they would all meet somewhere else next month. Joan and Agnes were hanged at Northampton on 22 July, 1612, denying guilt to the last.[6]

Whisked Out of Pinner (1592)

The reporter of a case in Pinner notes a class distinction that witches make: "Of wrathful witches this same pa[m]phlet tells/ How most of all on simple folke they worke."[7]

One of these simple folk was Richard Burt, who was walking to his master's barn one day with a mastiff when he startled a large hare. He tried to set the mastiff on it, but the great beast only whimpered and cowed behind

Burt's legs. Burt followed the hare to Mother Atkyns's house. Mother Atkyns was a charity case, but recently, when the squire's maids had been too busy churning butter to give her the milk she wanted, she had made the cream well up out of the churn and run into the drain. Then it was learned that she had made George Coulson's lambs frisk themselves to death. Truly, as the narrator says, "Witches are the most unprofitable creatures in the world." Of course Burt knew all about Mother Atkyns, so he blessed himself and said, "Avant witch!" This, says the author, was the beginning of his difficulties. The next time he met Mother Atkyns, about a month later, Burt, "...giving hir the time of the daye, like a perverse woman, like a perilous waspe, like a pestiferous witch, incensed with hate at the sight of him held downe hir head, not daigning to speake."

The following day Burt went to work in the barn, bringing his dinner of bread, butter, cheese, apple pie, and a bottle of the best beer. At 12 he took up his apple pie, but was interrupted by a black cat shaking and wadding some straw, and a voice that commanded him, "Come and leave thy vittels behind thee and thy knife also."

Still holding his pie, Burt was whisked into the air, over his master's fields, through a pond (where he lost his hat), then over Harrow's steeple into a dark place. Only flames were visible, but he was assailed with howling, filthy stenches, and such a heat that Burt, "minding a pennie hee had in his purse: looked round for an Alehouse where he might spend it."

The voice told Burt that he would be released if he promised to keep his experience secret. Burt refused because he knew his master would ask him where he had been, so he was thrown clear back to Pinner, scorched and coatless, with his tongue so twisted that he could not speak. His master did not recognize him at first, but sent for the parson and the squire. The parson reached into Burt's mouth and freed his tongue to tell his story. They fetched Mother Atkyns and scratched her until they drew blood. This treatment, as expected, cured Burt.

We are not told that she went to trial, but the author's verdict is:

"O rebels towards God: enemies to mankinde: catterpillars of a commonwealth, the fire is too good to consume them."[8]

Mother Sutton's Dip (1613)

Milton Mills, Bedfordshire, relieved Mother Sutton's poverty by making her the community swineherd. For 20 years the villagers had been satisfied with her work. She lived not far from the mill with her daughter Mary, who had three bastard children, including a boy named Henry. Mother Sutton's years had passed quietly. In the fields and barns around Milton Mills a rural calamity would occasionally impoverish a farmer: The beasts would miscarry, or get the staggers, or go into frenzies, but nobody blamed Mother Sutton.

Then one day she fancied some insult from miller Enger, who had always given her food. Mr. Enger's horses were found dead in his stable, some from no apparent cause, some strangled, some with their brains beaten out. Over the next two years, his swine would try to eat each other, even at their feed troughs. Others ran headlong into the mill pond and drowned themselves. Altogether, Enger lost about £200, uninsured.

Later, little Henry started throwing dirt, dung, and stones into the mill pond. An elderly servant of the miller boxed his ears, and he ran home crying to his mother and grandmother. The next day, the old man and a younger servant of Enger's started off for Bedford market with a cart of bagged grain. This was routine for them, marked this time only by a strange black sow that seemed to be stalking them, staying always in the fields, but keeping up with their horses in a quite nonporcine way. A mile short of Bedford, the black sow turned two or three times like a windmill. This feat so unhinged the horses' wits that they bolted, dragging the cart off its wheels and dumping the grain bags along the road. It was some time before the two men caught their horses, put the cart together, and laboriously collected the bags, but at last they sold their grain in Bedford.

The older servant sent his junior back home with the empty cart, keeping the other horse to catch up later, so he could have a quart or two with the lads. His story of the great black sow gave him stardom at the alehouse. On the way back home, the old man was rejoined by the black sow. When he and the sow caught up with the wagon, the horses bolted again and left the wheels behind.

He reported all this to Mr. Enger, who paid no attention, rightly supposing he was drunk. The old man was pretty sure who was behind all this, and a few days later, at his plowing, he told Mother Sutton and Mary what he thought of their pranks. As he stood at his plow, a great beetle or mallet came flying through the air and struck him in the chest so that for a while he was winded and nearly senseless. He was carried back to Enger's house and put to bed, where he spent some time in "grievous perplexity" and strange ecstasies, so distressing that his friends, out of pity, wished he would die.

That night, in the moonshine, Mary entered through his window and sat at the foot of his bed. She had brought her knitting, and sat clicking her needles, stopping now and then to peer into his face. He was terrified but could not move or cry out. She moved up to the side of the bed and, bending over him, told him if he would go to bed with her she would make him well. Then came a miraculous cure. He was able to reject Mary. Instantly he regained his power to move and speak, and scold her for her three bastards and abominable life. Mary and her knitting vanished out the window.

This time he was sober when he reported the latest to his master, but Enger wished to test the matter further. He confronted Mary in the fields that day and accused her of doing mischief in his house. He had a test in mind, to see what would happen when Mary and his old servant were brought together. When she denied any mischief, he tried to get her to go home with him. Not without a constable to make me, she shouted; but after a great struggle Enger and his servants forced her onto a horse and got her to the mill, even though she kept falling off all the way. Enger's experiment worked: Mary touched the old man on the neck and he immediately relapsed, worse than he had been before. This was something of a triumph for Enger, though not for his poor guinea pig of a servant.

After that, Enger's son of seven started shouting "Witch!" at the Sutton women and throwing rocks at them. The other little boy, Henry Sutton, overheard his mother and grandmother talking about the Enger boy, and what they would like to do to him. It was time for the two women to call up their familiars, named Dick and Jude. They gave Dick and Jude nourishment in the way witches do, and set them to tormenting little Enger. The boy fell into a miserable illness, and died after five days of torment. The grieving father, depressed and unsure what to do, was lapsing into lethargy when an old friend dropped by on his way to London. He knew just the procedure for such cases, having often seen it applied in the north country. It was a double test, and if a woman failed both, he said, "you may build upon it, that she is a Witch."

The next day Enger and several servants seized Mary in the fields again to bring her in for the tests. This was not easy. All the servants were stricken lame when they tried to bind her on horse back, but Enger, "taking courage and desiring God to bee his assistance," saved the day by beating her with a cudgel until she could hardly move. The servants suddenly recovered and carried her to the test. Enger closed his mill gates to raise the level of his pond. Mary's arms were tied in crossed position, and she was thrown into

Witches Apprehended, Examined and Executed, for notable villanies by them committed both by Land and Water.

With a strange and most true triall how to know whether a woman be a Witch or not.

Printed at London for *Edward Marchant*, and are to be sold at his shop ouer against the Crosse in Pauls Church-yard. 1613.

Mother Sutton's familiar, an agile black sow, sabotages Mr. Enger's grain wagon in the background. In the foreground, Mother Sutton and her daughter are failing their "strange and most true" test by floating on Mr. Enger's mill pond. The swimming dogs might be other familiars. Reproduced by permission of the Huntington Library, San Marino, California.

the pond. After an initial ducking she rose to the surface and floated. She had failed the first test. The servants fished her out. Some of the women inspected her and found a devil's mark on her left thigh. After that discovery, nasty little Henry told everybody that the mark showed where his mother fed various spirits shaped like cats and moles. It was clearly time for the second test. Mary's thumbs were bound crosswise to her toes. A long rope was tied about her waist so that servants holding the ends on shore could rescue her from drowning just in case she passed the test and sank. When she was thrown in again, she floated on an eddy, turning around and around. Just to be sure, the servants bounced the rope to sink her, but still she floated. She had failed again. Back on land, she still denied all accusations, but when Enger told her of Henry's testimony about overhearing her and her mother plotting revenge, she concluded that the Devil had deserted her, leaving her as it were stuck with the bill. She confessed, implicating her mother, who also confessed. Mother Sutton and Mary were tried at Bedford assizes on Monday, 30 March, 1613, and hanged the next day.[9]

The Devil Wags His Tail (1621)

The case of Elizabeth Sawyer began in a small way in Edmonton on a spring wash day in 1621, when Agnes Ratcleife laid down a bit of laundry soap beside her and Elizabeth's sow ate it. Agnes gave the sow a smack with her laundry beetle. It ran off, and Elizabeth told Agnes, You'll pay. That evening, at home with her husband, Agnes suddenly "fell very sicke, and was extraordinarily vexed, and in a most strange manner in her sicknesse was tormented." After four days of foaming at the mouth, she died. Agnes's solemn dying oath was that, if death came to her, it would have been Elizabeth Sawyer who caused it.

This was the last straw for the locals. Their cattle had been dying, and two infants put out to nurse had died. Elizabeth was the only likely suspect. To confirm their suspicions, they resorted to a well-known test, which was to tear a wisp of thatch from Elizabeth's roof, take it somewhere else, and burn it. If the inhabitant showed up there, she was guilty. Yes, Elizabeth showed up. The justice of the peace, Arthur Robinson, was above such superstitions. He gave no heed to this rustic experiment, but he was impressed by other *prima facie* evidence: Her face was pale and bloodless, and always looking down. Her body was crooked, having recently bent nearly double. Finally, she had a runaway tongue that kept cursing and blaspheming. When she was arrested, she called on the Devil to deliver her, but that wily one had fled, "leaving her to shift and answere for herselfe."

She was taken for trial before Heneage Finch, the recorder of London, and a jury in the Old Bailey. Agnes' dying words were presented in evidence by her husband. The defendant kept on swearing, but now she was cursing herself. The London jurymen retired for deliberation, but after a time they came back. They were uneasy and did not trust their own judgment; what should they do?

"Doe in it," replied the recorder helpfully, "as God shall put in your hearts."

Robinson, sitting on the bench with the recorder, was unwilling to take this risk. In his earlier investigations he had heard that she bore a private and strange mark (just as King James had written). At his suggestion the court appointed as inspector Margaret Weaver, a widow who worked in the Old Bailey, assisted by two grave-looking matrons hooked in at random off the street. Elizabeth did not take to them at all, but "Nicenesse they laid aside," and finished their work by force. They found the mark. After this, the hesitant jury convicted Elizabeth of witchcraft in Agnes's death, though they acquitted her of the deaths of any cattle or nursing infants. She was sentenced on Saturday, 14 April, 1621, to hang at Tyburn the following Thursday.

The Newgate minister, Henry Goodcole, interviewed Elizabeth on the Tuesday, and coaxed out her story. The Devil had first come to her eight years before, during one of her famous tantrums. He had said, "Oh! have I now found you cursing, swearing, and blaspheming? now you are mine." He told her not to be afraid, and if she wanted him to vex anybody to death, he would do it.

How? she asked. By pinching and scratching, he explained. Whenever he came to Elizabeth to say he was ready to do her bidding, he spoke like a person. When he reported back, usually in a week, he would bark. As a matter of fact, he always appeared as a dog, sometimes white, sometimes black. Goodcole asked her about her victims.

"I have bene by the helpe of the Divell, the meanes of many Christians and beasts death, the cause that moved mee to do it, was malice and envy, for if any body had angered me in any manner, I would be so revenged of them, and of their cattell. And do now further confesse, that I was the cause of those two nursechildren's death, for the which I was now indited and acquitted, by the Jury."

And Agnes Ratcleif?

"No, I did not by any meanes procure against her the least hurt."

Elizabeth's relations with the Devil over eight years had not been smooth. During his visits, he would suck her blood for about 15 minutes at a time. She once asked him why he did this, and got the prosaic answer that he needed the nourishment. Initially he let her select the part of her body that he would thereafter use: the upper inner thigh. Over the years he had left the mark that the matrons had found. There was never any pain involved. Answering the curious Mr. Goodcole, she said she never had to raise her clothing to accommodate the Devil. Difficulties arose when the dog (white or black) would occasionally discover her praying to God, and that would anger him. He taught her a little gibberish prayer to himself, "*santibiciter nomen tuum.*" No, she knew no Latin and did not know what the prayer meant. Nobody had taught her the words but the Devil. He would sometimes ask her if she had been praying to him. She would say, "Sometimes I did, sometimes I did not," and this annoyed the Devil, who warned her not to mock him. But the Devil did like to be petted, and then he would wag his tail.

Why did you lie to the court about all this?

"I did it thereby hoping to avoyd shame."

And this is true now?

"Yes, it is all truth, as I shall make answer unto almighty God."

And nobody has promised you your life to say it?

"No: I doe it to cleere my conscience, and now having done it, I am more quiet, and the better prepared, and willing thereby to suffer death, for I have no hope at all of my life, although I must confesse, I would live longer if I might."

Henry Goodcole tells his readers that he published this account only to buy himself some peace from those who were pressing him to tell his version. Ballad mongers had been selling a lot of nonsense about Elizabeth Sawyer, saying she had bewitched corn on the ground, and was attended daily by a ferret and an owl sporting before her, and had spirits visit her in prison. One ballad even had her bewitching Agnes into braining herself. The tabloid press has a long history. Goodcole would rather have kept silence, he said, because of the diversity of opinion on the whole subject of witchcraft, not only among the ignorant but among the learned.

"It is none of my intent here to discusse, or dispute of Witches or Witchcraft, but desire most therein to be dispensed withall."

What would Goodcole have written if the legal establishment did not govern his pen? This minister seems to have had fewer career options than the average cleric. At the age of 20, he had had to marry to give legitimacy to his expected child. This problem probably narrowed his prospects in church circles, already limited because he had not gone to university and had no church preferment. Being allowed by the Bishop of London to minister to the condemned of Newgate (and peddle pamphlets about them) was a lifesaver that he was not about to jeopardize.

The playwright Thomas Dekker was less inhibited. About 1623, he wrote a play called *The Witch of Edmonton*. Despite the title, the witch is not the main character. Dekker's Elizabeth Sawyer is an old woman persecuted by her neighbors until at last she calls on the Devil for revenge. She decided to become a witch because people were treating her like one. Dekker and the hesitant Old Bailey jurors show that credulity, though great, was not uniform nor universal.[10]

Lads Will Be Lads (1643)

Even as they neared the battlefield of Newbury, the roundhead troops of the Earl of Essex found time to forage for apples, plums, nuts, and berries in the woods, and to have a little horseplay. They started chasing each other, and in "waggish merriment" one of them scrambled up a tree. Looking down on the River Kennet, he saw something he had never seen before: a tall, slender woman skating on a board upon the surface of the river. The sight sent a chill through him. He called others up the tree to see her, and a couple of officers joined them. The woman was turning and winding, apparently for fun. At last she gave up her sport and landed near the soldiers, giving her board a kick that sent it across the river.

Bring her here, ordered the officers. Some of the soldiers were afraid, but others seized her by the arms and asked who she was. She would not speak. Our author said the soldiers and officers did not know what to do with her, "being it so apparently appeared she was a *Witch*." Because of this apparent appearance, the men did not feel free to loose her upon mankind. On the other hand, they were after all in an army, and felt awkward dragging a witch with them as they went to fight King Charles.

Let's shoot her then. A few of the best shots aimed carefully and fired. The woman caught the bullets in her hands and laughed. As proof of witchcraft, this was even better than the surfboard. They conferred and recalled that, if you cut the veins that cross the temples of the head, you can prevail against the strongest sorceress. When the woman heard this, she knew the Devil had deserted her. Crying, roaring, and tearing her hair, she made a valedictory prophecy:

"His Excellency the Earle of Essex shall be fortunate and win the field."

She would say no more. This time, a pistol shot under the ear worked as God meant it to do, and the army left her body behind as they went off to fulfill her prophecy and beat the King.[11]

XI

From Religion to Disaster

Many Catholic priests were executed at Tyburn, and today, on the Bayswater Road across from the site, a chapel preserves their memory. The attempt of a few Catholics in 1605 to blow up the king and parliament with gunpowder gave Protestant hostility a very long lease. The age witnessed not only this long struggle, but puritanical strains within the Church of England, and the appearance of splinter groups of excited amateurs democratically challenging the contemptuous experts. A minister said of his compatriots:

> It is like inough, that other Lands may match us, with sinnefull actions: but I thinke this Land can hardly find her match, for manyfolde and schismaticall opinions, some about discipline, some about doctrine, some about matter of faith, some about right adoration, whereof all may carrie some glosse, but most corrupt the text.... Saint Paul forewarned that which he foresaw, the easie and ready embracing of novelties, in wavering minds, & unstable heads, to the disturbance of the peace of the Church.[1]

Catholics versus Protestants

Doctrine at the Half Moon (1607)

On a January Sunday, 1607, 14 months after Catholic gunpowder had been safely hauled out of the cellars of parliament, Humphrey Lloyd and Thomas Morris were drinking wine in the Half Moon in Aldersgate Street, and having a religious discussion. Thomas, an off-duty yeoman of the guard, called Humphrey a dissembler and a Catholic. They called each other liars. Humphrey threw a cup of wine in Thomas's face. Thomas threw a bread roll at Humphrey. Friends separated them, and they made up by drinking to each other. After drinking to each other several more times, they started again. Thomas threatened "to bee even with Lloyd's bald pate." Humphrey said he "would try acquittance with the others Codsheade." The friends separated them and got them out of the Half Moon.

The next Wednesday their paths happened to cross in front of Lincoln's Inn. There was a sort of challenge to a duel, but they quarreled even over how to do that, and Humphrey ran his sword through Thomas, giving the corpse a few slashes for good measure.

At his trial, Humphrey Lloyd was found to have been implicated in the harebrained plot of a priest, William Watson, in 1603, to kidnap the king and force him to grant tolerance to all Catholics. Lloyd, a small fish, had been given a royal pardon. He did not get a second chance, and rode in one of the carts from the Old Bailey to Tyburn gallows. It was customary for these carts and their woeful cargo to halt at Saint Sepulchre, Newgate, for a prayer by its Protestant parson. Lloyd made his position clear by stopping his ears.[2]

A Happy Conversion (1618)

By his fourth visit to London, Francis Robinson felt he understood business in the big city. He stayed at the Swan by Charing Cross because it was near Whitehall Palace, where he was petitioning the council for a document to be issued under the great seal of England. This was a rather routine certificate empowering him to enforce a recent statute regulating victuallers, maltsters, and usurers, and before long he had it in hand.

In the meantime, he had met somebody named Morgan, also staying at the Swan. Morgan revealed that he was a Catholic. Robinson revealed that he had plans to make a lot of money. Together they moved out of the Swan to the Maidenhead Inn in the squalid neighboring parish of St. Giles. Robinson, who had just a country gentleman's smattering of law, made up a bogus "royal commission" requiring various merchants to hand over certain sums of money to him for delivery to some prestigious courtiers whom he listed. He had a scrivener write it up properly, and using his genuine great seal as a model he affixed a counterfeit seal to his forgery. This highhanded way of levying exactions would have raised eyebrows among the merchants affected. Later, when the king tried to raise large sums by similar means, he caused a huge constitutional uproar. Robinson's idea of a lot of money was not royal. In the course of the next month his scheme raised £28 5d.

Word of these levies soon got around, and Robinson was investigated by "spies"—now we would call them detectives. When a warrant was issued for his arrest, Robinson took fright and fled as far as Derby, but decided to return and defend himself, still denying everything. He was confident that as long as his forged commission lay hidden in a locked chest, there was not evidence enough to convict him. Somehow one of the detectives found the trunk and key, delivered (says Goodcole) by divine providence, or perhaps by friend Morgan to save himself. With this, Robinson and his defense crumpled. If only he had altered the text of his genuine sealed document, he would have been merely hanged as a forger. Unfortunately, faking the great seal was high treason, and the sentence included not only hanging but having one's bowels and private parts burnt before one's eyes, after which one's quarters and head were displayed at five locations. Sometimes this sentence was carried out in its full fury; at other times the hangman would let the culprit die of hanging before completing the sentence. We cannot be sure which way Francis Robinson died that Friday the 13th, 1618, only that in an unusual gesture he left legacies to the lord chief justice, who tried him, and to the attorney general. Goodcole does not trouble to tell us this detail because his interest lay on a different plane, the "Happy Conversion" of Robinson away from the Catholicism into which Morgan had enticed him.

Goodcole dedicated this pamphlet to the lord chief justice. Legacies and a dedication had made Friday the 13th a lucky day for the justice and attorney general, and apparently a happy conversion had made it a lucky day for Goodcole and (according to Goodcole) for Robinson.[3]

Newgate Protestants on Strike (1642)

The religious conflict must have reached deeply into men's minds, judging by a small incident in 1642, when Newgate prison was crowded with over 300 prisoners. These included seven Jesuits condemned to death, along with the usual contingent of persons awaiting execution for various crimes. The king reprieved the seven Jesuits:

"Wherupon did arise a tumultuous mutiny among the other Prisoners, who refused to dy without the Jesuits: but afterwards they were mitigated in a pacified tranquillity." The government achieved this tranquillity by hanging one token priest. Just how prisoners might have refused to die in this strike is not explained.[4]

Protestants versus Protestants

How Windows Lie (1631)

The sexton's wife, who did the dusting and cleaning in St. Edmund's Church, Salisbury, was well acquainted with the elderly man with the long staff. He was Henry Sherfield, the recorder of Salisbury and head of the church vestry.

"Woman, bring the Keys of the Church-Door, and let me into the Church," he told her. Once inside, he said, "Now Woman go about your business while I walk in the Church."

Instead, she watched him through the crack in the double door. In the twilight, he balanced himself on the back of a pew just under the south window. He stabbed at the medieval stained glass with his staff several times, breaking parts of it. Then he lost his balance and fell. She could not see him any more, but heard him groan. In a half hour she saw him limp painfully out of the church and hire a horse to take him home. The recorder was laid up for about a month.

It was no secret who had broken the window. A sympathizer threw a pitchfork through what was left of it. The growing aggressiveness of Puritans made the government sensitive to such acts. Sherfield was haled before the Star Chamber, a court in Westminster that dealt with potentially political matters touching the king's interest. Its power stemmed solely from the royal prerogative, and it was not conducted according to the common law. Much of its work was prosaic and even sensible, though it was fast becoming a symbol of tyranny. Its sessions were closed. There was no jury, and the judges were high royal officials. The prosecutor was the attorney general. Oddly, the Star Chamber allowed an attorney to defend Sherfield, which the common law courts would not have done in a criminal case. He was charged with breaking the church window, contrary to church government as established by the law, because he ought to have asked permission of the Bishop of Salisbury. Sherfield was not a Puritan at all, but a local pillar of the established church. The south window had been offending him for years. Some anonymous glazier had made it in the 13th century, to depict the biblical story of the creation.

Sherfield, a lawyer, saw a great deal that was wrong in the stained glass illustrations. The craftsman had mixed up the order of days of creation, so that the fourth came before the third, and the sixth before the fifth. Each day had a depiction of God the Father, making a total of seven. There are not seven Gods, but one. The artist had got Eve all wrong, showing her rising from Adam, when the fact was that she had been fashioned from a rib extracted from Adam. Sherfield did not think that God should be shown as "a little old Man in a blue and red Coat." God was even barefoot. He was shown using compasses to create the sun and moon, "as if he had done it according to some Geometrical Rules." Most offensive was the portrayal of God the Father in any form. Sherfield had come across a woman kneeling before the window; when he asked her why, she said she was kneeling before God. This window had been breeding idolatry.

There was little factual dispute at the trial. The prosecutor said that Sherfield had ignored a specific prohibition by the Bishop of Salisbury, but he could not find the prohibition. The defense lawyer said that Sherfield had permission from the vestry to destroy the window. The justices said that that was just like vestries, always going beyond their authority. In the end, the judges concluded that Sherfield should have asked the bishop's permission before breaking the window. The most severe recommendation, voted by some of the judges, was to deprive Sherfield of his recordership, fine him £1,000, and make him apologize publicly to the bishop. The least severe votes were to make him apologize privately before the bishop and any persons the bishop wished to invite. The actual sentence was that Sherfield retain his recordership, make a private apology and pay a fine of £500, with committment to the Fleet prison, presumably until the fine was paid.[5] The issue, even the concept, of vandalizing an antiquity or work of art never arose.

Not Conforming (1634)

To be safe from the Welsh, Shrewsbury huddles in a loop of the Severn. Eastward the English Bridge connected with fellow Saxons. Westward frowned the Welsh Bridge, its fortifications a monument to ancient fears and fights. All about are pre–English names, some of them even pre–Celtic. The ancient names included the sheltering river itself, towns like Clun, and families like ap Evan. A jingle claims that

> Clunton and Clunbury,
> Clungenford and Clun,

XI. From Religion to Disaster

> Are the quietest places
> Under the sun.

Outwardly, this was as true in the summer of 1633 as when A. E. Housman wrote it two and a half centuries later. The ap Evans family were industrious farmers, neither rich nor poor, though said to be the best off in Clun. They could read English but not Latin, and led quiet lives. Edward and Joan had married off five daughters and were living with their two unmarried sons, Enoch, 34, and John, 31. They had brought up their children piously, conducting prayers and Bible readings twice a day.

Enoch's brother was tall, affable, and content with the world as he found it. Enoch was dark, and stocky. He was serious, rather courteous than hostile, but moody and intense. His untrained but enquiring mind led him into energetic religious investigations. For the past two years he had been riding three or four miles to hear weekday sermons. In those days of religious ferment he would have picked up ideas from Puritans and various other sects. Those were the sort who were wont to hold weekday sermons, a practice that mainstream Anglicans like our author tended to regard as somewhat more curious and zealous than was really necessary or proper.

Whatever he learned from these sermons, Enoch held stubbornly to beliefs once he had admitted them into his private system. These beliefs included the undesirability of bishops, of making the sign of the cross at baptisms, and of kneeling. Whether he formed these ideas on his own, or received them from nonconformist preachers, was to become a matter of heated debate. He revealed a smattering of knowledge about predestination that he could only have acquired from others. On the other hand, his reason for standing instead of kneeling for communion sounds truly homegrown and mechanical, suiting a person who in his everyday life dealt with concrete things rather than abstractions. He said that the sanctity radiated by the host at communion reached the entire body of a standing person, but, you see, if you are kneeling, your legs from the knees down are in the spiritual shade, as it were, and miss out. On other occasions that called for kneeling, he preferred to sit and bow. It would appear that Enoch insisted on standing in the parish church of Clun. It is not clear how this eccentricity was treated by the old parson, Erasmus Powell, who had baptized both brothers more than three decades before. The rest of Enoch's family all knelt. Enoch gave undivided attention to the services, but when he disagreed with something he would frown, squirm, and stamp his feet.

These religious questions were discussed earnestly at the family table.

Joan, the mother, described as a strong character, was especially adamant, warning her son sternly that "the end of all these things would be nought." Brother John would take her side. On Sunday, the last day of June, their discussions grew more rancorous than usual. The brothers had never quarrelled in their lives. They even kept their money in a single chest without a dispute over amounts. This Sunday, for the first time, it occurred to Enoch that he might have to kill, not his mother who was calling him a "sorry fellow," but his wrongheaded brother.

Yet, for a few days, sunnier thoughts came to the fore. Thursday, 4 July, was market day at Knighton, three miles away. Enoch enjoyed a social quart now and then, and today he had one with a young woman, variously described as his wench and his betrothed. She agreed to meet him at about one o'clock in the morning in a room at an alehouse a mile from his home—to work on their marriage plans, Enoch was later to tell the clergyman who is his biographer. Enoch returned home from Knighton "very jocund and merry." The brothers, who had slept together from infancy, turned in at dark, about ten. John of course noticed Enoch's sleepless tossing and turning, waiting for one o'clock and bliss. John asked if Enoch would like company on the dark way to the alehouse, and Enoch invited him along. When they reached the alehouse and Enoch asked for the girl, the landlord told him no one of that name was there. Enoch had been stood up. His high spirits plummeted as he composed negative fancies of the girl rejecting him and being unfaithful. After some dithering, the brothers returned home at about four. By then the sun was rising, so they yoked their oxen and headed for the fields.

John had a habit of going into the house for an hour's nap during the day, lying on the great dining table with a cushion. This Friday, Enoch entered quietly with a large, sharp hatchet and aimed a blow at John's head. In an agony of internal conflict, Enoch hesitated midway, and only wounded John. The sudden horror that had held back his arm now drove it forward; he had to finish what he had started. With one sweep of the great hatchet he cut off John's head. Just then his mother came in from the next room to investigate the strange sounds, and Enoch swung his hatchet at her as well. This formidable woman of 72 said something like "Thou villain, what hast thou done?" though Enoch could not recollect her exact words. After some struggle Enoch was able to do what he had not planned, hack off his mother's head too, just inside the front door.

After bolting the doors, he put the two heads in a linen bag, soaking it in water, and tying it up neatly in an old russet jerkin so no blood would be noticed. He changed out of his bloody clothing. Then, instead of using the usual exits, he knocked a hole in the daub wall of the house and carried his wet bag of heads off to the fields. He had a vague hope of making people think that thieves had broken in. Outside, he hid his bundle under a pile of dried ferns kept for tinder, and walked on to see his cousin Howell. The cousin was out, and while Enoch waited for him he took out his Bible and read the first chapter of Isaiah. When the cousin came, Enoch borrowed his *Practice of Piety*. Leaving the Howells, Enoch came face to face with two of the maids from his house, at the head of the citizenry of Clun.

Enoch had deceived nobody. He was arrested and taken before the justice of the peace, Sir Robert Howard. At first Enoch denied everything, but eventually he confessed to Erasmus Powell. Sir Robert commited him to Shrewsbury jail to await trial. The constable and several citizens led him on the journey to Shrewsbury. When they passed his own home, he was allowed to say good-bye to his father. Some say his father refused to see him, others say he met him at the door.

His eldest sister did go to Enoch with tears running down her face, and asked, "Ah, brother Enoch, what moved you to take away the life of our deare mother and brother?"

Some said he made no reply, but her husband insisted that he said, "Peace foole, hold thy tongue, wee live in a false Church, and thou shalt see a change shortly."

Sundown caught the escort five miles short of Shrewsbury, so they stopped at Thomas Turner's alehouse in Powlderbach. The prisoner and his escort all sat down to a good dinner. Enoch was asked to say grace, "as most versed in matters of Devotion." After dinner they all settled down to a friendly chat by the social summer fire. The scene was so peaceful that only a waiter thought it necessary to be alert. It was he who noticed Enoch's face begin to cloud with anger, and who caught Enoch glancing at the long sharp spit that a maid had left by the fireplace. He was ready when Enoch lunged for the spit. After Enoch had been subdued, the constable decided it was bedtime. Enoch was sent up to his bed. A few of the escort stood guard downstairs, while the village of Powlderbach posted its own watch of three men in the street. For two hours quiet lay over the dark village. Then a great rumbling and rattling seemed to come down the dark street, like a heavy wagon. It frightened the watch and guards, but nobody could see anything. Enoch heard it too, and was so panicked that he threw off his shirt and ran naked down the stairs crying "O they murder me, they murder me, they murder me."

Protestants versus Protestants

Enoch ap Evan exits his dining room with the heads of his more orthodox mother and brother and is next seen gibbeted beside his front door. Bodleian Library, University of Oxford. Wood 365 (7).

The constable and his escort agreed that the stopover at Powlderbach was not bringing them the rest they had sought, so they pinioned Enoch's arms, put him back on his horse, and continued to Shrewsbury. Several times on the way they had to pause to retie the pinion, and rather than admit that they were not very good at knots they blamed some ghostly intervention, somehow related to the mysterious rumbling. It had been on the whole a supernatural day or two, for a black horse had ambled into the ap Evan house after the murders. Some clods said it was a neighbor's horse, but others said it was the Devil, reviewing his handiwork. At last the constable reached Shrewsbury, and was much relieved to hand Enoch over to the keeper of the jail, who loaded him with irons and lodged him in the common pen with the usual drunks, thieves, and debtors.

When the news spread through Shropshire and the diocese of Hereford, the growing religious division of the country was lit as if by lightning. The case of ap Evan became a shibboleth distinguishing the conventional Anglicans from the more puritanical Anglicans and radical nonconformists. The Reverend Peter Studley, a familiar champion of the established church in Shrewsbury, seized upon the case, spending many hours interviewing Enoch. In a long polemical work Studley hammered home his message:

See where nonconformity can take you. See the evil that separatists and Brownists can bring. See what happens when ignorant chandlers, tinkers, and housewives try to interpret and preach the Bible. Enoch ap Evan was misled and perverted by zealots to the destruction of himself and his family, and the hazard of his soul. The murders show what can happen when people go off into sects and set themselves up to question the authority of learned theologians. The dangers of heterodoxy are manifest. Remember the mason in Tewkesbury who converted part of a stone crucifix to a hog trough? His children became shapeless idiots, but still he did not repent, until the hogs went mad and died. Also, remember that nonconformist schoolmaster here in Shropshire, who castrated himself in broad daylight in his school.

Not so, argued others. Studley is taking liberties with the facts. Enoch alone dreamed up whatever fuzzy beliefs he holds. His deeds have nothing to do with any Puritan or independent theology. He is so unstable that once he had a fit of terror while he was drinking with a scrivener, just because he had never seen red ink before. Parishioners had heard Enoch tell his mother that a voice had called to him in church, saying, "Enoch, prepare." (She had told him, "Hold thy peace thou foole, I heard no such voyce, nor thou neither.") He was also afflicted with melancholy, so severely, it was said, that he had to be bled for it. A fourth proof of Enoch's distraction appeared when he was seen bathing naked in a stream.

Enoch was said to be a Brownist or separatist. Since this group evolved into what we know today as Congregationalists, it is well to remember that, in the early days, the details of their beliefs were in considerable flux, and, the sect being so democratic, its members' beliefs could vary from place to place. One or two of the earliest of them had been hanged for denying the royal supremacy in religion. There was an important level of society that could read English and not Latin or Greek. They tended to be yeomen and artisans, who read the English Bible and shunned the subtleties and speculations of the Latin and Greek fathers and scholastics. It was heady work to go back and discover the naked truths that had been obfuscated by the centuries of monkish glossing and superstition. For a time independents were treated with some mildness under Archbishop Whitgift, but now under Archbishop Laud toleration was at an end. Studley, who wrote up the case, was following the party line. The argument of the Laudians was that Enoch was sane but so ignorant that he was easily corrupted by unorthodox and zealous preachers. The argument of Puritans and independents was that Enoch was insane and quite on his own. If he had been a more sympathetic character, we might feel a little sorry for him. Persons on both sides of the debate pestered him in prison for statements that would help them prove either that he was an exploited dolt or that he was crazy.

Enoch never shed a tear in prison. One day when the hangman was visiting the prison, the five prisoners who were scheduled to meet him later were making remarks about him. Enoch said if he could kill the hangman he would be killing death. The minister got wind of this remark and told him it did not betoken a very Christian attitude. Enoch said he was just making a joke, and the minister said the same thing about making jokes. Enoch had his hair trimmed the day before he appeared for trial. Studley scolded him for this vanity (Studley, remember, was the non–Puritan), and told him it would have been more honest to go as a wild man.

On a lowering August day, Enoch was put on a horse to ride the 13 miles back home to Clun and the gallows that had been set up for him. He paused at a familiar inn in Bishop's Castle to take the sacrament. For a while the attending minister would not administer it because he refused to kneel. At last Enoch gave in, and the party proceeded on its way. The summer skies blackened. Enoch was hanged in a violent thunderstorm amid the shrieks of his sisters.

176   XI. From Religion to Disaster

The rest of his sentence was to hang in chains, a practice that, long after its disappearance, Housman's Shropshire lads were still calling "hanging sheep by moonlight." The judge, following custom, directed that Enoch's body be taken from the gallows and hung up in an iron frame at the scene of the crime, which in this case was his front door. The crime scene was also the home of the surviving members of the ap Evans family. The judge relented in response to a petition from the father and sisters, who had committed no crime and would after all be using the front door. Enoch and his iron frame were carted instead to the edge of the town of Welshpool, 70 yards from the nearest road, considerately placed so that the sister who traveled it daily could more easily look the other way as she passed.

Although public opinion had little outlet, local and family loyalties could be expressed in quiet ways. After 14 warm August days, some anonymous locals, armed with strong-smelling herbs and a metal file, gave Enoch's corpse a secret burial.[6]

Schism on the Ladder (1609)

The authorities did not suspect religious heterodoxy when they arrested Edward Wilson and Robert Tetherton for murdering a servant maid, Joan Wilson, in the course of a robbery in Sir Jerome Bowes's house next to Whitehall Palace. Their story is simple. They were betrayed by some gold buttons they had stolen there, and were captured in Chester awaiting a favorable wind to Ireland. Edward Wilson, once a servant of Bowes, knew the house and the maid. He completed the case against himself by writing to an unsympathetic relative requesting a perjured alibi. They were hanged in 1606 at Charing Cross, in sight of Sir Jerome's house.

The minister did not realize until the execution that Wilson was a Brownist. The execution ritual included at least one prayer at the ladder, in which the condemned and the crowd all joined. It also included all present saying the Lord's Prayer. Wilson refused to participate, and insisted on saying a silent prayer alone. To the minister this was clear evidence of Brownist beliefs. He did not link the sect to the crime, but the episode at Charing Cross stirred him to the editorial comment above, on English heterodoxy.

To tell this plain story, the author made allusions to over a score of classical writers and mythical characters, including Agrippina, Alectos, Cicero, Cleonice, Herodotus, Horace, Julius Caesar, Lalius, Leonidas,

Megera, Nero, Pausanias, Pindar, Plato, Prometheus, Romulus, Scipio, Tesiphon, Titius, Virgil, and Xenophon. The church fathers Augustine and Chrysostom also helped him with his case, and from the Bible he drew the enlightening examples of Abel, Abraham, Adam, Cain, David, Eve, Isaiah, Job, Jonah, Jude, Naaman, Nahum, Paul, Pilate, Rebeccah, Stan, Solomon, and Uriah. This, like many gallows accounts, was a sermon.[7]

An Anabaptist Drunk (1643)

Even the most tenuous connection between a culprit's crime and his heterodoxy could make it the target for a sermon. Two recently converted Anabaptists went drinking with a solicitor one day in London. One does not connect modern Baptists with getting drunk, but these were Anabaptists, and one of them, John Faulkner, made his living as a "strongwater man," selling spirits. The other, a salter named Francis Deane, had a wealthy sister in law, a widow whose affairs were being handled by a solicitor named Daniel. Finding either the widow or her money attractive, the solicitor had proposed marriage to her. On a January day, Daniel and Deane, accompanied by Faulkner, discussed the proposal over their drinks. Deane did not like it because he had a better bid from a gentleman in Watford who was worth £2,000 a year. As the drinking progressed, the discussion became a quarrel. By about eight or nine that night the solicitor was saying that if he did not marry the widow he would see to it that they ended up without a groat. In Elbow Lane, Deane somehow got a poleax and killed Daniel with it. He was arrested a little later, along with Faulkner, who had most foolishly made himself an accessory after the fact by hiding Deane and suggesting he flee to the king's forces in Oxford. They were hanged at Tyburn on 17 April, 1643.

The author appends to this quite secular case an Anabaptist sermon, titled "Wash and Be Cleane," setting out the basic beliefs of the sect. The sermon likens London's Bow and Hackney rivers to the Jordan, and argues that people should have only nicknames until they are adults. To the author, these are amusing demonstrations of the fringe character of the sect, and somehow relevant to the crime.[8]

XII

Conclusion

> My friend, judge not me,
> Thou seest I judge not thee.
> Betwixt the stirrup and the ground
> Mercy I asked, mercy I found.
> —William Camden (1551–1623), *Epitaph for a Man Killed by Falling from His Horse.*

The Christian doctrine expressed in this equestrian's epitaph also entered the hanging ceremony, even if its origins are lost deep in pagan centuries. Changing "stirrup" to "ladder" would make it a fit epitaph for many of those in this book. A pirate at Execution Dock was probably not minting a new simile when he likened his ladder to Jacob's ladder to heaven. Of course clerics would tend to exaggerate the religious features of executions, but their evidence cannot be discarded solely on the anachronistic 18th-century analogy of festive executions and gleeful mobs. Those were the great-grandchildren or great-great-grandchildren of our spectators.[1] Times change.

Great events tell us to end here. Civil war, the beheading of a king, and the downfall of lords and bishops were about to work their transformations. When these institutions reappeared after 1660, they were altered. Soon after came the great plague and, for London, the great fire.

Threads

Certain threads weave through these accounts. One was fecklessness, reflecting a certain innocence. An ax murderer is invited to say grace over supper with his guards, and lounge by the fire, near the poker. Murderers chat about their guilty knowledge and then are surprised to be arrested. One tears up his bloody kerchief in front of witnesses when somebody comments on it. A jailer who must know he is liable for escapes fails to notice that his young prisoner is thinner than the space between bars. Protestants threaten not to die without at least a token Catholic, but have no idea how they could refuse. A thug tries to get a dentist to extract the teeth from a skull that has already been identified, and a minister attributes his failure to the refusal, not of the dentist, but of his instruments. A father tries to pin murders on his son, when common sense has told the neighbors to blame the laborer. A woman and her lover break her husband's neck and appropriate his savings, and people believe her story of a visit from the Devil. Bungling conspirators poison pets and a little girl instead of their target, and then one of them gets an unintended quarter's reprieve because the sheriff does not deliver her death warrant in time.

No wonder such people were also fatalistic. Yet so was a clever and ambitious man like Bishop Atherton. His is a good example of the disintegration of a person with good prospects, the very sort of demonstration to confirm fatalists in their beliefs. We have seen others disintegrate: Bartram went dotty with age, Fitz before he had that excuse. Rowse the fishmonger collided with mid-life crisis just as he achieved his dream of suburban respectability, and rapidly came apart.

Another thread is kindness. People who saw whipping and branding as the natural order of things were yet neighborly. Some keep putting a drunk widow to bed. A man gives up his bed to a raving stranger and is killed for it, and then his neighbors give the murderer-suicide one of their best grave sites. Pious people flock to an articulate penitent, and try to get her pardoned. Beggars survive only because of donors who are moved by pity and religion to acts of undeductible charity.

Tragedy abounded, in its sloppy journalistic sense of "misfortune," but not many of the actors in these cases were tragic in the sense of having been brought low by some flaw that would normally have been a virtue. The Glanfield girl's quite normal virtue was fidelity to the man she and her parents expected her to marry, and had made a de facto husband. Her disaster was the arbitrary imposition of a de jure husband. Mrs. Vincent's and Elizabeth Barnes's maternal solicitude had fatal results because mental isolation had distorted this virtue.

The aroma of alcohol pervades many of our cases. People drank ale, beer, and wine more commonly than spirits, which would have been whisky and brandy but not rum or gin. They compensated for the lower alcohol content with gargantuan consumption, but these drinks were both drug and food to them. Laborers needed something in the dawn's light to keep them going until noon. We call it calories, and they called it beer. Not having heard of calories, they did not worry that theirs were "empty." While Billingsgate fish market still operated (until recently), a pub across the street bore a sign proclaiming that it could serve beer in the early morning, by special act of Parliament. This legislation allowed generations of nimble porters and eponymously foul-mouthed fishwives to drink their absolutely essential breakfasts here.

Close contact would have made violence so real that persons would not enter it lightly. In general, most of the ways Elizabethans could hurt each other were still so intimate and messy that people could not help knowing the immediate consequences of what they did. The traditional weapons, knives and swords, were ready at hand and must have been drawn in innumerable boozy brawls and macho fits too dull to come down to us. Common sense suggests that sober men would rather not cut or be cut, for both were mortally risky. A body of courtesies grew to reduce unwanted confrontations. Quarrels over status account for the elaborate rules of precedence at court and elsewhere. Violence in the wide and status-conscious radius of the monarch's presence drew special attention from the marshalsea court. An Irish Captain Cosbie quarreled with the Irish Lord Brook at Elizabeth's court. Cosbie stabbed him to death in Wandsworth, and was hanged there. His simple deed attracted attention for occurring too near the queen, and for his effrontery toward a lord.[2] Handguns may have seemed unmanly or unfair to Elizabethans, who passed several laws to prohibit them. Old Bartram had no business owning a pistol. His murder of Sir John Tyndal is the only one in this book involving firearms, but they were used in 16 percent of homicides in Hertfordshire at about this time.[3] In that rural environment we would expect more hunting pieces than handguns.

Women figure in these accounts as victims, offenders, or subjects of contention. They often seem doomed by some fatal loyalty. Elizabeth Abbott steadfastly refused to endanger her accomplice husband. The Glanfields' daughter and Alice Fortune were disloyal to their enforced husbands only as a reciprocal of their loyalty to their lovers. Mrs. Vincent and Elizabeth Barnes killed their children purely out of love for them. Old Doublets' cleaving to Double Diligence was as simple as it was terminal.

We would call the women passive, but in their culture they were called patient (a virtue) or obedient (a divine obligation). Sir John Fitz imposed his trulls on Lady Fitz. Her "patience" was commended by a narrator who would doubtless have condemned any other possible course as disobedience. Rowse's successive wives had to share the house with his paramour. Their vehement objections were certainly not passive, but the first is said to have died of a broken heart, and the second to have welcomed her wayward mate when at last he came broken home. Mrs. Caverley, in trying to remedy her situation, worked always within the rigid frame of obedience. Obedience could also account for the apparent complacence of the wives of the Vicar Gwin and Bishop Atherton. The line between obedience and culpable personal passivity is so unsettled, even after the Nuremberg trials, that it seems pretentious to seek retroactive clarification across four centuries.

Perhaps it is more practical to think of the women as proactive or reactive. It was Mrs. Vincent who decided to kill her children, not any priest; hers alone her proactive disobedience of her husband, of her former religion, and of the religion she had adopted. Margaret Ferneseed too was proactive. So at first were the wives she seduced into prostitution. Robbing her maid was the free choice of the Windsor gamekeeper's wife, though perhaps murdering her, and certainly cutting her up, were reactions to the situation she had created. Probably Anne Saunders actively sought some kind of adulterous event, out of pique and boredom, without at first being sure of its outcome. Of course her later ingenious tactics to save herself were reactive. Anne Potter was at first highly proactive, urging her master to kill her mistress, and planning to benefit from the murder by wedding him. To flee the county after his disappointing marriage to the neighboring widow was reactive. It is interesting to speculate whether on her death bed she confessed him straight into the noose for her own salvation, or because that was the first time revenge was safe.

The Rye fisherman's wife thought she had a choice: Either leave her husband in debtor's jail, or make herself a pauper with all its irretrievable consequences. Her real choice, which she had no way of knowing, was to free the incurable loser or to be murdered. The amateur hooker of Bishopsgate reacted first to her accidental pregnancy by seeking abortion, and then to her failure to find it by murdering her newborn. Alice Fortune had nothing in life but her poor and powerless lover. She was given away by her bored keeper to a worse keeper, and she reacted fatally. The pious and ladylike Elizabeth Caldwell got onto a slippery slope. First came her husband's neglect. Next came seduction by her neighbor, whose insistence on marriage suggests that his intentions were acquisitive if not predatory. Then she was badgered into a murder plot. Nothing worked as she wished until she reacted to her condemnation with an eloquent repentance that brought her popular affection and support.

Two of the women at least are truly puzzling, surely in part because the male authors did not try to know about them. There is the widow who remained dependent on her predator neighbor as, over time, he picked off her four children. Did she have nothing to say about their deaths and disappearances, or was it the narrator who deprived her of a voice? Or did she stupidly believe the hardly credible reports of the predator's henchmen about where her children had gone? Or was she terrorized into passivity? Her other neighbors were long terrified into silence by the community bully, but silence would have been easier for them than for her. What isolation might have kept her from knowing where to turn? After all, somebody in the family knew enough to start proceedings in court against the predator. We know that she had not simply vanished, because at the end she appeared and identified a son's bones.

Murkier yet is Castlehaven's countess. Just how voluntary was her sex with Antil and Skipwith? Would she have condescended to either if she were not the hostage of Skipwith, who controlled her very food? Did she accept these base men merely in a desperate bid for security in a prison full of perilous surprises? Two rogues, but sane rogues, in bedlam? Or perhaps sex with Antil and Skipwith was a price she was resigned to paying in the hope of forestalling any novel experiments by her imaginative spouse. Antil and Skipwith were evidently superior on some kind of scale to the rapist Broadway, whose attack made her try suicide. If she had wished, she could have testified in such a way as to accuse Antil and Skipwith of rape.

And how did she regard her daughter and fellow hostage Elizabeth? Was Elizabeth a sacrifice who might save her mother, or a daughter whom she might protect by self-sacrifice? All we hear is the countess's brief testimony at her husband's trial that she was raped, and her reaffirmation at Broadway's trial, from which she departed "with as much privacy as might be in her coach," leaving a trail of silence.

A few crimes show family unity. The Smithwickes, for example, murdered the parson to recover a family asset, and in subsequently defending themselves showed continued solidarity. In Caverley's quirky mind, he was a family man. He resented his enforced marriage as the invasion of his family by a more powerful family. He murdered his wife and children because they were invaders. The immediate motive for his crime was family duty, to rescue his brother from debtor's prison. There is no more dramatic demonstration of the force of family unity than the election of a defendant to be pressed to death. Whether the head of a family liked his descendants or not, the desire to continue the name and the line sustained him through substantial terminal torture. Caverley and Jeffrey Bowndes chose this course.

More often, we find families engaged in nearly every possible permutation of conflict. To resolve triangles, wives murdered husbands, and husbands wives. A husband killed his wife to get out of jail. Fanaticism lured a man to fratricide and matricide. The steadfast enmity of a wife and husband ended with her successfully conspiring to have his skull bashed. A husband opposed his wife's religion, a cause for which she strangled their children. A father had his children's throats cut because they hampered his finding a rich wife. Either through stupidity, terror, or some unnatural paralysis, a mother continued to consort with the predator who did away with her children as each reached majority.

Finally, the mansion at Fonthill Gifford must have sheltered more dysfunction per square foot than any other in the realm. The father helped a servant rape his wife. She had two paramours, how voluntarily is uncertain, who were also lovers of her husband's. Her husband married off her first paramour to one of his own daughters. Her second, piqued when she gave away their infant, became the paramour of her daughter after an initiation supervised by the girl's stepfather, though he had married her to his son. The son recognized his father's enmity and terminated the whole menage by telling the king. Castlehaven could have refused to plead. He would not have avoided scandal, but he would have saved his son's estate. Obviously his interest in the continuity of his line was shaky.

Justice

Readers must decide for themselves what miscarriages of justice have been revealed. To some it is *ipso facto* a miscarriage to execute a priest or a witch, or for that matter anybody at all. Many will suspect that suggestible and confused persons were seduced by some prestigious figure in a cassock to translate the general guilt of mankind into a specific confession.

We have seen why our authors, routinely fulsome in their praise of judges and prosecutors, could not have questioned the justice of any sentence. They would go as far as to report denials, then treat them as the work of the Devil. Denials were failure, confessions success. A confession of crime tended to be treated as conclusive, an assumption logically supported by the fact that a false confession made no religious sense. The ministers look like adjuncts of the prosecutor's office. They were often instrumental in eliciting information and inducing a public confession. Alongside the common lawyers' formal presumption of innocence stood the clerics' conviction that we are all sinners.

The learned Bishop Atherton did not hold his prosecutors to precise details, but instead accepted a holistic justice, knowing more about his life than anybody else. Seeing how holistic justice missed Elizabeth Barnes and her treacherous tailor, we feel sure that a stiff dose of compulsory child support would have brought truer justice to the tailor, Elizabeth, and of course their little daughter. But in this kind of case we still often fail.

Certain notions were inherently dangerous to justice. One of the most obvious errors, elevated to a legal tenet, was that no rape has occurred if pregnancy results, because only a willing woman can conceive.[4] In one witchcraft case, a dying person's opinion was taken as evidence of fact. Another procedural problem would have been how to keep a brand on a defendant's hand or face from being prejudicial before a jury. In those pre-scientific times, forensic evidence was cluttered with errors. Investigators, including physicians, tended to assume that swelling meant poison. They also believed that dead victims would bleed, blush, or wink in the presence of their murderers. This belief was held equally by the guilty, however, and sometimes helped break them down and reveal the truth. Other quaint forensic techniques rested on beliefs that poison breaks Venetian goblets, and that if a section of lung floats when dropped into water, its owner had been born alive.[5]

Insanity was necessarily dealt with crudely by society and the law. Few of our cases appear to involve madness. Whether Sir John Fitz was insane by the standards of the time will never be known. Nobody seems to have asked whether the Earl of Castlehaven was insane, though his aunt was. Religious partisans debated fiercely whether Enoch ap Evan was insane, their purpose being, not to find the truth about his state of mind, but to embarrass or exonerate his sect. We consider him insane because he beheaded his brother for no communicable reason, but if we ask whether his fanaticism was the product of his madness we enter treacherous ground. We would be applying orthodoxy as a test of sanity, as in those recent workers' paradises where political unorthodoxy led to psychiatric treatment. Mrs. Vincent was mistaken about her own faith when she murdered her children, but there is no indication that she was delusional.

We think the Witch of Edmonton was delusional because her doggy little Devil is incredible to us. The sometimes compassionate Henry Goodcole, her spiritual counsellor, was careful not to subscribe to her belief, but neither did he treat it as evidence of insanity. We can, however, imagine some of the London jurors asking each other, "She's a right nutter. What do we do?" No examples appear of witches being thought insane.

Ghosts enjoyed some acceptance, certainly enough for playhouse audiences. Reporting them would have been unlikely to cast doubts on anyone's sanity. Lambert's high and mighty spirits certainly were not enough to prove his madness, but in any case his treatment by a Dutch court martial does not tell us what his experience would have been in England.

The mentally impaired were treated with the same sometimes brutal pragmatism that much of society experienced in one form or another. Lunatics, like cripples, could get begging licenses, and become the Tom o'Bedlams familiar in literature. Among the propertied classes, effective legal machinery could be brought to protect an insane owner's property (and his heirs) from his mistakes. Madmen were restrained according to how much trouble they caused. A parish would not have gone out of its way to do so because of the expense. Once a madman was locked up, his treatment would be somewhat callous because that was cheaper. As for criminal responsibility, society had for centuries recognized that only the sane could be felonious; one who obviously did not know what he was doing, like a child or lunatic, was incapable of felony. One who acted under a delusion would be excused from criminal responsibility only if what he thought he was doing would have been lawful, not if it would have been unlawful. Thus a person who killed under the delusion that the victim was a bear bore no criminal responsibility. But if his delusion was that the victim was his wicked uncle, it did not excuse him. All this was pretty homespun. Elizabethans did not know much about criminal insanity, but at least they did not pretend to much knowledge.

As justice delayed is justice denied, we must concede to the Elizabethans the virtues of speed. The time that lapsed between crime and arrest depended of course on external factors such as the ease or difficulty of detection. The crudity of the resources available was offset by the simplicity of the crime and criminals. This simplicity encouraged amateur detectives such as those who consulted over the corpse of Ferneseed and the skeletons of the Leeson heirs. Justices of the peace were not quite amateurs. They solved the murder of Parson Trat despite elaborate efforts to deceive them. They also solved the murder of Parson James with a competent *ruse de guerre*. On the other hand, tracing a musician's broken neck and emptied strong box to the Devil was not detection's finest hour.

XII. Conclusion

The time that lapsed from arrest to trial was governed outside London by the quarterly assizes, so that the normal wait would be a maximum of three months, and usually much less. In special cases this would stretch to a year or more, as when the justice replaced a corrupt grand jury in the Trat case. At the Old Bailey the rhythm was faster.

The time that lapsed from sentence to execution was commonly a few days. Pregnancy of course would alter this schedule, as would respites and pardons. As the only relief from the rigidity of the law, royal pardons intruded fairly often into the system. They must often have represented genuine mercy in a hard case, but our examples of pardons were the mischievous work of courtiers brokering the mercy of the chronically impecunious Stuart kings. Certainly this was true of the pardons of Francis Cartwright and John Fitz.[6] A notorious beneficiary of this system was Dr. Lambe, an habitual criminal who prospered amidst reprieves and pardons. His case so blatantly violated the precept that justice must be seen to be done, that it ruptured the system, bringing first Lambe's lynching and then a failure to prosecute a single member of the lynch mob.

This extreme example of delay shows its evil effects, but also sets off the usual dispatch that so distinguished criminal from civil justice. It was not unusual to hang an offender about a fortnight after his or her arrest. Browne's wait from arrest to execution was 16 days, Strangwich's nine.

Speaking of justice, we might be unjust if, like tourists visiting our ancestors, we assess them according to the learning that we have acquired the easy way, by precept rather than experience. It took time to observe that toleration would not attract plagues and lightning. It took time for the Leeuwenhoeks, Brunos, and Newtons to rot the pilings of superstition. After that, while piety and prudence still prevented jurists from denying the existence of witchcraft, they could say, Yes, there is witchcraft, but we have never seen a credible case. Moderns feel superior to superstition, but how many of us would be bright enough and brave enough to defy social pressure and leave its smothering comforts?

Coarsening

Writers and sensitive witnesses like Dickens were concerned with the corruption of humanity wrought by public executions. These spectacles, never quite avoidable, did not corrupt Sidney, Shakespeare, or Milton. Shakespeare gives us more than 300 references to hanging. Most of them are just dismissive, as in "Hang him slave." Not surprisingly, his only truly nasty reference is in butcherly *Titus Andronicus* (V i 51): "First hang the child, that he may see it sprawl." There must be some significance in the fact that the vast majority of his hanging references are in the comedies or in comic parts of the histories.

Evidence

Those poor cartloads of condemned persons are on the far side of huge changes. The ways we have of knowing them are few. One way is asking ourselves what we would do and feel in their carts. What parallel can we know from our experience that would bridge the gap? Perhaps a big-city emergency room (even just a television version, if that is all we have experienced). It would provide the sights and sounds of dismay, and also the quiet people, numbed by shock, or busy concentrating on the merciful promise they had been taught since infancy, or stoic Horatios who are not Fortune's slave. It has been said that the condemned, whether liked or hated, were sustained by custom and the crowd to show a certain bravery, the last public assertion of self.[7] Fine. We too believe in the efficacy of cheering sections. On the melancholy three miles from Newgate to Tyburn once stood a hospital where the condemned prisoners were offered something called St. Giles' Bowl of Ale, "thereof to drinke at their pleasure, as to be theyr last refreshing in this life."[8] We too believe in the efficacy of a good slug at such moments. But these are only sparks in the gloom, and in the long run we do not know how we would act in the poor cartload. The method does not work well, then, but the reason is that we are something of a mystery to ourselves.

All our knowledge of the past is circumscribed by the erratic survival of evidence. The stone age might have been the wood age, and we would almost certainly wonder at its bygone craft and art, if wood were not so perishable. Organic evidence survives irregularly. In Europe we study mostly skeletons, but in Egypt mummies and in Central Asia ice people, because they are what is left. Elizabethan London would be different in our histories if the great fire had not destroyed evidence. We recently learned a little more about Shakespearean theatre when archaeologists discovered a layer of hazelnut shells where the groundlings stood in the *Globe*—shells that have not perished.[9]

Evidence is affected by changes in terms too subtle for the dictionaries.

XII. Conclusion

For instance, we do not always know when an Elizabethan is trying to be funny. Again, our notion of privacy has changed enough to distort our view of at least one event. The open sex that went on in the Castlehaven household offended his contemporaries, but they viewed the openness partly in the light of their kind of privacy, not ours. Family, servants, and guests shared bedrooms and sometimes beds at home, and strangers shared beds at inns. Privies with plural seats facilitated seamless conversation. The Essex annulment trial suggests how slight was the expectation of privacy. To prove that they had never had sex, the young Earl and Countess of Essex called the testimony of four servants and seven acquaintances, males and females ranging in age from 16 to 60. These had all seen the two naked in bed at various times, but no sign of sexual activity (which the earl called "Motions or Provocations"). There was so little privacy that failure to see signs of sexual activity was taken as evidence that there had been none.[10]

The fate of evidence can be illustrated topographically, by revisiting sites. Tyburn is marked only by a modern round tablet in the paving of a traffic island next to Marble Arch. Wapping's Execution Dock, undistinguished, is overlooked by a pub of unknown antiquity which may or may not have been a tavern in 1609. Wormewall Wood, the sad picnic site of unreachable trees and inadequate streams, is now no more but the A219 highway and its inorganic adjuncts. The Tower of London has shed its Iron Gate. Across the busy pavements, the site of Margaret Ferneseed's slummy brothel lies by an upscale hotel at St. Katherine's Dock. Smithfield is clean and under vast roofing, but still handles much of London's beef. The present Old Bailey stands on the site of Newgate prison. It might perhaps have been called the New Bailey because the old Old Bailey had stood just south of it. An addition recently built on the site of the old Old Bailey is of course newer than the new Old Bailey, but both are still the Old Bailey. Only with some inner eye can anyone look at a London pavement and see, a yard or so below the surface, the forgotten cellar, the rubbish pit and its clay pipes, the hearth, the well, or the crypt of St. Botolph's, Billingsgate, across the street from where Ann Saunders sat in her doorway waiting for adventure.

The countryside has been kinder than London to its antiquities. St. Edmund's, Salisbury, where a work of art so offended a vestryman, is now an art center. Behind the Georgian facades of suburban Ewell lurk Tudor houses similar to the fishmonger Rowse's. The churches of those ill-starred parsons, Storre, Trat, and James still stand. Chester Castle still frowns over the Dee, Shrewsbury Castle over the Severn. Village streets usually follow their ancient courses, and a few village inns still serve customers after four centuries.

Some relics have taken sanctuary in archaeological museums. Some of the human relics have found sanctuary in Westminster Abbey, for example one of Castlehaven's judges, Lord Dorset, who went a few months after the trial to lie there. The Duke of Buckingham rests beneath his pompous oversize monument a few yards from his doting King James, who somewhat illogically has no monument at all, and who was long lost until a search party went down to find him in 1867. Nor does James's daughter, the Queen of Hearts, have a monument. She lies with her grandmother Mary Queen of Scots and dozens of other Stuarts.[11]

On Tower Hill, the site of the upmarket scaffold is marked by a monument listing its distinguished victims. Some are famous historical figures, like Bishop Atherton's protectors, Archbishop Laud and the Earl of Strafford, but in its neutral way it is also a memorial to the Earl of Castlehaven. Whether we are ready or not, forgiving Time heals by indifference.

Appendix A

Shakespeare's Purse

It is impossible to produce a consistent translation of Elizabethan and Jacobean money into modern pounds or dollars. Authors over the intervening years have told us that money was ten or a hundred times its present worth. They were only guessing. Even if they had been right at the time they wrote, their estimates would subsequently have been eroded by inflation. Efforts to improve on them can be frustrating. We could apply some standard, for instance the cost of bread, and compare how many loaves a pound bought then and now. Bread prices were set and published. So were beer prices. Strong beer typically cost a penny a quart, weak beer a half penny, so that we could also work out a beer standard. A gold standard gives us the following scale: The pound of 1603 contained 171.9403 grains of gold. Today's pound (1999) trades for a varying amount of gold, typically 2.65 grains. By this standard, the pound of 1603 equals about £65 of 1999, or $104. Calculations of this sort are only convenient perspectives. A haircut standard would give quite different values.

Elizabethan money needs another translation as well. One British and six American generations have grown up unfamiliar with its arithmetic: a pound had 20 shillings, a shilling 12 pence, and a penny four farthings. Thus farthings were added up according to base four arithmetic, pennies base 12, shillings base 20, and pounds base ten. The shilling was particularly handy for trade, for unlike decimal money it was easily divided into halves, thirds, quarters, sixths, and twelfths. This allowed simple calculations in the head; for those of greater complexity, merchants and exchequer clerks were fast on the abacus. An abacus can be designed for any number system, and it appears that people had a specialised abacus handling pounds, shillings, and pence.[1] For them, a decimal system had no advantage at all. Dependence on the abacus was increased by the general practice of keeping accounts in Roman numerals.

Merchants also used a money of account, the mark, which was two thirds of a pound. An amount like 13 shillings and four pence becomes less odd when we realize that this is one mark.

The only currency was coins. The main coins that Shakespeare would have carried in his purse were either gold or silver. The gold coins were a sovereign of 20 shillings, a half-sovereign or angel, and a half angel. People seem also to have had nobles, worth six shillings eight pence (that is, half a mark), that had not been coined for a century, and a variety of foreign gold. The silver coins were a crown of five shillings, a half crown, a shilling, a sixpence, a groat or fourpence, threepence, a half groat, a penny, a three-farthing piece that Shakespeare used as a metaphor for skinniness, and a half penny too small to bear a portrait. Farthings had disappeared except as tokens, because they would have had to be too tiny if they were silver and the populace mistrusted the government too much to accept many base metal coins at a time.

Popular mistrust of the coinage arose from its having been debased by Henry VIII and Edward VI, though later coinage was restored in silver or gold content. Consequently people discounted certain coins and referred to them specifically: for example, not just a shilling, but an "Edward shilling."[2]

Appendix B
"Appeal" by Next of Kin

In the case described in Chapter 2 ("Jeopardies"), Francis Cartwright's murder of William Storre had left Mrs. Storre and her two children destitute. Despite the pardon, she had one remaining legal recourse. Over the centuries, private vengeance had evolved from a duty and a right to something of an antiquity. "Revenge is a kind of wild justice," wrote Sir Francis Bacon, adding like a civilized prosecutor, "which the more man's nature runs to, the more ought law to weed it out."[1] On the grounds that the king's peace was broken by a murder, retribution was increasingly monopolized by his courts. Yet it was still legally possible for the next kin of the victim as a private person (appellant) to "appeal" an alleged murderer (appellee), that is, to charge him with the crime and force him to a trial. If the appellant was an able-bodied male, the appellee could either challenge him to wager of single combat in person, or elect to face an ordinary jury. But if the appellant was not an able-bodied male (for instance, an old man, handicapped, or a woman) then the appellee could not elect trial by battle and was stuck with trial by jury. This quaint survival had two important peculiarities. First, the king had no power to pardon the appellee. Second, no plea of double jeopardy was available; even if the appellee had been acquitted in one of the king's courts, he must still face either battle or a second jury.

Trial by combat took place in an open area of 60 square feet. On one side sat the justices of common pleas in scarlet robes. The combatants were dressed in armor, but were bare-headed, bare from the elbows down, and bare from the knees down except for red sandals. Each was armed with a baton an ell (45 inches) long, and a square leather shield. The battle began at sunrise and continued until one was killed or one surrendered by crying "Craven!" If the battle was still undecided when the stars came out that evening, the appellee won. A lawyer in the more rational 18th century commented, "The nature of this trial is, a presumptuous appeal to providence, from an expectation that heaven would unquestionably give the victory to the innocent or injured party."[2]

This remedy looked as if it had been made exactly for the poor widow Storre. She had to appear in person at Westminster, justices of the peace having no authority to receive appeals, and there she went, despite the expense and inconvenience. Alas, on a mere technicality of form, as Cartwright himself admitted later, the appeal was cancelled, by a writ called a *ne recipiatur*.

Mrs. Storre's appeal was not the last example of this ancient practice. Occasional cases followed for the next 50 years, falling into disuse after 1653. Although it was defended in theory during the 18th century by a judge and by Edmund Burke, it was practically forgotten by 1819. In that year, more than two centuries after Mrs. Storre's disaster, one Ashford was incensed when a jury acquitted Abraham Thornton of murdering Ashford's sister. Somehow he dug up the old practice and appealed Thornton of murder. The appeal put lawyers into turmoil. They were embarrassed to find that it was still law. Abraham Thornton's counsel came up with just the right reply: Thornton challenged Ashford to wager by battle. Ashford, weighing the risks and benefits, declined to fight and thereby killed his appeal. In the new age of steam and science, parliament lost no time passing a statute that ended both appeals and trial by battle.[3]

Notes

Introduction

1. Stephenson and Marcham, eds., *Sources of English Constitutional History*.... New York and London, 1937. pp. 387–390.
2. *The Laws Respecting Women*.... London, 1777. Reprint, 1973. p. 10. Joan R. Kent, *The English Village Constable, 1580-1642*.... Oxford, 1986. pp. 58–59.
3. Sir Edward Coke, *Les Reports*. [Part I]. Londini [London], 1600. Corbet's Case.
4. Cynthia Herrup, *The Common Peace*.... Cambridge, 1987. pp. 68–81. J.S. Cockburn, ed., *Crime in England, 1550–1800*. Princeton, N.J., 1977. p. 59 et passim. J.H. Baker, *An Introduction to English Legal History*. 2nd ed., London, 1979. p. 23.

I. Issues of Crime and the Time

1. E.M.W. Tillyard, *The Elizabethan World Picture*. New York, n.d. pp. vii, 94–99.
2. Laudanum could be bought legally on the open market, but was probably not widely known. *These Oils, Waters, and Other Compositions*.... [London], 1585. Broadside, 1 p. Robert Parker Sorlien, ed., *The Diary of John Manningham ... 1602–1603*. Hanover, N.H., 1976. p. 82. Manningham writes of laudanum as if he had just heard of it.
3. John Aubrey, *Brief Lives*, ed. by Oliver Lawson Dick, London, 1950. p. 11. David Harris Wilson, *King James VI & I*. London, 1956. pp. 337, 384. Michael B.Young, *King James and the History of Homosexuality*. New York, 2000. 221 pp. Otto J. Scott, *James I*. New York, 1976. 472 pp. Leon Radzinowicz, *A History of English Criminal Law and Its Administration from 1750*. New York, 1948. vol. I, p. 307.
4. Cynthia Herrup, *The Common Peace*.... Cambridge Studies in Early Modern British History. Cambridge, 1987. pp. 168–171.
5. J.S. Cockburn, "The Nature and Incidence of Crime in England, 1559–1625...," in his *Crime in England, 1550–1800*. Princeton, N.J., 1977. pp. 55–58.
6. Sir Matthew Hale, quoted in *Encyclopaedia Britannica* (11th ed.) under "Abortion." Sir William Blackstone, *Commentaries on the Laws of England*. Philadelphia, 1772, vol. IV, p. 198. "Misprision" at this time had the sense of "misde-

meanor," but calling it either appears to have been an innovation imposed by Justice Coke. John M. Riddle, *Eve's Herbs*. Cambridge, 1997. pp. 130–131.
   7. Blackstone, *Commentaries*.... vol. IV, p. 388.
   8. *The Laws Respecting Women*.... London, 1777. Reprint, London, 1973. pp. 423–426. Quote from p. 348.
   9. Steven H. Gifis, *Law Dictionary*. New York, 1984, under "Abortion."
   10. London. *Orders Appointed to Be Executed in the Cittie of London, for Setting Roges and Idle Persons to Worke, and for Relief of the Poore*. London, n.d. [15] pp.

II. Removing Obstacles to Wealth

   1. For Shakespeare's arms, see Arthur Charles FoxDavies, *A Complete Guide to Heraldry*. New York, 1978, p. 285.
   2. *Two Notorious Murders*.... London, 1595. 10 pp.
   3. *Sundrye Strange and Inhumane Murthers Lately Committed*.... London, 1591. [12] pp.
   4. *The Examination, Confession, and Condemnation of Henry Robson, Fisherman of Rye*. London, 1598. [8] pp.
   5. *The Manner of the Cruell Outrageous Murther of William Storre*.... Oxford, 1603. [9] pp. Francis Cartwright, *The Life, Confession, and Heartie Repentance of Francis Cartwright*.... London, 1621. [32] pp. *Three Bloodie Murders*.... London, 1613. [19] pp.
   6. *Two Most Unnatural and Bloodie Murthers*.... London, 1605. 8 pp. Discussed in Dolan, *Dangerous Familiars*.... p. 41.
   7. Thomas Cooper, *The Cry and Revenge of Blood*.... London, 1620. 63 pp.
   8. J.H. Baker, *An Introduction to English Legal History*. 2nd ed. London, 1979, pp. 112–113.
   9. The story of this murder was written, probably by a clergyman known only as "C.W.," as *The Crying Murther Contayning the Cruell and Most Horrible Butchery of Mr. Trat*.... London, 1624. [23] pp. The publisher, Nathaniel Butter, was just at this time introducing the idea of the newspaper to England. Butter understood the importance of freshness in news, and as early as 1605 published (in handset type, remember) an account of a murder only a day or two after it occurred. Text in modern spelling in Marshburn and Viele, *Blood*.... p. 40.
   10. In heraldry, the Irish national color was a special blue known as Irish blue. Green came to symbolize the Irish nationalist movement about 1800. *The Encyclopaedia of Ireland*. Dublin, 1968. p. 171.

III. Murdering Children for Their Own Good

   1. *Two Most Unnatural and Bloodie Murthers*.... London, 1605. 28 pp. Summarized in Marshburn, *Murder*...; discussed in Dolan, *Dangerous Familiars*, pp. 153–159. *Dictionary of National Biography*. London, 1949–50. Under "Caverley," and Brooke. Two plays were written about this tragedy: George Wilkins, *The Miseries of Inforst Mariage*.... London, 1607. This is rather a comedy than anything else. The other is *A Yorkshire Tragedy*.... London, 1609. The play is falsely attributed on its title page to William Shakespeare.

2. *A Pittilesse Mother*.... [London, 1616]. [9] pp. Discussed in Dolan, *Dangerous Familiars*, pp. 148–150.
  3. John Rowse, *The Unnatural Father*.... London,1621. [19] pp.
  4. Henry Goodcole, *Nature's Cruell Step-Dames*.... London, 1637. 20 pp. Discussed in Dolan, *Dangerous Familiars*, p. 162.

IV. Murdering to Resolve Triangles

  1. *Sundrye Strange and Inhumane Murthers Lately Commited ... of Master Page of Plymouth*.... London, 1591. [12] pp. *Two Horrible and Inhumane Murders*.... London, 1607. [17] pp. Summarized in Marshburn, *Murder*....; modern spelling text in Marshburn and Velie, *Blood*....
  2. Arthur Golding, *A Briefe Discourse of the Late Master George Saunders*.... London, 1573. [16] pp. Summarized in Marshburn, *Murder*.... This was made into a play, *A Warning for Faire Women*.... London, 1599.
  3. *A True Relation of the Most Inhumane and Bloody Murther, of Master James*.... London, 1609. [17] pp. Summarized in Marshburn, *Murder*....
  4. Lawrence Southerne, *Fearfull Newes from Coventry, or a True Relation and Lamentable Story of One Thomas Holt*.... London, 1642. 8 pp. Thomason Tracts E146 No. 3.
  5. Henry Goodcole, *Nature's Cruell Step-Dames*.... London, 1637. 20 pp.
  6. *The Apprentices Warning-piece*.... London, 1641. 6 pp. Thomason Tracts E173 No. 22
  7. *Murther, Murther, or a Bloody Relation*.... London, 1641. 6 pp.
  8. Henry Goodcole, *The Adulteresses Funerall Day*.... London, 1635. [13] pp.
  9. Clinton H. Thienes and Thomas J. Haley, *Clinical Toxicology*. Philadelphia, 1972. Robert H. Dreisbach, *Handbook of Poisoning: Diagnosis and Treatment*. 8th ed. Los Altos, Calif., 1974. Robert A. Lewis, *Lewis' Dictionary of Toxicology*. Boca Raton, Fla., 1998. 1,127 pp. See under "Mercury poisoning" and related entries.
  10. Gilbert Dugdale, *A True Discourse of the Practices of Elizabeth Caldwell on the Parson of T. Caldwell*. London, by James Roberts for John Busbie, 1604. [27] pp.
  11. Sollum Emlyn, ed., *A Complete Collection of State-trials*.... XXIV. London, 3rd ed., 1742. The Proceedings against Sir John Hollis ... in the Star-Chamber for Traducing the Publick Justice, November 10, 1615.... pp. 333–338. Hollis and two others were fined and given a year in prison for riding up to Tyburn and unofficially cross examining Weston, one of Overbury's poisoners, just as he was about to be hanged. Their object was probably to vindicate their master the Earl of Somerset, another of the culprits. Needless to say, they made Weston's spiritual preparations more difficult, but their offense was contempt of court.

V. Robbery on Land

  1. *The Apprehension, Arraignment, and Execution of E. Abbot*. London, 1608. [21] pp. Summarized in Marshburn, *Murder*....
  2. *Three Bloodie Murders*.... London, 1613. [19] pp.
  3. *The Arraignment of John Selman*.... London, 1612. [17] pp.

4. *Bartholomew Faire or Variety Fancies*.... London, 1641. 5 pp.
5. Henry Goodcole, *Heaven's Speedy Hue and Cry*.... London, 1635. [22] pp. Summarized in Marshburn, *Murder*.... *Murder upon Murder*.... London, [1635]. A ballad, 2 pp. Ballad in modern spelling in Marshburn and Viele, *Blood*....
6. H. Pecham, *The Art of Living in London, or a Caution How Gentlemen, Countreymen and Strangers*.... [London], 1642. [7] pp. Thomason Tracts E145 No. 20.
7. Thomas Harman, *A Caveat for Common Cursetors Vulgarly Called Vagabones*.... London, 1567. [10] pp.
8. William Shakespeare, *Coriolanus*, I.v.
9. *A Bloody New-Yeares Gift, or a True Declaration of the Murther of Maister Robert Heath. Whereunto is Annexed, Sundry Exploits of Tendance*.... London, 1609. [15] pp.
10. Robert Greene, *The Black Bookes Messenger, 1592. "Cuthbert Conny-Catcher," the Defense of Conny-Catching*. R[obert] G[reene], *The Blacke Bookes Messenger. Laying Open the Life and Death of Ned Browne One of the Most Notable Cutpurses, and Conny-Catchers, That Ever Lived in England*.... London, 1592. [26] pp. Robert Greene, *The Black Bookes Messenger, 1592. "Cuthbert Conny-Catcher," the Defense of Conny-Catching. 1592*. Elizabethan and Jacobean Quartos, ed. by G.B. Harrison. New York, [1966], p. vii.
11. *The Life and Death of Gamaliel Ratsey*.... [London], n.d. [43] pp.
12. *The Life, Apprehension, Arraignment, and Execution of Charles Courtney, Alias Holice, Alias Worsley*.... London, 1612. [22] pp.

VI. Robbery at Sea

1. J.E. Thomson, *Mercenaries*.... Princeton, 1994. 219 pp. J.E. Neale, *Queen Elizabeth*. New York, [1957]. pp. 355–356.
2. D.H. Willson, *King James I and VI*. London, 1956. p. 274.
3. *The Lives, Apprehensions*.... London, [1608]. [28] pp.
4. "Turkish" included Tripoli, Tunisia, Algeria, or Morocco. Turkish suzerainty over these places was variable.
5. N. Williams, *The Sea Dogs*.... London, 1975. pp. 25 & 165.

VII. Fraud and Blackmail

1. N.L., *A True Relation of the Grounds, Occasion, and Circumstances, of the Horrible Murther Committed by John Bartram*.... London, 1616. [20] pp. *The Examination of John Bartram*.... London, 1616. [4] pp.
2. John Darrel, *The True Relation of the Grievous Handling of William Sommers*.... London, 1641. [6] pp. Samuel Harsnett, *A Discovery of the Fraudulent Practices of John Darrel*.... London, 1599. 324 pp. *Dictionary of National Biography*. Under "Darrel, John" and "Harsnett, Samuel."
3. *The Laws Respecting Women*.... 1777. Reprint, London, 1973, p. 344.
4. *The Arraignment & Burning of Margaret Ferne-Seede*.... London, 1608. 11 pp. *The Lives, Apprehension, Arraignment & Execution of Robert Throgmorton*.... London, 1608. [21] pp. Summarized in Marshburn, *Murder*....
5. *The Life and Death of Griffin Flood Informant*.... London, 1623. [19] pp.

VIII. From Sex to Disaster

1. A scholarly and entertaining guide is Eric Partridge, *Shakespeare's Bawdy*, especially his Introductory, pp. 1–48. Censorship of play performances, administered quite differently, as we have seen, from that of printed matter, was probably more permissive in this regard. On the stage, one could talk bawdy; in books, sexual detail usually required the prophylactic of Latin or Greek.

2. *The Just Reward of a Debauched Cavallier*.... [London], 1643. [5] pp. Thomason Tracts E101 No. 21.

3. *The Bloudy Book*.... London, 1605. [41] pp. Summarized in Marshburn, *Murder*....

4. John Gerard, *Gerard's Herball, the Essence thereof Distilled by Marcus Woodward*. New York [1985], *passim*. John M. Riddle, *Eve's Herbs*.... Cambridge, [1997], pp. 182–184.

5. Philip Ziegler, *The Black Death*. London, 1969, p. 158.

6. *Deeds against Nature, and Monsters by Kinds*.... London, 1614. [11] pp.

7. *Deeds against Nature, and Monsters by Kinds*.... London, 1614. [11] pp.

8. Thomas Bayly Howell, *Cobbett's Complete Collection of State Trials*.... London, 1809–1826. Vol. III, No. 137, "The Trial of Mervin Lord Audley...." cols. 401–426.

9. *The Mirrour of Justice*.... Cited in Howell's *Cobbett's Complete Collections of State Trials*.... vol. III, cols. 401–402. The law may have been enforced more rigorously against sodomy committed on minors. On the complaint of their parents, Humphrey Stafford was convicted of buggering Richard Robinson, about 17, and Nicholas Crosse, about 13, so that they needed surgical attention. Stafford was hanged after walking in procession from King's Bench prison to the gallows in Southwark, the very pattern of the penitent gentleman. *The Arraignment, Judgement, Confession, and Execution of Humphrey Stafford*.... London, 1607. [17] pp. See also Sir William Holdsworth, *A History of English Law*, London, 1924, vol. IV, p. 504.

10. *The Laws Respecting Women*.... 1777. Reprint, London, 1973. p. 323.

11. The *Dictionary of National Biography* places the son's birth in "about 1617" and has him marrying his stepsister at 13 or 14. Frances Dolan gives his age as 15 in November, 1630, and mentions a report that the couple did not live together after the execution. To be sure, they had no surviving children. A new edition of the account was published in 1679, the year in which Elizabeth died.

12. *The Arraignment and Conviction of Mervyn Lord Audley*.... London, 1642. 12 pp. This copy is missing the account of the execution. The pamphlet omits some details that are in Cobbett and the manuscript mentioned below, including the earl's "three woes" speech. Even so, it was probably printed from the manuscript. The pamphlet and the manuscript have "Antil" for "Ampthill," and "Blawdma" for "Blandina," a visual error not in the manuscript. *Harleian MSS*, 2194, folios 78:90. This manuscript appears to be the basis for the book above and for the account in *State Trials* below. It includes farewell letters from the earl to his son and sisters. The account in Cobbett's *State Trials* follows this manuscript closely, with a few corrections, but omits the farewell letters. Gt. Britain, Public Record Office, *Calendar of State Papers, Domestic, 1629–1631*, p. 371. Gt. Britain, Public Record Office, *Calendar of State Papers, Domestic, 1631–1633*, p. 20. *Dictionary of National Biography*. Under "Touchet." Lady Eleanor Touchet Davies Douglas wrote numerous pamphlets, some perhaps vaguely alluding to this case. She was the sister of George

Touchet, first Earl of Castlehaven, therefore an aunt of Mervyn, the second earl, and not, as Frances Dolan states, his sister. (*Burke's Peerage*; also *Dictionary of National Biography*.) Lady Eleanor is an exasperating source. Her writings include many incoherent religious pamphlets, which are listed in the Bibliography. Perhaps her last publication was *Bethlehem Signifying the House of Bread: or War*.... n.p., 1652, 12 pp. These show her to be not merely eccentric, "verging on madness," as the *Encyclopaedia Britannica* (11th ed.) describes her, but quite dotty. In this last text, the Bethlehem to which she alludes is actually London's Bedlam.

13. Nicholas Barnard, *The Penitent Death of a Woefull Sinner*.... Dublin, 1641. 36 pp. Nicholas Barnard, *A Sermon Preached at the Buriall of the Said John Atherton*.... Dublin, 44 pp. *The Life and Death of John Atherton Lord Bishop of Waterford and Lysmore*.... London, 1641. 6 pp.

14. *Articles Ministered by His Majesties Commissioners ... against John Gwin*.... London, 1641. 5 pp.

IX. Corruption

1. Michael B. Young, *King James and the History of Homosexuality*. New York, 2000. 221 pp.

2. Beatrice White, *Cast of Ravens*.... London, 1965. 260 pp.

3. Lowry Charles Wimberley, *Folklore in the English and Scottish Ballads*. New York, 1965. pp. 33–98.

4. *A Briefe and True Relation of the Murther of Mr Thomas Scott*.... London, 1628. 10 pp. *Dictionary of National Biography*. Under "Scott, Thomas."

5. George Eglisham, *The Forerunner of Revenge*.... Franckfort, 1626. 22 pp. Gt. Britain, Public Record Office, *Calendar of State Papers, Domestic*.... 1625–1626. "Gabriel Browne to a priest in Spain," 20 May, 1626, p. 337. Gt. Britain, Public Record Office, *Calendar of State Papers, Domestic*.... 1629–1631. "Andrew Herriott to Nicholas," 18/28 Jan., 1630, p. 168. Gt. Britain, Public Record Office, *Calendar of State Papers, Domestic*.... 1627–1628. "George Eglesham, Doctor of Physic, to a 'Right Reverend Father,'" 27 May, 1627, p. 192. *Strange Apparitions*.... London, 1642. 8 pp.

6. Johann Oberndoerffer, *The Anatomyes of the True Physition*.... London, Arthur Johnson, 1602. 43 pp.

7. Gt. Britain, Public Record Office, *Calendar of State Papers, Domestic*. 1628–1629, 18 June, 1628, pp. 94 and 169; 21 June, 1628, p. 172.

8. Donald Rumbelow, *I Spy Blue*.... London, 1971, pp. 48–49. Rumbelow cites Repertories of the Court of Aldermen stating that the king himself rode to the scene, arriving too late to save Lambe.

9. Thomas Randolph, *Poems*.... Oxford, 1638. pp. 53–57.

10. *A Briefe Description of the Notorious Life of John Lambe*.... [London?], 1628. 21 pp. See also *Dictionary of National Biography* under "Lambe, John"; and A.L. Rowse, *Simon Forman*, London, 1974.

X. Shades and Witches

1. *The Complete Justice*.... London, 1638. p. 275.

2. John Cotta, *The Triall of Witch-craft, Shewing the True and Right Methode of the Discovery: With a Confutation of Erroneous Wayes*. London, 1616. pp. [1–4].

3. Arthur Johnson, *The Witches of Northamptonshire*.... London, 1612. p. [2].
4. G.B., *A Most Wicked Worke of a Wretched Witch*.... London, 1592. 6 pp.
5. The *Malleus Maleficarum* (or *Hexenhammer*), a guide for the Inquisition, was not translated into English until 1928. Gregory Zilboorg, *The Medical Man and the Witch During the Renaissance*. New York, 1969. pp. 237–239.
6. Arthur Johnson, *The Witches of Northamptonshire*.... London, 1612. pp. [7–12].
7. G.B., *A Most Wicked Worke of a Wretched Witch*.... London, 1592. 6 pp.
8. *Ibid*.
9. *A Briefe and True Relation of the Murther of Mr Thomas Scott*.... London, 1628. 10 pp. *Dictionary of National Biography*. "Scott, Thomas."
10. Henry Goodcole, *The Wonderful Discovery of Elizabeth Sawyer a Witch, Late of Edmonton*.... London, 1621.[25] pp. Discussed in Dolan, *Dangerous Familiars*, pp. 210–212. Thomas Dekker, *The Witch of Edmonton*, 1623.
11. *A Most Certain, Strange, and True Discovery of a Witch Being Taken by Some Parliament Forces*.... [London], 1643. 7 pp. Thomason Tracts E69 No. 9.

XI. From Religion to Disaster

1. *A True Report of the Horrible Murther, Which Was Committed in the House of Sir Jerome Bowes*.... London, 1607. [46] pp. A Catholic, Inigo Jeanes, [sic] beat his father to death for warning him of the severity of the laws. Inigo botched his effort to disembowel himself and lived long enough to implicate 15 of his Catholic friends. George Closse, *The Parricide Papist*, London, 1606. [20] pp.
2. *A True Report of the Arraignment, Tryall, Conviction, and Condemnation, of a Popish Priest*.... London, 1607. [28] pp.
3. Henry Goodcole, *A True Declaration of the Happy Conversion, Contrition, and Christian Preparation of Francis Robinson*.... London, 1618. [22] pp.
4. *The Prisoner of New-Gates Condemnation*.... London, for H. Blunon, 1642. 6 pp.
5. Sollom Emlyn, ed., *A Complete Collection of State-trials and Proceedings for High-treason*.... London, 3rd ed., 1742. XXIII. Proceedings in the Star-Chamber against Henry Sherfield Esq., Recorder of Salisbury, for breaking a painted Glass-Window in the Church of St Edmonds ... the 6th of February 1632....
6. *A True Relation of a Barbarous and Most Cruell Murther Committed by One Enoch ap Evan*.... London, 1634. [17] pp. Peter Studley, *The Looking-Glasse of Schisme*.... 303 pp., and *A Refutation of Such Calumnies*.... [84] pp. Both London, 1634. Summarized in Marshburn, *Murder*....
7. *A True Report of the Horrible Murther*.... London, 1607. [46] pp.
8. *The Arraignment, Tryall, and Confession of Francis Deane a Salter*.... London, 1643. [6] pp.

XII. Conclusion

1. Ordinary executions of the 18th century are described in William B. Thesing, ed., *Executions and the British Experience from the 17th to the 20th Century*.... Jefferson, N.C., McFarland, [1990]. 180 pp. Gallows scenes are artistically encap-

sulated by Hogarth. See for example Sean Shesgreen, *Engravings by Hogarth*, N.Y. 1973. no pp. (100 engravings).

2. *The Manner of the Death and Execution of Arnold Cosbie, for Murthering the Lord Boorke*.... London, 1591. [5] pp. Copy owned by the Bodleian Library. *The Araignment ... of Arnold Cosbye: Who Wilfully Murdered the Lord Burke*.... London [1592]. [14] pp. Copy owned by the British Library.

3. J.S. Cockburn, "The Nature and Incidence of Crime in England 1559–1625: A Preliminary Survey," in his *Crime in England, 1750–1800*, cited above, pp. 58–59.

4. *The Complete Justice*.... London, 1638. pp. 185–186.

5. R.W. Malcolmson, "Infanticide in the Eighteenth Century," in J.S. Cockburn, ed., *Crime in England, 1550–1800*. Princeton, N.J., 1977. p. 200.

6. The pardoning of pirates worked at a different level. When it involved no homicide, the crime was essentially commercial. The victims were often willing or eager to compound, recover as much as possible, and perhaps stick another victim with the rest of the bill.

7. Ronald Blythe, *Divine Landscapes*. New York, 1986. p. 62.

8. John Stow, *A Survey of London, Reprinted from the Text of 1603*.... Rev. ed., Oxford, 1971. vol. II, p. 91. Although the hospital was dissolved by Henry VIII, one alehouse or another along the way continued the practice. Leon Radzinowitz, *A History of English Criminal Law*.... New York, 1948. Vol. I, p. 173.

9. Martin Clout, "The Evaluation and Scheduling of the Globe Theatre Estate." *London Archaeologist*, VI (Summer, 1992) pp. 407–414.

10. Sollom Emlyn, *Complete Collection of State Trials*.... I, 315–324. To be sure, the verdict was influenced by the king's desire to let the child-countess have her annulment so she could marry his favorite, who was heterosexual when the exigencies of his career permitted.

11. H.F. Westlake, *The New Guide to Westminster Abbey*. Oxford, 1917. 53 pp. Lady Antonia Fraser, *Mary Queen of Scots*. New York, 1970. pp. 552–555.

Appendix A: Shakespeare's Purse

1. *Encyclopaedia Britannica*. 11th ed., vol. XIX, p. 867c.

2. George C. Brooke, *English Coins from the Seventh Century to Our Day*. 3d ed. London, 1950. pp. 192–197.

Appendix B: "Appeal" by Next of Kin

1. Sir Francis Bacon, *The Essays of Sir Francis Bacon*, Cambridge, 1907. p. 15.

2. *The Laws Respecting Women*.... 1777. Reprint, London, 1973. pp. 7–10. J.H. Baker, *An Introduction to English Legal History*. 2nd ed. London, 1979. pp. 107, 413–414, 429.

3. Sir William Blackstone explains appeals in his *Commentaries on the Laws of England*. Vol. IV, pp. 310–312. In Cartwright's time it was no longer customary for the relatives of a victim "to drag the appellee to the place of execution," though in Blackstone's time the custom still prevailed "among the wild and untutored inhabitants of America."

Works Cited

Previous Studies

Some pamphlets and books cited in this work have been visited before. In 1971, Joseph H. Marshburn performed helpful detective work in discovering and identifying scores of pamphlets and broadsides on murder and witchcraft, adding to his bibliographical work concise summaries of many of them, strengthened with research among official records in London. (Joseph H. Marshburn, *Murder and Witchcraft in England, 1550–1640, as Recounted in Pamphlets, Ballads, Broadsides, & Plays.* Norman: University of Oklahoma Press, 1977. 187 pp.)

Two years later, he and Alan R. Velie reprinted a few of them in modern spelling. (Joseph H. Marshburn and Alan R. Velie, *Blood and Knavery: A Collection of English Renaissance Pamphlets and Ballads of Crime and Sin.* Rutherford, N.J.: Fairleigh-Dickinson University Press, 1973. 215 pp.)

In 1994, Frances Dolan published an analysis of domestic murder and witchcraft in the literature of the 16th and 17th centuries. She offered a feminist viewpoint and examined the social assumptions of the authors. (Frances E. Dolan, *Dangerous Familiars, Representations of Domestic Crime, 1550–1700.* Ithaca: Cornell University Press, 1994. 253 pp.) The present book also includes cases not found in any of these studies. From time to time, an article employing one of these cases may appear in psychology, law, or other journals.

The originals of these contemporary books and pamphlets are held chiefly by the Bodleian Library of Oxford University, the British Museum (now the British Library), the Huntington Library in California, the Folger Shakespeare Library in Washington, and the Cambridge University Library. In the 1930s, a gigantic project was launched to rescue the contents of English printed books, from the first, in 1475, to 1700, by copying them onto microfilm. After over 60 years it still goes on. Microfilm copies have in turn been sold to numerous libraries, making this treasure available throughout the world. It is these films that have been used for some of this book. The bibliography acknowledges the owner of the original. "S.T.C." and "Wing" refer to the numbers in the printed catalogues:

Pollard, Alfred W., and G.R. Redgrave, comp. *A Short-Title Catalogue of Books Printed in England ... 1475–1640,* London: Bibliographical Society, 1956. 609 pp.

Wing, Donald, comp. *A Short-Title Catalogue of Books Printed in England ... 1641–1700.* New York: Columbia University Press, 1945–51. 3 vols.

Publications of the 17th Century and Before

The Apprehension, Arraignment, and Execution of E. Abbot. London: [H. Ballard] for H. Gosson, 1608. [21] pp. S.T.C. No. 23. [Harvard University]

The Apprentices Warning-Piece, Being a Confession of Peter Moore, Formerly Servant to Mt. Bidgood, Apothecary in Exeter, Executed There the Last Assizes, for Poysoning His Said Master.... London, 1641. 6 pp. Thomason Tracts E173 No. 22. [British Library]

The Arraignment & Burning of Margaret Ferne-Seede, for the Murther of Her Late Husband.... London: Henry Gosson, 1608. 11 pp. S.T.C. No. 10826. [British Library]

The Arraignment and Conviction of Mervyn Lord Audley.... As Also the Beheading of the Said Earle Shortly After on Tower Hill. London: For Tho. Thomas, 1642. 12 pp. Wing No. A3473. [British Library]

The Arraignment, Examination, Confession and Judgment of Arnold Cosbye: Who Wilfully Murdered the Lord Burke, Neere the Towne of Wandsworth, on the 14. Day of This Present Month of January and Was Executed the 17. of the Same Month. 1591. London: For Edward White [1591]. [14] pp. S.T.C. No. 5813. [British Library]

The Arraignment, Judgement, Confession, and Execution of Humphrey Stafford, Gentleman, Who on the Tenth of This Present Month of June, 1607, Suffered at Saint Thomas Waterings. London: By E.A. and A.I. for F.B., 1607. [17] pp. S.T.C. No. 23131. [British Library]

The Arraignment of John Selman, Who Was Executed Neere Charing Crosse the 7 of January, 1612. London: By W.H. for Thomas Archer, 1612. [17] pp. S.T.C. No. 22183. [Huntington Library]

The Arraignment, Tryall, and Confession of Francis Deane a Salter, and of John Faulkner a Strong-water Man (Both Anabaptists, and Lately Received into That Sect) for the Murther of One Mr. Daniels Soliciter.... London: For Richard Harper, 1643. [6] pp. Thomason Tracts E97 No. 13. [British Library]

Articles Ministered by His Majesties Commissioners for Causes Ecclesiasticall. Presented to the High Court of Parliament against John Gwin, Vicar of Cople in the Country of Bedford, Wherein is Discovered His Lascivious Wenching, Drunkennness, and Wanton Life, and Most Vild and Unbecoming Courses, Most Unfit for His Function. London: For V.V., 1641. 5 pp. Thomason Tracts E177 No.20. [British Library]

B., G. *A Most Wicked Worke of a Wretched Witch, (the Like Whereof None Can Record These Manie Yeares in England.) Wrought on the Person of One Richard Burt, Servant to Maister Edling of Woodhall in the Parrish of Pinner ... 1592....* London: For William Barley. 6 pp. S.T.C. No. 1028. [Lambeth Library]

Barnard, Nicholas. *The Penitent Death of a Woefull Sinner, Or, The Penitent Death of John Atherton Executed at Dublin the 5. of December. 1640....* Dublin: Society of Stationers, 1641. 36 pp. Thomason Tracts E176 No. 3. [British Library]

———. *A Sermon Preached at the Buriall of the Said John Atherton. The Next Night after His Execution, December the Fifth, 1640. In Saint Johns Church in Dublin....* Dublin, 44 pp. Thomason Tracts E176 No. 4. [British Library]

Bartholomew Faire or Variety of Fancies, Where You May Find a Faire of Wares, and All to Please Your Mind.... London, 1641. 5 pp. Wing No. B980, Thomason Tracts E173 No. 6. [British Library]

A Bloody New-Yeares Gift, or a True Declaration of the Murther of Maister Robert Heath. Whereunto is Annexed, Sundry Exploits of Tendance, Otherwise Called Double Diligence, Servant unto Derrick the Hangman, Who with His Consort (Old Doublets)

Was Executed at Tyborne in January Last Past, 1609. London: For B. S[utton] and W.B., 1609. [15] pp. S.T.C. No. 13018.3. [Huntington Library]

The Bloudy Book, or the Tragicall End of Sir John Fites (alias) Fitz. London: For Francys Burton, 1605. [41] pp. S.T.C. No. 10930. [British Library]

A Briefe and True Relation of the Murther of Mr Thomas Scott Preacher of Gods Word and Bachelor of Divinitie.... London: For Nath. Butter, 1628. 10 pp. S.T.C. No. 22106. [British Library]

A Briefe Description of the Notorious Life of John Lambe, Otherwise Doctor Lambe. Together with His Ignominious Death. "Printed in Amsterdam" [London?], 1628. 21 pp. S.T.C. No. 15177. [British Library]

Cartwright, Francis. *The Life, Confession, and Heartie Repentance of Francis Cartwright for His Bloudie Sinne of Killing One Master Storr, Master of Arts, and Minister of Market Raisin in Lincolnshire....* London: For Nathaniell Butter, 1621. [32] pp. S.T.C. No. 4704. [Folger Library]

Climsell, Richard. *A Cruell Murther Committed Lately upon the Body of A. Gearsy.* [London], 1635. 2 pp. S.T.C. No. 5418. [British Library]

Closse, George. *The Parricide Papist....* London, 1606. [20] pp. S.T.C. No. 5441.2. [British Library]

Coke, Sir Edward. *Les Reports. [Part I].* Londini [London]: in aedibus Thomas Wright. 1600. Corbet's Case. S.T.C. No. 5493. [Huntington Library]

The Complete Justice. A Compendium of the Particulars Incident to Justices of the Peace, Either in Sessions or Out of Sessions. Gatheerd Out of the Statutes, Reports, Late Resolutions of the Judges, and Other Approved Authorities.... London: By the Assignes of J. More Esquire, 1638. 277 pp. S.T.C. No. 14888. [Cambridge University Library]

Cooper, Thomas. *The Cry and Revenge of Blood Expressing the Haynousness of Wilfull Murther....* London: By Nicholas Oakes for John Wright, 1620. 63 pp. S.T.C. No. 5698. [Huntington Library]

Cotta, John. *The Infallible True and Assured Witch.* London, 1625. 135 pp. S.T.C. No. 5838. [British Library]

———. *The Triall of Witch-Craft, Shewing the True and Right Methode of the Discovery: With a Confutation of Erroneous Wayes.* London, 1616. S.T.C. No. 5836. [Bodleian Library.]

Dalton, Michael. *The Country Justice, Conteyning the Practices of the Justices of the Peace Out of Their Sessions....* London: For the Society of Stationers, 1618. 370 pp. S.T.C. No. 6205. [Library of Congress]

Darrel, John. *The True Relation of the Grievous Handling of William Sommers of Nottingham Being Possessed with a Devill. Shewing How He Was First Taken, and How Lamentably from Time to Time He Was Tormented and Afflicted....* London: By Tho. Harper, 1641. [6] pp. Wing No. D253. [British Library]

Deeds against Nature, and Monsters by Kinds: Tryed at the Gaol Deliverie of Newgate, at the Sessions in the Old Bayly.... London: For Edward Wright, 1614. [11] pp. S.T.C. No. 809. [Bodleian Library]

Dekker, Thomas. *The Belman of London.* London, 1608. S.T.C. No. 6480. [British Library]

A Detection of Damnable Driftes, Practized by Three Witches Arraigned at Chelmisforde in Essex, at the Assizes There Holden, Whiche Were Executed in Aprill. 1579. London: For Edward White. [16] pp. S.T.C. No. 5115. [British Library]

Douglas, Lady Eleanor Touchet Davies. *Bethlehem Signifying the House of Bread: or*

War. Whereof Informs Whoso Takes a Small Roul to Taste Cures Forthwith Distraction in the Supreamest Nature; with Some Vertue Indu'd. n.p., 1652. 12 pp. Wing No. D1978. [Bodleian Library]

———. *From the Lady Eleanor Her Blessing to Her Beloved Daughter, the Right Honorable Countesse of Huntingdon The Prophet Daniels Vision: Chap. 7. In the First Years of Belchazar Rex, &c.* [London], 1644. 38 pp. Thomason Tracts E10 No. 1. [British Library]

———. *The Lady Eleanor Her Appeale to the High Court of Parliament.* n.p., 1641. 20 pp. Thomason Tracts E172 No. 33. [British Library]

———. *The Star to the Wise. 1643. To the High Court of Parliament ... Shewing Cause to Have Her Book Licensed, Being the Revelations Interpretation*. London, 1643. 20 pp. Thomason Tracts E76 No. 28. [British Library]

———. *A Warning to the Dragon and All His Angels*. n.p., 1625. 106 pp. S.T.C. No. 904. [British Library]

———. *The Word of God to the City of London....* London, 1644. Wing No. D2018. [British Library]

Dugdale, Gilbert. *A True Discourse of the Practices of Elizabeth Caldwell on the Parson of T. Caldwell.* London: By James Roberts for John Busbie, 1604. [27] pp. S.T.C. No. 7293. [Huntington Library]

Eglisham, George. *The Forerunner of Revenge. Upon the Duke of Buckingham for the Poysoning of the Most Potent King James of Happy Memory King of Great Britain, and the Lord Marquis of Hamilton, and Others of the Nobilitie....* Franckfort, 1626. 22 pp. S.T.C. No. 7548. [Emmanuel College, Cambridge]

The Examination, Confession, and Condemnation of Henry Robson, Fisherman of Rye. London: By Felix Kingston for R.W., 1598. [8] pp. S.T.C. No. 21131. [Bodleian Library]

The Examination of John Bartram ... before Sir Francis Bacon ... and Sir Henry Yelverton.... London: By John Beale, 1616. [4] pp. Bound with L.,N., below.

Golding, Arthur. *A Briefe Discourse of the Late Master George Saunders, a Worshipfull Citizen of London, and of the Apprehension, Arraignment, and Execution of the Principal and Accessaries of the Same.* London: Henry Bynneman, 1573. [16] pp. S.T.C. No. 11986. [British Library]

Goodcole, Henry. *The Adulteresses Funerall Day: in Flaming, Scorching, and Consuming Fire: Or the Burning Down to Ashes of Alice Clarke Late of Uxbridge ... in West Smithfield, on Wensday the 20. of May, 1635. for the Unnatural Poisoning of Fortune Clarke Her Husband....* London: By N. & I. Oakes, 1635. [13] pp. S.T.C. No. 12009. [Harvard University]

———. *Heaven's Speedy Hue and Cry after Lust and Murther.... Written by H. G. Their Daily Visiter, at the Time of Their Imprisonment, and Severall Days of Execution.* London: By M. and I. Okes, 1635. [22] pp. S.T.C. No. 12010. [British Library]

———. *Nature's Cruell Step-Dames, or Matchless Monsters of the Female Sex....* London: For Francis Coules, 1637. 20 pp. S.T.C. No. 12012. [Folger Shakespeare Library]

———. *A True Declaration of the Happy Conversion, Contrition, and Christian Preparation of Francis Robinson, Gentleman, Who for Counterfeiting the Great Seale of England was Drawen, Hang'd, and Quartered at Charing-Crosse, on Friday Last, Being the Thirteenth Day of November, 1618.* London: By Edw. Allde, 1618. [22] pp. S.T.C. No. 12013. [British Library]

———. *The Wonderful Discovery of Elizabeth Sawyer a Witch, Late of Edmonton, Her Conviction and Condemnation and Death. Together with the Relation of the Divels Access* to Her, and Their Conference Together. London: For William Butler, 1621. [25] pp. S.T.C. No. 12014. [British Library]

G[reene], R[obert]. *The Blacke Bookes Messenger. Laying Open the Life and Death of Ned Browne One of the Most Notable Cutpurses, and Conny-Catchers, That Ever Lived in England....* London: By John Danter, 1592. [26] pp. S.T.C. No. 12223. [Huntington Library]

Harman, Thomas. *A Caveat for Common Cursetors Vulgarly Called Vagabones....* London: By William Gryffith, 1567. [10] pp. S.T.C. No. 14438. [Bodleian Library]

Harsnett, Samuel. *A Discovery of the Fraudulent Practices of John Darrel, Bachelor of Arts, in His Proceedings Concerning the Pretended Possession of William Somers at Nottingham: of Thomas Darling the Boy of Burton at Caldwell: and of Katherine Wright at Mansfield....* London: By John Wolfe, 1599. 324 pp. S.T.C. No. 12883. [Huntington Library]

Hutton, Luke. *The Blacke Dogge of Newgate: Both Pithie and Profitable to All Readers.* London, 1597? [39] pp. S.T.C. No. 14029. [Huntington Library]

———. *Luke Hutton's Lamentation: Which He Wrote the Day before His Death, Being Condemned to Be Hanged at Yorke This Last Assizes for His Robberies and Trespasses Committed. To the Tune of Wandering and Wavering.* London: For Thomas Millington, 1598. 1 page folio. S.T.C. 14032. [Huntington Library]

Johnson, Arthur. *The Witches of Northamptonshire. Agnes Brown. Joane Vaughan. Arthur Bill. Hellen Jenkinson. Mary Barber. Witches. Who Were All Executed at Northampton the 22. of July Last. 1612.* London: For Arthur Johnson, 1612. S.T.C. No. 3907. [Bodleian Library]

The Just Reward of a Debauched Cavallier: Or, the Wicked and Divellish Intentions of One Thomas Browne a Late Cavallier, and Now a Prisoner in New Gate.... [London]: For J. Jackson, 1643. [5] pp. Thomason Tracts E101 No. 21. [British Library]

L., N. *A True Relation of the Grounds, Occasion, and Circumstances, of the Horrible Murther Committed by John Bartram, Gent., upon the Body of Sir Thomas Tyndal of Lincolns Inne....* London: By John Beale, 1616. [20] pp. S.T.C. No. 14054. [Huntington Library]

The Life and Death of Gamaliel Ratsey a Famous Thief of England, Executed at Bedford the 26th of March Last Past, 1605. [43] pp. (The Bodleian copy has only a manuscript title page that omits place and date of publication.) S.T.C. No. 20753. [Bodleian Library]

The Life and Death of Griffin Flood Informant.... London: For I.T., 1623. [19] pp. S.T.C. No. 11090. [British Library]

The Life and Death of John Atherton Lord Bishop of Waterford and Lysmore within the Kingdom of Ireland, Borne Near Bridgewater in Somersetshire. Who for Incest, Buggery, and Many Other Enormous Crimes, After Having Lived a Vicious Life, Dyed a Shameful Death, and Was on the Fifth of December Last Past, Hanged on the Gallows Greene at Dublin, and His Man John Childe Being His Proctor, with Whom He Had Committed the Buggery, Was Hangd in March at Bandon Bridges, Condemned Thereunto at the Assizes at Corke. London: 1641. 6 pp. Thomason Tracts E176 No. 6. [British Library]

The Life, Apprehension, Arraignment, and Execution of Charles Courtney, Alias Holice, Alias Worsley, and Clement Slie Fencer: With Their Escapes and Breakings of Prison: As Also the True and Hearty Repentance of Charles Courtney with Other Passages Worthy of Note and Reading. London: For Edward Marchant, 1612. [22] pp. S.T.C. No. 5848. [British Library]

The Lives, Apprehension, Arraignment & Execution of Robert Throgmorton. William Porter. John Bishop. Gentlemen.... London: Henry Gosson, 1608. [21] pp. S.T.C. No. 24053. [Bodleian Library]

The Lives, Apprehensions, Arraignments, and Executions of the 19 Late Pyrates. Namely: Capt. Harris, Jennings, Longcastle, Downes, Haulsey, and Their Companies. As They Were Severally Indited on St. Margarets Hill in Southwarke, on the 22 of December Last, and Executed the Fryday Following. London: For John Busby the Elder, [1608]. [28] pp. S.T.C. 21681. [Huntington Library]

The Manner of the Cruell Outrageous Murther of William Storre.... Oxford: Joseph Barnes, 1603. [9] pp. S.T.C. No. 23295. [Huntington Library]

The Manner of the Death and Execution of Arnold Cosbie, for Murthering the Lord Boorke. Who Was Executed at Wandsworth Townes End on the 27. of Januarie 1591. With Certain Verses Written by the Said Cosby in the Time of His Imprisonment, Containing Matter of Great Effect, as Well Touching His Life as Also His Penitence before His Death. [London]: For William Wright, 1591. [6] pp. S.T.C. No. 11936. [Bodleian Library]

Marchant, Edward. *The Life, Apprehension, Arraignment, and Execution of Charles Courtney.* London, 1612. [21] pp. S.T.C. No. 5878. [British Library]

A Most Certain, Strange, and True Discovery of a Witch Being Taken by Some Parliament Forces as She Was Standing on a Small Planck Board and Sayling on It over the River at Newbury.... [London]: By John Hammond, 1643. 7 pp. Thomason Tracts E69 No. 9. [British Library]

Murder upon Murder, Committed by Thomas Sherwoode, Alias Countrey Tom, and Elizabeth Evans, Alias, Canbrye Bess.... London: For T. Langley by Thomas Lambert, [1635]. A ballad, 2 pp. S.T.C. No. 22431. [Bodleian Library]

Murther, Murther, or a Bloody Relation.... London: For Tho. Bates, 1641. 6pp. Wing No. M3084. [British Library]

Oberndoerffer, Johann. *The Anatomyes of the True Physition, and Counterfeit Mountebanke....* London: Arthur Johnson, 1602. 43 pp. S.T.C. No. 18759. [British Library]

Orders Appointed to Be Executed in the Cittie of London, for Setting Roges and Idle Persons to Worke, and for Releefe of the Poore. London: By Hugh Singleton, n.d. [15] pp. S.T.C. No. 16390. [Bodleian Library]

Pecham, H. *The Art of Living in London, or a Caution How Gentlemen, Countreymen and Strangers, Drawn by Occasion of Businesse, Should Dispose of Themselves in the Thriftiest Way, Not Onely in the Citie, But in All Other Populous Places. As Also the Direction for the Poorer Sort That Come Thither to Seeke Their Fortunes.* [London]: For John Gyles, 1642. [7] pp. Thomason Tracts E145 No. 20. [British Library]

A Pittilesse Mother. That Most Unnaturally at One Time, Murthered Two of Her Owne Children at Acton.... [London, 1616]. [9] pp. S.T.C. No. 24757. [Harvard University]

The Prisoner of New-Gates Condemnation.... London: For H. Blunon, 1642. 6 pp. Thomason Tracts E143 No. 21. [British Library]

Randolph, Thomas. *Poems: With the Muses Looking-Glasse; and Amytas.* Oxford: Leonard Lichfield for Francis Bowman, 1638. pp. 53–57. S.T.C. No. 20694. [British Library]

Ratsey, Gamaliel. *The Life and Death of Gamaliel Ratsey.* n.p., 1605. [43] pp. S.T.C. No. 20753. [Bodleian Library]

Rowse, John. *The Unnatural Father....* London: For I. T. and H.G., 1621. [19] pp. S.T.C. No. 23808a. [British Library]

Southerne, Lawrence. *Fearfull Newes from Coventry, or a True Relation and Lamentable Story of One Thomas Holt of Conventrey a Musician: Who through Covetousness and Immoderate Love of Money, Sold Himself to the Devill, with Whom He Made a Contract for Certain Yeares. And Also of His Most Lamentable End and Death, on the 16. Day of February, 1641. To the Terror and Amazement of the Inhabitants Thereabouts....* London: For John Thomas, 1642. 8 pp. Thomason Tracts E146 No. 3. [British Library]

Strange Apparitions, or the Ghost of King James, with a Late Conference between the Ghost of That Good King, the Marquesse Hamiltons, and George Eglishams, Doctor of Physick, unto Which Appeared the Ghost of the Late Duke of Buckingham, Concerning the Death and Poysoning of King James and the Rest. London: For J. Aston, 1642. 8 pp. S.T.C. No. S5880. [British Library].

Studley, Peter. *The Looking-Glasse of Schisme: Wherein by a Briefe and True Narration of the Execrable Murders, Done by Enoch ap Evan, a Downe-Right Separatist, on the Bodies of His Mother and Brother, with the Cause Mooving Him Thereunto, the Disobedience of that Sect, against Royal Majesty, and the Lawes of Our Church Is Plainly Set Forth.* London: By R.B. for Thomas Alchorne, 1634. 303 pp. S.T.C. No. 23403. [University of Illinois]

——— . *A Refutation of Such Calumnies as the Virulent Malice of Schismaticall Fellowes, Hath Scattered Abroad to Deprave the Credit and Truth of This Historie.* London: By R.B. for Thomas Alchorne, 1634. [89] pp. Bound with the second edition (1635) of his Looking Glass. S.T.C. No. 23404. [University of Illinois]

Sundrye Strange and Inhumane Murthers Lately Commited ... of Master Page of Plymouth, Murthered by the Consent of His Own Wife.... London: By Thomas Scarlet, 1591. [12] pp. S.T.C. No. 18286.5. [Lambeth Palace Library]

These Oils, Waters, and Other Compositions.... [London], 1585. Broadside, 1 p. S.T.C. No. 14601. [British Library]

Three Bloodie Murders: The First by Francis Cartwright upon William Storre..., the Second, Committed by Elizabeth James, on the Body of Her Mayde..., the Third, Committed upon a Stranger.... London: For John Trundle, 1613. [19] pp. S.T.C. No. 18287. [Bodleian Library]

A True and Most Dreadfull Discourse of a Woman Possessed with a Devill: Who in the Likenesse of a Headlesse Beare Fetched Her out of Her Bedd ... May Last. 1584. At Dichet in Sommersetshire.... London: For Thomas Nelson. [11] pp. S.T.C. No. 5681. [Folger Library]

A True Relation of a Barbarous and Most Cruell Murther Committed by One Enoch ap Evan.... London: By N. Okes, 1634. [17] pp. S.T.C. No. 10582. [Bodleian Library]

A True Relation of the Most Inhumane and Bloody Murther, of Master James Minister and Preacher of the Word of God at Rockland in Norfolke.... London: For R. Bonian and H. Walley, 1609. [17] pp. S.T.C. No. 14436. [British Library]

A True Report of the Arraignment, Tryall, Conviction, and Condemnation, of a Popish Priest, Named Robert Drewrie.... Also, the Tryall and Death of Humphrey Lloyd, for Maliciousie Murdering One of the Guard.... London: For Jefferie Chorlton, 1607. [28] pp. S.T.C. No. 7261. [Huntington Library]

A True Report of the Horrible Murther, Which Was Committed in the House of Sir Jerome Bowes, Knight, on the 20. Day of February, Anno Dom. 1606.... London: By H.L. for Mathew Lownes, 1607. [46] pp. S.T.C. 3434. [British Library]

Two Horrible and Inhumane Murders Done in Lincolnshire, by the Husbands upon Their

Wives.... London: For John Wright, 1607. [17] pp. S.T.C. No. 4768. [British Library]

Two Most Unnatural and Bloodie Murthers. The One by Master Caverley, a Yorkshire Gentleman, Practised upon His Wife, and Committed uppon His Two Children, the Three and Twentie of Aprill 1605. The Other by Mistris Browne, and Her Servant Peter.... London: By V.S. for Nathaniel Butter, 1605. 28 pp. S.T.C. No. 18288. [Bodleian Library]

Two Notorious Murders. One Committed by a Tanner on His Wives Sonne.... London: For William Blackwall and George Shaw, 1595. 10 pp. S.T.C. No. 18209. [British Library]

W., C. *The Crying Murther Contayning the Cruell and Most Horrible Butchery of Mr. Trat....* London: Nathaniel Butter, 1624. [23] pp. S.T.C. No. 24900. [British Library]

A Warning for Faire Women ... As It Hath Beene Lately Diverse Times Acted by the ... Lord Chamberlaine His Servants. London: Valentine Sims for William Aspley, 1599. S.T.C. No. 25089. [Huntington Library]

Wilkins, George. *The Miseries of Inforst Mariage. As It Is Now Played by His Majesties Servants....* London, 1607. S.T.C. No. 25635. [British Library]

Witches Apprehended, Examined and Executed for Notable Villanies by Them Committed Both by Land and Water. With a Strange and Most True Triall How to Know Whether a Woman Be a Witch or Not. London: For Edward Marchant, 1613. [19] pp. S.T.C. No. 25872. [Huntington Library]

The Whole Life and Death of Long Meg, of Westminster. London: For A. Veale, 1582. 24 pp. S.T.C. No. 17782. [British Library]

A Yorkshire Tragedy, Not So New As Lamentable and True. Acted by His Majesties Players at the Globe.... London: By R. B. for T. Pavier, 1609. S.T.C. No. 22340. [British Library]

Later Publications

Aubrey, John. *Brief Lives.* Ed. by Oliver Lawson Dick. London: Butterworths, 1950. 408 pp.

Baker, J. H. *An Introduction to English Legal History.* 2nd ed. London: Butterworths, 1979. 477 pp.

Blackstone, Sir William. *Commentaries on the Laws of England.* Reprint of first American edition, Philadelphia: 1772. 4 vols.

Blythe, Ronald. *Divine Landscapes.* New York: Viking, 1986. 254 pp.

Brooke, George C., *English Coins from the Seventh Century to the Present Day.* 3rd ed. London: Methuen, 1950. 300pp.

Burke's Genealogical and Heraldic History of the Peerage, Baronetage, and Knightage.... 105th ed. London: Burke's Peerage, 1970.

Clout, Martin. "The Evaluation and Scheduling of the Globe Theatre Estate." *London Archaeologist,* VI (Summer, 1992): 407–414.

Cockburn, J.S., ed. *Crime in England, 1550–1800.* Princeton, N.J.: Princeton University Press, 1977. 364 pp.

Cromartie, Alan. *Sir Matthew Hale, 1609–1676: Law, Religion, and Natural Philosophy.* Cambridge Studies in Early British Modern History. Cambridge, New York: University Press, Cambridge, 1995. 264 pp.

The Dictionary of National Biography. London: Oxford University Press, 1949–50.
Dolan, Frances E. *Dangerous Familiars: Representations of Domestic Crime, 1550–1700*. Ithaca: Cornell University Press, 1994. 253 pp.
Dreisbach, Robert H. *Handbook of Poisoning: Diagnosis and Treatment*. 8th ed. Los Altos, Calif.: Lange Medical Publications, 1974. 517 pp.
Emlyn, Sollom, ed. *A Complete Collection of State-trials and Proceedings for High-treason....* 3rd ed. London. 1742. 6 vols.
The Encyclopaedia of Ireland. Dublin: A. Figgis, 1968. 463 pp.
Fraser, Antonia. *Mary, Queen of Scots*. New York: 1970. 613 pp.
Gerard, John. *Gerard's Herball, The Essence thereof Distilled by Marcus Woodward*. New York: Crescent, 1985. 303 pp.
Gifis, Steven H. *Law Dictionary*. New York: Barron's, 1984. 524 pp.
Great Britain. Public Record Office. *Calendar of State Papers, Domestic Series 1547–1704 Preserved in the Public Record Office*. London: Longman's, 1856–1872. Years 1626–1627, 1627–1629, 1629–1631, and 1631–1633.
Greene, Robert. *The Black Bookes Messenger, 1592*. "Cuthbert Conny-Catcher," the *Defense of Conny-Catching. 1592*. Elizabethan and Jacobean Quartos. 1922–1926. Ed. by G. B. Harrison. Reprint, New York: Barnes & Noble, 15 vol.
Herrup, Cynthia. *The Common Peace: Participation and the Criminal Law in Seventeenth-Century England*. Cambridge Studies in Early Modern British History. Cambridge, New York: Cambridge University Press, 1987. 232 pp.
Hibbert, Christopher. *Tower of London*. New York. 1980. 172 pp.
Holdsworth, Sir William. *A History of English Law*. London 1924. 16 vols.
Howell, Thomas Bayly. *Cobbett's Complete Collection of State Trials and Proceedings for High Treason and Other Crimes....* London, Hansard, 1809–1826. Vol. III, No. 137, "The Trial of Mervin Lord Audley...."
Kent, Joan R. *The English Village Constable, 1580–1642: A Social and Administrative Study*. Oxford: Clarendon, 1986. 325 pp.
The Laws Respecting Women as They Regard Their Natural Rights, or Their Connections and Conduct.... 1777. Reprint, London: Oceana, 1973. 449 pp.
Lewis, Robert A. *Lewis' Dictionary of Toxicology*. Boca Raton, Fla.: Lewis Publishers, 1998. 1,127 pp.
McNeill, William H. *Plagues and Peoples*. Garden City, N.Y.: Anchor, 1977. 340 pp.
Neale, J. E. *Queen Elizabeth: A Biography*. Garden City, N.Y.: Doubleday, 1957. 424 pp.
Partridge, Eric. *Shakespeare's Bawdy*. rev.ed. New York: Dutton, 1969. 223 pp.
Radzinowicz, Leon. *A History of English Criminal Law and Its Administration from 1750*. New York: Macmillan, 1948. 3 vols.
Riddle, John M. *Eve's Herbs: A History of Contraception and Abortion in the West*. Cambridge: Harvard University Press, 1997. 341 pp.
Rowse, A.L. *Simon Forman: Sex and Society in Shakespeare's Age*. London: Weidenfeld and Nicolson, 1974. 315 pp.
Rumbelow, Donald. *I Spy Blue: The Police and Crime in the City of London from Elizabeth I to Victoria*. London: Macmillan, 1971. 250 pp.
Scott, Otto J. *James I*. New York: Mason/Charter, 1976. 472 pp.
Shesgreen, Sean, ed. *Engravings by Hogarth*. New York: Dover, 1973. no pp. (100 engravings).
Sorlien, Robert Parker, ed. *The Diary of John Manningham of the Middle Temple, 1602–1603*. Hanover, N.H.: University Press of New England, 1976. 467 pp.

Stephenson, Carl, and Frederick George Marcham, eds. *Sources of English Constitutional History*.... New York and London: Harper, 1937. 906 pp.
Stow, John. *A Survey of London, by John Stow. Reprinted from the Text of 1603*.... rev. ed., Oxford: Clarendon, 1971. 2 vols.
Thesing, William B., ed. *Executions and the British Experience from the 17th to the 20th Century: A Collection of Essays*. Jefferson, N.C.: McFarland, 1990. 180 pp.
Thienes, Clinton H., and Thomas J. Haley. *Clinical Toxicology*. Philadelphia: Lea & Febiger, 1972. 459 pp.
Thomson, Janice E. *Mercenaries, Pirates, and Sovereigns*. Princeton, N.J.: Princeton University Press, 1994. 219 pp.
Tillyard, E.M.W. *The Elizabethan World Picture*. New York: Vintage, n.d. 116 pp.
Westlake, H.F. *The New Guide to Westminster Abbey*. Oxford, 1917. 53 pp.
White, Beatrice. *Cast of Ravens: The Strange Case of Sir Thomas Overbury*. London: J. Murray, 1965. 260 pp.
Williams, Neville. *The Sea Dogs: Privateers, Plunder and Piracy in the Elizabethan Age*. London: Weidenfeld and Nicholson, 1975. 278 pp.
Willson, David Harris. *King James I and VI*. London: J. Cape, 1956. 480 pp.
Wimberly, Lowry Charles. *Folklore in the English and Scottish Ballads*. New York: Ungar, 1965. 466 pp.
Young, Michael B. *King James and the History of Homosexuality*. New York University Press, 2000. 221 pp.
Ziegler, Philip. *The Black Death*. London: Collins, 1969. 331 pp.
Zilboorg, Gregory. *The Medical Man and the Witch During the Renaissance*. New York: Cooper Square, 1969. 215 pp.

Index

Abbott, Elizabeth 74ff
Acton 46
Addle Hill 109
Aldersgate 90, 165
Aldgate 76
Algiers, Dey of 25
Alley, Daniel 118ff
Ampthill 125ff
ap Evans family 170ff, 184
Arthur, John 121ff
Arundel, Earl of 125
Ashby de la Zouche, Leicestershire 108
Ashford, Kent 19
Ashford, __ 194
Athelstan, King 128
Atherton, John, Bishop 132ff, 179, 181, 184
Atkyns, Mother 156
Audley, Lord *see* Castlehaven, Earl of
Austin, Cirill 35ff
Avery, __ 154

Bacon, Sir Francis 11, 73, 79, 107, 193
Baker, Andrew 34ff
Baltimore Bay, Ireland 93, 96
Banister, Sir Robert 79
Barbican 149
Barnes, Elizabeth 51ff, 179, 184
Barry, Leonard 79
Barthelmew, Mrs. 77
Bartram, John 106ff, 179, 180
Battersea 51

Battie, John 73
Beane, John 58
Bedford 87, 157, 160
Bedford, Earl of 60
Belcher, Mrs. 154
Bergen op Zoom 138
Berwick on Tweed 24
Bethlehem (Bedlam) Hospital 120
Bidgood, Humphrey 69
Billingsgate 58, 188
Bishop, Captain 91ff
Bishop, John 111
Bishop's Castle, Salop 175
Bishopsgate 151
Blackstone, Sir William 13
Blandford, Dorset 34
Blandina 127
Bloomsbury 80
Blundell, Jane 49ff
Boulton, Master 20
Bowes, Sir Jerome 176
Bowndes, Jeffery 71ff, 183
Bracton, Henry de 128
Brentwood, Essex 75
Bridewell 15
Brigandine (parson) 37
Bristol, Somerset 91, 93, 102
Broadway, Giles 125ff
Brooke, Lord 39ff, 180
Brooks, __ 134
Browne, __ 26ff, 186
Browne, Agnes 154
Browne, George 57ff
Browne, Ned 83
Browne, Thomas 113ff

Brussels 143
Brydges, Elizabeth 125ff, 182
Buckingham, Duke of 136ff, 189
Burke, Edmund 194
Burs, maid 69
Burt, Richard 155ff

Caldwell, Elizabeth 71ff, 181
Caldwell, Thomas 71ff
Cambridge 87
Canberry Bess 80ff
Canterbury 19
Carlisle, Earl of 125
Cartwright, Francis 22ff, 186, 193
Cash family 61ff
Castlehaven, Countess of 125ff, 182
Castlehaven, Earl of 122ff, 182, 184, 189
Caverley, Yorkshire 39
Caverley family 39ff, 181, 182
Chambers, Thomas 17
Chancery Lane 128
Chandos, Lord 125
Charing Cross 79, 166, 176
Charles I, King 128ff, 138ff
Cheapside 80
Chester 73, 100, 188
Chichester, Sir Arthur 99ff
Childe, John 132ff

213

214 Index

Cholmsly, Lady Mary 73
Christ's Hospital 14
Clanricard, Earl of 98
Clarke, Alice 70ff
Claxton, Thomas 81
Clement, "Trusty" Roger 57ff
Clerkenwell 80
Clink, Southwark 143
Cloth Fair 80
Clun, Salop 170
Coke, Sir Edward 77
Colchester, Essex 101
Coleman Street 149
Compton, Lady 140, 147
Cople, Beds 133
Corbet's Tie, Essex 17
Cork, Ireland 132
Cornhill 58
Cornwall 101, 103
Cosbie, Captain 180
Cotta, John 153
Courtney, Charles 88ff
Courtney, Sir William 118
Courtney family 117
Coventry, Earl of 122ff
Coventry, Warwickshire 67
Cow Cross 80
Cox, Mrs. 76
Creech, Somerset 33
Creechurch 74, 76, 77
Croydon, Surrey 50
Cuffe (justice of the peace) 33ff

Danby, Earl of 125
Daniel (solicitor) 177
Darling, Thomas 107ff
Darrel, John 107ff, 153
Davies, Lady Eleanor 130
Davy family 134
Deal, Kent 25
Deane, Francis 177
Dekker, Thomas 163
Derby 167
Derby, Earl of 60, 125
Derrick, hangman 82
Dighton, constable 47
Dorset, Earl of 125, 189
Doubleday, Edmond 79
Downes, Captain 101ff
Downes, Elizabeth 143
Drake, Sir Francis 56

Drewrie, Elizabeth 57ff
Dublin 99, 132
Duck Lane 79, 109
Dudley, Lord 125
Duncalfe (father of E. Caldwell) 71
Dunkirk 95
Dunnage, Suffolk 27
Dunster, Somerset 38

Eastbridge, Suffolk 26
Edmonton 160
Edward VI, King 15, 192
Eglisham, George 139ff
Elbow Lane 177
Elizabeth I, Queen 4, 49, 57ff, 91, 95, 117
Elizabeth, Queen of Bohemia 138ff, 189
Enger (miller) 156ff
Epping, Essex 17
Essex, Countess of see Somerset, Countess of
Essex, Earl of 125, 135, 163ff, 188
Evans, Richard 51ff
Ewell, Surrey 47, 188
Exchange 58
Exeter, Devonshire 56

Faulkner, John 177
Felton, John 151
Ferneseed, Anthony 109ff
Ferneseed, Margaret 109ff, 181, 188
Finch, Heneage 161
Fitz, Sir John 116ff, 179, 184, 186
Fitz, Lady 181
Fitzpatrick, Lawrence 125ff
Fleet Prison 169
Fleet River 15
Fleet Street 128
Flood, Griffin 112ff
Fonthill Gifford, Wiltshire 125
Forman, Simon 146
Fortune, Alice 70f, 181
Fortune Theatre 149
Fowcks family 134
Fowey, Cornwall 101
Fulham 51

Gardner (pawnbroker) 89

Gibraltar 25, 92
Glanfield family 55ff, 179
Glasier (cellmate of Robson) 19
Globe Theatre 4, 187
Golden Lane 149
Golding, Peter 26ff
Gondomar, Count 138
Goodcole, Henry 51ff, 71, 79, 88, 131, 161, 167, 184
Goodrich, Alice 107
Goring, Lord 125
Grantham, Lincolnshire 25
Graygoose family 17
Green (servant) 127
Greene, Robert 83
Greenwich 57
Guildhall 59
Gwin, John 133ff, 181

Hal (ship owner) 100ff
Hale, Sir Matthew 13
Half Moon Tavern 165
Hall, Isabel 71ff
Halsworth, Suffolk 29
Hamcotes, Sir Richard 62
Hamilton, Marquess of 141ff
Hamton, Ann 69
Harris, James 91ff
Harsnett, Samuel 108, 153
Harwood, Margaret 69
Hawkins, Sir Richard 25
Heath, Sir Robert 125
Henry VIII, King 11, 15, 128, 192
Hereford, Diocese 174
Herriott, partner of Eglisham 144
Holborn 81
Holland, Earl of 125
Holt, Roland 80
Holt family 67ff
Holton, Lincolnshire 61
Houndsditch 81
Housman, A.E. 170
Howard, Sir Robert 172
Howell family 172
Hutton, Matthew, Archbishop of York 25, 108
Hyde Park 90

Index

Ilminster, Somerset 38
Islington 122

James, Elizabeth 78
James family 63ff, 185
James I, King 4, 11, 24, 45, 53, 79, 89ff, 107, 117, 136ff, 153, 189
Jennings, Captain 92ff
Jonson, Ben 4, 128, 149

Kennet, River 163
Kensington 51
Key, publican 45
Killingworth, __ 74ff
King Street 143
King's Bench Prison, Southwark 146
Kingston, Middlesex 118
Knighton, Salop 171

Lambe, John 144ff
Lambert, John 136ff, 185
Lambeth 108
Lancashire 108
Land (servant) 29ff
Laud, William, Archbishop of Canterbury 133, 175, 189
Leeson family 29ff, 185
Limerick, Ireland 98
Lincoln (farmer) 17
Lincoln's Inn 106, 166
Lloyd, Humphrey 165ff
Lockey, James 92
London Bridge 4, 104
Long Oarsbie, Lincolnshire 62
Longcastle, Captain William 100ff
Lowe, curate 62ff
Lusty Jack 117

Malaga, Spain 25
Manchester, Earl of 125
Marble Arch 188
Market Deeping, Lincolnshire 84
Market Rasen, Lincolnshire 21
Marlowe, Christopher 4
Matthewson (shipmaster) 102

Mell (defrocked chaplain) 59ff
Middle Rasen, Lincolnshire 62
Mill Hill, Suffolk 29
Milton, John 1
Milton Mills, Bedfordshire 156
Montague, Sir Henry 90
Moor Fields 81, 113
Moore, John 100
Moore, Peter 69
Moorgate 149
Morgan (companion of Robinson) 166ff
Morgan (parson) 28ff
Morris, Thomas 165ff
Mowse, Jennet 62

Newbury, Berkshire 163
Newgate Prison 6, 12, 46, 59, 75, 77, 79, 83, 89, 90, 163, 167, 187
Newton family 61ff
Nonesuch Palace, Surrey 75
North, Lord 125
Northampton 154
Norton (landowner) 29ff
Nottingham 107

Old Bailey 12, 161, 166, 188
Old Cleeve, Somerset 32
Old Doublets 82ff, 180
Old Jewry Street 149
Otterhampton, Somerset 33
Overbury, Sir Thomas 135
Oxford 109

Page (husband of Miss Glanfield) 55ff
Paternoster Row 3
Paulet (servant) 127
Paul's Cross 2
Pecham, Henry 82
Peckham, Surrey 109
Pie Corner 80
Pinner 155
Plymouth, Devonshire 55, 101, 102
Porter, William 111

Potter, Anne 61ff, 181
Poultry Compter 149
Powell, Erasmus 170ff
Powlderbach, Salop 172
Priddis, Robert 55ff
Purser family 134

Ratcleife, Agnes 160ff
Ratsey, Gamaliel 84ff
Richmond, Duke of 143
Rigge (killed by Francis Cartwright) 25
Ring Cross, Islington 81
Roberts (justice of the peace) 47
Robinson, Arthur 160ff
Robinson, Francis 166ff
Robson, Henry 19ff
Rochester, Kent 57
Rockland, Norfolk 63
Rotherhithe, Surrey 116
Roup, Captain 92ff
Rowse, John 49ff, 179
Rumford, Essex 17
Rye, Sussex 19

Sacheverell, clergyman 34ff
Safi, Morocco 100
St. Audrey's, Somerset 33
St. Bartholomew's Hospital 14
St. Botolph's Billingsgate 188
St. Decuman, Somerset 33
St. Dunstan's in the East 58
St. Edmund's, Salisbury 168, 188
St. Faith's 2
St. Giles 166, 187
St. Gregory's 2
St. Katherine's Dock 188
Saint John, Sir William 94
St. Leonards Houndsditch 62
St. Malo, France 93
St. Martin's in the Fields 130
St. Mary Cray 58
St. Mary's, Nottingham 108

St. Pancras 80
St. Paul's Cathedral 2
St. Thomas' Hospital 14
Salisbury, Bishop of 168ff
Salisbury, Wiltshire 125
Sanders, Sir Edward 76
Saunders, Anne 57ff, 188
Saunders, George 57ff
Saunders, Sir William 155
Savill, Sir John 43
Sawyer, Elizabeth 160ff
Scambler, Martha 120ff
Scott, Thomas 136ff
Seager, Joan 147
Selman, John 79
Sergeant's Inn 128
Shakespeare, William 1, 16, 186, 187
Sherfield, Henry 168ff
Sherwood, Country Tom 80ff
Shipman, John 102
Shipman, Thomas 102
Shoe Lane 79
Shooter's Hill 57
Shorthose (robber) 85ff
Shrewsbury 169, 172
Shrewsbury Castle 188
Skellington, Walter 87
Skipwith, Henry 126f
Slanning, landowner 117
Slie, Clement 89
Smithfield, West 59, 79
Smithwicke family 34ff, 182
Snell, robber 85ff
Somers, William 107ff
Somerset, Countess of 135, 188
Somerset, Earl of 135
Southampton, Earl of 143
Spalding, Lincolnshire 84
Starkie, Nicholas 108
Stone, Tom 55ff
Storre, William 22ff, 193
Strafford, Earl of 125, 133, 189
Strand 76

Strangwich, George 55ff, 186
Stuart, Lady Arabella 45
Studley, Peter 174ff
Sutton, Mrs. 74
Sutton family 156ff
Swan Inn 166
Swansea, Wales 102
Swinnerton, Mabel 148

Tanfield, Sir Lawrence 36
Taunton, Somerset 34
Taverner, William 100
Tavistock, Devonshire 55
Temple Bar 89
Temple Stairs 90
Tendance, "Double Diligence" 82ff, 180
Tetherton, Robert 176
Tewkesbury, Gloucestershire 174
Thetford, Norfolk 67
Thomond, Earl of 98ff
Thornton, Abraham 194
Throgmorton, Robert 111
Tomkins, Captain 102
Touchet, Frances 125ff
Touchet, George 125ff
Touchet, James 125
Touchet, Mervyn see Castlehaven, Earl of
Touchet, Mervyn, Jr. 125ff
Tower Hill 130, 189
Tower of London 110, 135, 188
Trat, parson 33ff, 185, 186
Tunis 92, 95
Turner, Anne 136
Turner, Thomas 172
Twickenham 120
Tyburn 121, 122, 131, 161, 166, 177, 187
Tyndal, Sir John 106, 180, 181

Utrecht 136
Uxbridge 70

Vaughan, Joan 154
Vincent, Jarvis 46ff
Vincent, Margaret 46ff, 179, 181, 184

Wakefield, Yorkshire 45
Walker, Alice 34ff
Wapping 104, 188
Warwick Lane 90
Waterford, Ireland 132
Watson, William 166
Weaver, Margaret 161
Welshpool, Wales 176
Wentworth, __ 27
Westminster 69, 148, 168
Westminster Abbey 189
Westminster Hall 122, 130, 141
Weston, Lord 125
White (servant) 70ff
White Lion Prison, Southwark 76, 77, 78, 111
Whitechapel 75
Whitecross Street 149
Whitehall 79, 166, 176
Whitgift, John, Archbishop of Canterbury 175
Willesden 46
Wilson, Edward 176
Wilson, Joan 176
Windham (justice of the peace) 33ff
Windmill Tavern 149
Windsor 78
Windsor, Lord 146, 148
Winstock, Devonshire 116
Woolwich 58
Worcester Castle 146
Worcester, Earl of 125
Worlish (servant) 29ff
Wormewall Wood 51, 188
Wright, Katherine 108
Wright family 17
Wye, Anthony 100ff

Yarmouth, Norfolk 32

www.ingramcontent.com/pod-product-compliance
Ingram Content Group UK Ltd.
Pitfield, Milton Keynes, MK11 3LW, UK
UKHW041954140426
5217IPUK00015B/800